Alliance Security Dilemmas in the Iraq War

Alliance Security Dilemmas in the Iraq War

German and Japanese Responses

Natsuyo Ishibashi

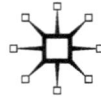

ALLIANCE SECURITY DILEMMAS IN THE IRAQ WAR
Copyright © Natsuyo Ishibashi, 2012.

All rights reserved.

First published in 2012 by
PALGRAVE MACMILLAN®
in the United States—a division of St. Martin's Press LLC,
175 Fifth Avenue, New York, NY 10010.

Where this book is distributed in the UK, Europe and the rest of the world, this is by Palgrave Macmillan, a division of Macmillan Publishers Limited, registered in England, company number 785998, of Houndmills, Basingstoke, Hampshire RG21 6XS.

Palgrave Macmillan is the global academic imprint of the above companies and has companies and representatives throughout the world.

Palgrave® and Macmillan® are registered trademarks in the United States, the United Kingdom, Europe and other countries.

ISBN: 978–0–230–33733–6

Library of Congress Cataloging-in-Publication Data

Ishibashi, Natsuyo.
   Alliance security dilemmas in the Iraq War : German and Japanese responses / Natsuyo Ishibashi.
     p. cm.
   ISBN 978–0–230–33733–6 (hardback)
   1. Iraq War, 2003–2011—Diplomatic history. 2. United States—Military relations—Germany. 3. Germany—Military relations—United States. 4. United States—Military relations—Japan. 5. Japan—Military relations—United States. 6. Germany—Military policy. 7. Japan—Military policy. 8. Alliances. I. Title.

DS79.761.I75 2012
956.77044′32—dc23
                                                                         2012011141

A catalogue record of the book is available from the British Library.

Design by Newgen Imaging Systems (P) Ltd., Chennai, India.

First edition: September 2012

For My Mother
with full of love and humor

Contents

List of Figures and Tables — ix
Acknowledgments — xi
Abbreviations and Foreign Terms — xv

1. Introduction — 1
2. Background — 27
3. Regional Security Environments and US Security Commitment: East Asia versus Europe — 41
4. Alliance Institutions: NATO versus US-Japan Security Treaty — 85
5. Military Institutions: Bundeswehr versus Self-Defense Forces (SDF) — 105
6. Alternative Explanations — 139
7. Conclusion — 171

Notes — 177
Index — 207

Figures and Tables

Figures

5.1	Military Expenditures of Germany and Japan in Constant (2009) US$ m., 1988–2010	118
5.2	Military Expenditures of Germany and Japan as Percentage of Gross Domestic Product, 1988–2009	119
5.3	Number of US Military Personnel in the FRG and Japan (1976)	130
5.4	Number of US Military Personnel in the FRG and Japan (2001)	130

Tables

1.1	German and Japanese Participation in Overseas Operations	7
1.2	List of Interviews in Germany	21
1.3	List of Interviews in Japan	22
5.1	Number of US Military Personnel in the FRG	129
5.2	Number of US Military Personnel in Japan	129
6.1	The Results of June 2000 and November 2003 Lower House Elections in Japan	161
6.2	The Results of September 1998 and September 2002 Bundestag Elections in the FRG	162

Acknowledgments

This book is based on my dissertation that I completed at Indiana University Bloomington in May 2010. It was a long journey for me to write up this book. I could not have completed this long journey without help from many people. First, I would like to express my gratitude to my dissertation advisor, Gregory Kasza. Kasza-sensei was always generous and helped me as much as he could when I was conducting dissertation research. Without his help, I would not have been able to accomplish this difficult task.

I also would like to express my sincere thanks to the people who agreed to meet with me for interviews in Germany and Japan. Without their kindness and generosity, I would not have been able to complete my dissertation. Indeed, the most interesting part of my dissertation research was conducting interviews. It was truly interesting and exciting for me to meet with them and ask them questions. Again, I would like to express my gratitude to all my German and Japanese respondents who kindly opened their door and shared their time with me. Their kindness was great encouragement for me to do research.

Next, I would like to thank the German Academic Exchange Service (DAAD), Indiana University (IU) Graduate Exchange Program, and Matsushita International Foundation for their generous financial support for my dissertation research. I was able to conduct field research in Germany thanks to the support of the DAAD and the IU Graduate Exchange Program. It was a revolutionary experience for me to go to Berlin and live there. Until summer 2006, I had never stepped foot in Europe. At first, I ignorantly thought that Germany was like the United States. However, Germany was a completely different country from the United States. The language was different, the history was different, the food was different, the lifestyle was different, and everything was different! In addition, although Germany and Japan share a lot of similarities (e.g., antimilitarist cultures), they are also different in many aspects. (For e.g., Japan does not have the East-West problem, because it was not divided after the end of World

War II.) By doing field research in Germany, I was able to recognize a lot of interesting differences and similarities among the three countries, not just in terms of their foreign policies, but also in terms of domestic political, social, economic, and cultural aspects.

I am also grateful to Dr. Verena Blechinger-Talcott, chair of the Institute of Japan Studies at Free University of Berlin. She kindly wrote a letter to the DAAD for me in fall 2005. In fact, she sent the letter to my address in Bloomington by express mail before the deadline. (The German express mail is very expensive!) Without her help, I would not have been able to get the DAAD fellowship. I also would like to thank Andreas Hoffmann-san, who worked as my research assistant. He helped me a lot when I was conducting interviews in Berlin.

Then, I would like to express my thanks to the Social Science Research Council (SSRC) Japan Studies Dissertation Workshop and the European Association for Japanese Studies (EAJS) Workshop for Doctoral Students for giving me precious opportunities to improve my dissertation. I learned a lot from the participants in the two workshops. I would especially like to thank Ellis Krauss and Christine Yano (SSRC), and Paul Midford (EAJS) for their comments on my dissertation proposal, their guidance on how to conduct interviews, and introducing me to useful source materials.

In addition, I would like to thank my dissertation committee members—Jeffrey Hart, Richard Rubinger, and Robert Rohrschneider—for their critical comments on my dissertation, as well as Rebekah Tromble for editing my dissertation. I learned a lot from many corrections in my paper.

I am also deeply grateful to the Japan Program at the Department of Sociology and Political Science, Norwegian University of Science and Technology (NTNU) for offering me a generous postdoctoral position, which enabled me to revise my dissertation and turn it into a publishable book. I would like to thank my *senpai* (senior colleagues) at NTNU—Paul Midford, Ola Listhaug, Marit Reitan, and Sabrina Ramet—for their kind support and encouragement. I especially owe it to Paul that I was able to complete this book. He is my great *senpai*.

Finally, I would like to express my full gratitude to my mother Kimiko Ishibashi. She has supported me whenever, wherever, and whatever! No matter how deeply I became depressed, her humor always cheered me up. She is a great source of my energy. This book is for her.

As a final note, although I am in debt to many people for helping me write this book, I alone take full responsibility for shortcomings found herein.

NATSUYO ISHIBASHI
Trondheim, Norway
February 2012

Abbreviations and Foreign Terms

ANRE	Agency for Natural Resources and Energy
ASDF	Air Self-Defense Force [J]
ATSML	Anti-Terrorism Special Measures Law [J]
BND	Federal Intelligence Service (Bundesnachrichtendienst) [G]
Bundestag	German National Parliament
Bundeswehr	German Armed Forces
CDU	Christian Democratic Union [G]
CJOEP	Coordinated Joint Outline Emergency Plan [J]
CSCE	Conference on Security and Cooperation in Europe
CSF	Costal Safety Force [J]
CSU	Christian Social Union [G]
Die Linke	Left Party [G]
DPG	Defense Policy Guide [G]
DPJ	Democratic Party of Japan (Minshutō)
DPRI	Defense Policy Review Initiative
ESDI	European Security and Defense Identity
ESDP	European Security and Defense Policy
EU	European Union
FDP	Free Democratic Party [G]
FOST	Flag Officer Sea Training (Portland/Plymouth in Great Britain)
FRG	Federal Republic of Germany (West Germany 1949–1990; unified Germany 1990–present)
FRY	Socialist Federal Republic of Yugoslavia
GDR	German Democratic Republic (East Germany)
GSDF	Ground Self-Defense Force [J]
IFOR	(NATO-led) Implementation force (in Bosnia-Herzegovina)
ISAF	(NATO-led) International Security Assistance Forces (in Afghanistan)
JCG	Japan Coast Guard
JCP	Japan Communist Party
JSC	Joint Staff Council (in the SDF) [J]
JSP	Japan Socialist Party

Abbreviations and Foreign Terms

JDA	Japan Defense Agency (The JDA was renamed the Ministry of Defense in 2007.)
KEDO	Korean Peninsula Energy Development Organization
KFOR	(NATO-led) Kosovo Force
KLA	Kosovo Liberation Army
Kōmeito	Clean Government Party [J]
KSK	Kommando Spezialfräfte (German Special Operations Forces)
LDP	Liberal Democratic Party [J]
METI	Ministry of Economy, Trade and Industry [J]
MOD	Ministry of Defense [G] [J]
MOF	Ministry of Finance [G] [J]
MOFA	Ministry of Foreign Affairs [J]
MSDF	Maritime Self-Defense Force [J]
NATO	North Atlantic Treaty Organization
NDPG	National Defense Program Guideline [J]
OAF	Operation Allied Force (NATO's operation against Serbia in 1999)
OEF	Operation Enduring Freedom (in and around Afghanistan)
PKOs	Peacekeeping operations
SACLANT	Supreme Allied Commander Atlantic (Norfolk, Virginia) (Supreme commander of NATO)
SDP	Social Democratic Party [J]
SDF	Self-Defense Forces [J]
SFOR	(NATO-led) Stabilization Force (in Bosnia-Herzegovina)
SPD	Social Democratic Party [G]
UNSC	United Nation Security Council
USARJ	US Army Japan
USFJ	United States Forces Japan
USMC	US Marine Corps
WMD	weapons of mass destruction

[G] = German; [J] = Japanese

Note: In my book, Japanese names are written as surname first and given name second, according to the Japanese custom. (For e.g., my name is Natsuyo Ishibashi in English; however, in my book, my name would be written as Ishibashi Natsuyo.)

1

INTRODUCTION

I. RESEARCH QUESTION AND ITS SIGNIFICANCE

This book explains why the Federal Republic of Germany (FRG) opposed the US invasion of Iraq in 2003, whereas Japan supported it, despite the two countries' many similarities. Public opinion in both countries was predominantly negative toward the US attack on Iraq; both countries were long-term allies of the United States; and both countries were called "civilian powers" in a sense that they have developed cultures of antimilitarism as a result of their devastating experiences in World War II and had a strong preference for avoiding the use of force to settle international conflicts.[1] Employing Glenn H. Snyder's concept of alliance security dilemma constituted by the twin fears of abandonment and entrapment,[2] I argue that the two countries pursued opposite policies toward the Iraq War because the level of Germany's fear of entrapment in the war was higher than Japan's. The two countries' alliance security dilemmas with the United States during the 2002–2003 Iraq crisis were derived from: (1) the nature of regional tensions and conflicts in the 1990s, along with US management and commitment to the regions, (2) the type of alliance institutions to which each country belongs (the US-Japan Security Treaty versus NATO), and (3) the characteristics of their military institutions (Japanese Self-Defense Forces versus German Bundeswehr).

The question of the two countries' divergent policies toward the Iraq War is important in both practical and theoretical senses. In a practical sense, this question is important for the United States' future foreign policy goals. Both the FRG and Japan have been loyal allies of the United States since the early 1950s, and the United States has projected its power over Europe and Asia through these important regional intermediary states.[3] Japan and Germany are the third- and fourth-largest economies (as of 2010),[4] and have the sixth- and seventh-largest defense budgets in the world, respectively.[5] Therefore, they can make substantial contributions to US overseas efforts, if they decide to do so. By understanding why the FRG and Japan pursued different policies toward the US war in Iraq, US policymakers will be better able to determine how to obtain support and cooperation from such allies, as well as to avoid misunderstanding and confrontation going forward.

In the theoretical sense, the two countries' opposite policies toward the Iraq War have important implications for both constructivism and realism—especially for the debate over the "normalization" of the two countries' military activities since the end of the Cold War. Constructivists such as Thomas U. Berger and Peter J. Katzenstein have made great contributions to the field of international relations by discovering the importance of political culture in explaining state behavior after the end of the Cold War. They argued that, contrary to realists' predictions, neither Japan nor the FRG tried to pursue great power status or to challenge the United States after the end of the Cold War, even though they were the second- and third-largest economies, respectively, in the 1990s. Both Japan and the FRG developed a culture of antimilitarism following the end of World War II and continued to be reluctant to participate in international military affairs, even after the collapse of the Soviet Union. Thus, constructivists concluded that cultural norms—not a balance of power among states in an anarchic world, as the realists claim—was the most significant explanatory variable for state behavior.[6]

Although the constructivists brought a new perspective into the field of international relations in the 1990s, Japan's and the FRG's different responses to the Iraq War have raised a question about the effectiveness of the constructivists' explanation about state behavior. Why did Japan and the FRG, both of which were supposed to have a culture of antimilitarism, pursue a different policy toward the US war in Iraq in 2003? If political culture is as significant a variable for explaining state behavior as the constructivists claim, Japan and the FRG should have behaved in the same way during the Iraq crisis of 2002–2003. Yet the FRG opposed the US attack on Iraq, whereas Japan supported it.

The question of the two countries' different policies toward the Iraq War also has important implications for the debate concerning the "normalization" of Germany and Japan since 1990. While realists coming from an elitist perspective maintain that Germany and Japan have been moving toward normalization—that is, toward a willingness to exercise "strategically offensive military power overseas"[7]—others from the constructivist and pluralist perspectives have argued that main components of the two countries' foreign policies have remained unchanged since the early 1950s.

German foreign policy experts considering the impact of the culture of reticence in foreign policy behavior—experts such as Hanns W. Maull, Adrian Hyde-Price, Peter Rudolf, Sebastian Harnisch, Kerry Longhurst, Franz-Josef Meiers, and Alister Miskimmon[8]—have stressed the continuity of German security policy since the Cold War era: Germany continues to have a "strong preference for nonmilitary solutions" and pursues "multilateralism," they argue.[9] In contrast, Rainner Baumann and Gunther Hellmann have pointed out important contributions made by certain political elites—particularly Chancellor Gerhard Schröder and Foreign Minister Joschka Fischer—to Germany's normalization. They argue that Germany's participation in the 1999 Kosovo Conflict was "the result of a deliberate strategy of German decision-makers who wanted the use of force to become an accepted means of German foreign policy right from the beginning,"[10] and their strategic ambitions "have produced the far-reaching changes in German attitudes and behavior towards the use of force which we can observe today."[11] In short, Baumann and Hellmann suggest that Germany—under active elite leadership—has been moving toward a normal country that is willing to "'take over more responsibility' by contributing to international military operations."[12]

Similarly, "reluctant realist" Japan experts—experts such as Michael J. Green, Christopher W. Hughes, Eliss Krauss, Kenneth B. Pyle, and Richard J. Samuels—have argued that the process of Japan's normalization (in Samuels's term, the process of "whittling away at the Yoshida Doctrine" by Japanese security strategists[13]) started in response to a series of external events in the 1990s (the 1990–1991 Persian Gulf War, the revelation of North Korean nuclear weapons development in 1994, the Taiwan Straits Crisis in 1996, etc.), and was accelerated by the strong leadership of Prime Minister Koizumi Jun'ichiro in the period 2001–2006.[14] According to Hughes and Krauss, for example, it "was Koizumi who smashed long-standing taboos and created the conditions for ending Japan's foreign and security policy inertia,"[15] and under his leadership, "Japan seemed to have transformed itself into a willing and active US ally."[16] Hughes also explains a series of modernization efforts undertaken by the Self-Defense Forces (SDF) in the 1990s and 2000s, including the Maritime Self-Defense Force's (MSDF's) procurement of "three *Osumi*-class transport ships with flat decks for the landing of transport helicopters and an integral rear dock for the operation of hovercraft capable of landing tanks" and the Air Self-Defense Force's (ASDF's) in-fight refueling capabilities.[17] Each of these measures, Hughes argues, signaled the SDF's ambition to project its power overseas. In addition, Hughes points out the significance of the 2004 National Defense Program Guideline (NDPG) for Japan's normalization. Not only did it add new emphasis on "global" security interests that corresponded with those of the United States in the "arc of instability" from the Middle East to East Asia, he contends, but it also advocated that the SDF should increase interoperability with UN and US forces. The NDPG, according to Hughes, indicates that Japan is considering expanding its security role to the Middle East as well as increasing its alliance cooperation with the United States.[18] Furthermore, Hughes maintains that even after Koizumi left office, Japan remains on the long-term trajectory of normalization.[19] Pyle shares this view and predicts that the new direction taken by Koizumi in Japanese foreign policy will not change, even if his successor, Abe Shinzo, and the Liberal Democratic Party (LDP) stumble in the future.[20]

On the other hand, scholars with constructivist and pluralist views, such as Andrew L. Oros and Paul Midford, have stressed the continuity of Japan's foreign policy from the Cold War era.[21] Oros, for example, denies the emergence of a new security identity resulting in the "normalization" of Japanese security practice. Instead, he argues that "Japan's postwar security identity," composed of three tenets—"no traditional armed forces, no use of force by Japan except in self-defense, no Japanese participation in foreign wars"—will continue to shape its policy for many years to come.[22] Despite a series of recent security policy innovations in Japan, according to Oros, the SDF is still focused on self-defense and does not engage in combat operations abroad.[23] The SDF's engagement in combat missions is strictly limited to the defense of Japan.[24] Although the SDF's overseas activities were expanded under the Anti-Terror Special Measures Law (October 2001) and the Iraq Special Measures Law (July 2003),[25] the actions taken under these laws still constitute humanitarian assistance and rear-area support for US forces.[26] And even in such rear-area support, the SDF is "prohibited from supplying weapons or ammunition, or *even transporting them within foreign territory*, and from refueling or serving combat vehicles, ships, or aircraft."[27]

Likewise, Midford suggests that public opinion can mold and constrain the government's plans for SDF deployment overseas, thereby placing a limit on how far hawkish elites can go to normalize Japan. He argues that the Japanese public was never truly pacifist, but "defensive realist." The majority of Japanese have never rejected the use of force for the sake of territorial defense. However, members of the public do not support offensive uses of force for promoting political goals—such as promoting democracy or human rights, suppressing terrorism, or countering weapons of mass destruction (WMD) proliferation—abroad. They believe that such goals can be more effectively achieved through nonmilitary means.[28] Midford identifies two different kinds of security-related attitudes among the postwar Japanese public: defensive realism and antimilitarist distrust ("distrust of the military and the state's ability to control it"[29]). According to Midford, antimilitarist distrust has declined over time as a result of successful demonstration effects of the SDF's noncombat humanitarian activities overseas in UN Peacekeeping operations (UNPKOs) since 1992, whereas attitudinal defensive realism has persisted. He suggests that some people have misinterpreted the decline of antimilitarist distrust among the public as an indication of a rise in the influence of hawkish elites. But the persistence of defensive realism and the rejection of the use of offensive force among the Japanese public continue to constrain hawkish elites' attempts to dispatch the SDF to combat missions abroad.[30] Midford writes in detail about the "reversing course" being forced upon military policy as a result of a backlash in public opinion since 2006, which, for example, has made it more difficult for the LDP to extend the MSDF's refueling mission in the Indian Ocean and which demonstrates that there is a limit on what Japanese elites can do to normalize their country's security policy.[31]

My comparative study of Germany's and Japan's responses to the Iraq War contributes to this debate over the two countries' normalization processes. Japan supported the US invasion of Iraq, whereas Germany opposed it because Germany's normalization process since 1990 has proceeded more rapidly than that of Japan. Because of its progress toward normalization, the likelihood of becoming entrapped in the US-led war was higher for Germany than Japan. Indeed, Germany's normalization was occurring as a direct result of its military responsibilities toward NATO (and more specifically toward the United States as the dominant force within NATO). As I explain in detail in the next section, Germany's normalization process was a result of its participation in the operations to intervene in a series of civil wars in former Yugoslavia after the end of the Cold War, the alliance obligation under NATO's Article 5 (collective self-defense clause), the transformation in the 1990s of NATO from an alliance for the territorial defense of the member states to a force primarily used for out-of-area peacekeeping operations (PKOs), and the willingness of the Bundeswehr to participate in overseas missions and work with its NATO troops as a result of its long-term socialization with them. It has been very difficult for Germany to reconcile these moves toward military normalization with its preexisting and widespread culture of antimilitarism. Despite the moves toward normalization, the German public still holds a deep skepticism about the efficacy of the use of force to solve international conflicts.

Throughout the Cold War period, the security policies of both countries were focused on territorial defense. Neither the SDF nor the Bundeswehr were ever dispatched overseas. Since the end of the Cold War, however, the Bundeswehr has been transformed from a territorial defense force to an expeditionary force for out-of-area operations, while the SDF's primary mission has remained territorial defense, with overseas PKOs only a secondary mission. Not only has Germany dispatched many more troops overseas than Japan (see table 1.1), but the Bundeswehr has also participated in offensive military operations abroad, while the SDF's overseas activities have remained humanitarian reconstruction efforts, and the SDF has never participated in combat operations. Moreover, 53 German soldiers have already died in Afghanistan (as of December 12, 2011),[32] while no SDF soldiers have died in overseas operations since the PKO bill was passed in 1992. Japan's normalization since the end of the Cold War, therefore, has not deviated from the existing political norms, namely, Oros's three tenets of postwar Japan's "security identity" (no traditional armed forces, no use of force by Japan except in self-defense, no Japanese participation in foreign wars) and Midford's "attitudinal defensive realism."

On the other hand, Germany had to face the disparity between the progress of its normalization process and the domestic political culture of antimilitarism. In spite of normalization, political risks associated with losing lives of soldiers and indigenous civilians in overseas operations have remained major concerns at home. Although Germany is far ahead of Japan in the process of normalization, it still lags behind its Western allies. To be sure, as Baumann and Hellmann have noted, Chancellor Schröder and Foreign Minister Fischer strongly pushed Germany toward normalization during the 1999 Kosovo Conflict. Still, sending ground troops to Kosovo remained out of the question for Schröder.[33] Moreover, the leader of Christian Democratic Party (CDU), Angela Merkel, supported the US decision to attack Iraq in March 2003 when the CDU was out of the government. Yet she has not tried to change the policies that the Social Democratic Party (SPD) pursued since becoming chancellor in 2005. In spite of bitter criticism

Table 1.1 German and Japanese Participation in Overseas Operations

Year	Germany	Year	Japan
1990–1991	200 soldiers and 18 fighter jets to Turkey as part of a NATO contingent		
1991–1992	Medical troops to PKO in Cambodia (UNAMIC)	1991	MSDF (4 minesweeping ships, 1 supply ship, 1 flag ship) to the Persian Gulf.
1992–1996	Naval forces ("no combat operation") to monitor embargo against FRY (Operation Sharp Guard)	1992–1993	606 soldiers (6 cease-fire monitor; 600 engineering unit) to UNTAC, Cambodia
1993–1994	Supply and transport units to Somalia (UNOSOM II)	1993–1995	Some 50 soldiers (transport units) to ONUMOZ, Mozambique.
1993–1995	Logistical support only (airlifts of Sarajevo, etc.) to Bosnia-Hercegovina (UNPROFOR)		
1993–1995	Air-force personnel as part of AWACS unit; No participation in NATO air strikes to Bosnia-Hercegovina to monitor no-fly zone; NATO air strikes against FRY		
1994–	10 medical officers and military observers as part of UN peacekeeping force to Georgia (UNOMIG)	1994	378 soldiers (260 medical; 118 airlift) to Rwanda.
1995–1996	Some 3,000 noncombat ground troops to Croatia (IFOR)	1996–	Some 40 soldiers to UNDOF.
1996	Some 3,000 ground troops (including combat troops) to Bosnia-Herzegovina		
1998–	Some 8,000 ground troops to Kosovo/FRY to participate unarmed OSCE-led Kosovo verification mission and in NATO air strikes	1999–2000	113 soldiers (air transport unit) to East Timor.
2001–	Some navy ships (3 frigates, 1 fast patrol boat group, and 4 supply ships) to OEF, Horn of Africa.	2001 (Oct)	Air transport (138 soldiers) for relief operation for Afghanistan refugees
2002–	Some 3,000 (5,323 in 2011) to ISAF, Afghanistan and Uzbekistan.	2001–2009	MSDF oil supply ships to the Indian Ocean.
		2004–2006	600 troops to Iraq (humanitarian reconstruction)
		2004–2008	Some 200 ASDF personnel to Kuwait (Transportation of materials for the humanitarian and reconstruction assistance)

Source: Rainer Baumann and Gunther Hellmann, "Germany and the Use of Military Force: 'Total War', the 'Culture of Restraint' and the Quest for Normality," *German Politics* 10, no. 1 (2001): 67; Ministry of Defense, *Defense of Japan* (Tokyo: Ministry of Defense, 2007), 577–578.

from NATO allies (namely, the United States, Canada, and Britain), she has firmly refused to send troops to southern Afghanistan, where intense conflicts between NATO troops and Taliban have been under way. As a result of this cautiousness, the number of German casualties in Afghanistan (53) is much smaller than those of other major NATO allies, such as the United States (1,852), Britain (391), and Canada (158).[34] As we can see, then, because of the progress toward normalization, the likelihood of Germany becoming entrapped in a US-led overseas war became high. At the same time, however, the preexisting, widely shared political norm of antimilitarism has put a brake on Germany's normalization process.

II. Arguments

With the concept of alliance security dilemma constituted by the twin fears of abandonment and entrapment, I argue that Japan supported the US preventive war on Iraq, whereas the FRG opposed it, because Japan's fear of entrapment in the war was lower than that of the FRG. Glen H. Snyder defines alliances as "formal associations of states for the use (or nonuse) of military force, intended for either the security or the aggrandizement of their members, against specific other states, whether or not these others are explicitly identified."[35] States form an alliance for the following benefits: a reduced probability of being attacked (deterrence), greater strength in case of attack (defense), and prevention of the ally's alliance with their adversary (preclusion). However, alliances also entail risks and costs upon states: the increased risk of war and reduced freedom of action resulted from the commitment to the alliance partner.[36] Snyder argues that states' alliance behavior after forming an alliance can be explained by the "alliance security dilemma" constituted by the twin fears of "entrapment" and "abandonment." States fear both being abandoned by their ally and being dragged into a war over the ally's interests that they do not share. States thus continuously engage in bargaining with their allies in order to avoid these two fears and, at the same time, to try to preserve their alliance.[37]

The fear of entrapment is an important element for explaining state alliance behaviors, especially those of regional great powers with cultures of antimilitarism (Japan and Germany) allied with a global power (the United States). Izumikawa Yasuhiro argues that Japanese antimilitarism consists of three elements: pacifism, antitraditionalism, and the fear of entrapment.[38] Although Constructivists have treated antimilitarism as a monolithic normative factor, Izumikawa suggests that it also includes a realist factor: the fear of entrapment. He explains that Japanese security policy is severely constrained when pacifists succeed in appealing either to the public's fear of entrapment or to the domestic political norm of antitraditionalism.[39] When the Japanese public is experiencing the fear of entrapment, it tries to pressure the Japanese government not to adopt an active security policy. As a result, the government tries to limit its alliance commitments to the United States. On the other hand, when the public's fear of entrapment is low, the government can enjoy relative freedom to pursue an active security policy. According to Izumikawa, a state's fear of entrapment will increase "when its ally is involved in regional conflicts that could eventually entrap the former in an unwanted war," or "when it regards its ally as overly aggressive and its ally's adversary as on the defensive."[40] For example, Izumikawa writes that Prime Minister Sato Eisaku announced the Three Nonnuclear Principles (Japan will not possess, produce, or allow the introduction of nuclear weapons on its territory) in 1967 because Sato was concerned about increasing public fear of entrapment in the Vietnam War, as well as about criticism against the government from antitraditionalists over the Three-Arrow Plan (the Defense Agency's secret table exercise for US-Japan military cooperation in the event of an emergency in the Korean Peninsula).

Scholars often argue that a source of a state's alliance security dilemma stems from international structural factors, and a state's fear of entrapment can be simply cancelled out by the presence of a high level of external threats. Izumikawa, for example, suggests that Japan supported the US-led war on terrorism following 9/11 and the Iraq War in 2003 because external security threats—the rise of China and North Korea's development of nuclear weapons and missiles capabilities—heightened the Japanese people's threat perception, thereby reducing their fear of entrapment in a US-led war. In case of the Iraq War, Izumikawa writes, "many Japanese considered their country's support for the United States undesirable but inevitable if Japan was to avoid US abandonment on other issues such as North Korea."[41]

I do not deny that the North Korean nuclear development and the rise of China are threats to Japan. It is true that, as Christopher Hughes writes, Japan's dispatch of the SDF to the Indian Ocean and to Iraq was "the price" that it "had to pay in order to obtain the assistance of the US in facing down North Korea, and most especially China."[42] However, I argue that Japan's alliance security dilemma with the United States is not simply derived from the external threats from North Korea and China. Japan's fear of entrapment in the US-led war in the Middle East in 2001–2003 was lower than that of Germany because: (1) there were no actual military conflicts in East Asia in the 1990s—as a result, Japan had never had a difficult experience participating in a U.S.-led regional military conflict before 9/11; (2) Japan's alliance obligation was fairly limited under the US-Japan Security Treaty; and (3) the characteristics of the SDF lessened the likelihood of Japan's entrapment in a US-led overseas war.

Although structural realist scholars predicted that Asia would become a dangerous place, with increasing arms races and power politics after the end of the Cold War, Asia has in fact been stable. There have been no major conflicts in the region since the 1978–1979 Vietnam-Cambodia-China war.[43] Muthiah Alagappa even writes, "Asia is much more stable than the Asia of the past and indeed more stable than several other regions of the world today (Eastern Europe, the Middle East, Africa)."[44] To be sure, the relative stability in East Asia in the 1990s does not mean that there was no potential for major conflict in the region or were no threats to Japan during that time. Not only was there a series of crises in East Asia in the 1990s that heightened the Japanese people's threat perceptions (such as the revelation of North Korean nuclear weapons development in 1994, China's nuclear test in 1995, the Taiwan Strait Crisis of 1996, the North Korean missile tests passing over Japanese airspace in1998, the North Korean spy ship incident of 1999, and so on), but Japan has also continued to face territorial disputes with all its neighbors. (These included disputes over the Northern Islands with Russia, the Senkaku Islands with China and Taiwan, and the Takeshima Islands with South Korea.) Nevertheless, these crises and territorial disputes did not escalate into the eruption of full-fledged war.

Stability in East Asia in the 1990s did not rest solely on the US security role. Factors such as growing economic interdependence among Asian states,[45] continuing consolidation of Asian countries as modern-nation states, and the development of a normative structure suggesting that disputes should be settled without recourse to war in Asia also played a prominent role.[46] Yet, not only did the United States' restrained behavior contribute to regional stability, but its security commitment to Japan also kept Japan's alliance security dilemma with the United States relatively low. Victor Cha, for example, argues that the United States' security commitment is more important than the level of external threat to explain a "quasi-alliance" relationship between Japan and South Korea. Cha writes:

> [I]n alliances where weaker partners are highly dependent on a common patron, the common patron's security commitment is a better

determinant of alliance behavior between the two weaker partners than the level of external threat. In other words, the pressures that the external threats put on alliance behavior are not linear. Instead, threats have to be filtered through perceptions of allied promise or patron commitment before one can explain or predict behavior.[47]

Japan's alliance security dilemma was not a simple product of the external threats from North Korea or China. Rather, it had to do with how the United States—Japan's "patron"—behaved in East Asia and the strength of the security commitment that the United States showed to Japan. The US military power was overwhelmingly preponderant in East Asia in the 1990s,[48] and the United States restrained its military power and used it only for defense and deterrence.[49]

The US strategy in the Asia Pacific was to maintain the status quo and uneasy stalemate rather than pursuing a dramatic strategy to resolve security problems.[50] China's and North Korea's possession of nuclear weapons also discouraged the United States from pursuing drastic measures to solve regional problems.[51] Moreover, although the United States and Japan experienced "alliance adrift" in the early 1990s,[52] they announced the revision of the US-Japan Guidelines for Defense Cooperation in April 1996 in order to strengthen their alliance. More fundamentally, the United States would never give up its security commitment to Japan because the commitment itself prevents Japan from acquiring nuclear weapons. A nuclear-armed Japan would inevitably escalate tensions and lead to a dangerous arms race in East Asia.[53] These two components—general stability in East Asia and a restrained but secure security commitment from the United States—therefore combined to keep Japan's alliance security dilemma (both its fear of entrapment and abandonment) low.

In contrast, although Germans expected that Europe would become a peaceful place after the end of the Cold War, they had to face difficult questions about how to solve a series of civil conflicts after the breakup of Yugoslavia in 1990. On the one hand, Germany was surrounded by friendly nations after the fall of Berlin Wall, and has faced no direct threats to its territorial integrity. As Josef Janning and Thomas Bauer describe, after "being exposed like South Korea," with the end of the Cold War, Germany suddenly became "embedded like Kansas."[54] Consequently, traditional territorial defense in an alliance context became unlikely, and NATO's Article 5 collective security guarantee no longer seemed vital for Germany.[55] Right after the end of the Cold War, therefore, German policymakers thought that, in order to maintain peace and stability in Europe, it would be sufficient to build "cooperative security governance," consisting of interlocking and functionally diverse institutions (such as the OSCE, the EU, the Council of Europe, and other regional or subregional organizations), and NATO would be one of the integral elements of such governance.[56]

Yet a series of intractable civil wars in former Yugoslavia—especially the 1999 Kosovo War—destroyed this optimistic view. Facing the atrocities committed by the Serb forces in Kosovo, German political leaders concluded that the conflict could not be solved without using force. In particular, US military commitment was indispensable.[57] SPD-Green leaders tried to convince their party members and the public that it was necessary for Germany to take part in the NATO-led air campaign against Serbia by using the logic of "never again Auschwitz."[58] Consequently, as Detlef Puhl's study on German public opinion about Kosovo shows, throughout Operation Allied Force (OAF), polls constantly showed a clear "'yes' for participation in the NATO [air] operation." However, the same study also showed "a resounding 'no' for any operation implying the use of ground forces."[59] Likewise, Jeffrey Lantis observed that the German public was rather calm and did not oppose the government's decision to participate in the NATO-led air campaign against Serbia in March 1999. Nor did significant soul-searching debates take place in the Bundestag (parliament). By April, however, public support for OAF seemed to decline as the media began to report the scale of humanitarian tragedy in and around Kosovo and the prospect of sending ground troops to end the war seemed to grow.[60] Therefore, Chancellor Gerhard Schröder was able to obtain public support for German participation in the NATO-led air campaign, but it was politically impossible for him to send ground troops to Kosovo. Fortunately, Germany did not have to send its ground troops since Serbian president Slobodan Milosevic agreed to withdraw his troops from Kosovo in June 1999. However, as we can see, although Germany was freed from direct external threats after the fall of the Berlin Wall, Europe was unstable in the 1990s, and Germans had to agonize over the civil conflicts in former Yugoslavia.

Although German political leaders thought—both before and after the war—that the conflict in Kosovo could not be solved without US forces, their experience of participating in OAF was a strained and stressful one. Their agony during the operation seemed to stem from the fact that the traditional German foreign policy based on multilateralism no longer served its culture of reticence or its new national interests in the post–Cold War environment.[61] Under the bipolar structure of the Cold War, Germany's commitment to multilateralism reflected the importance Germans place on "never alone" and "never again."[62]

Being a member of Western institutions (such as the EC/EU and NATO), Germany tried to refrain from pursuing *Sonderweg* (special way) in order to avoid repeating its mistakes before 1945. During the Kosovo War, however, German political leaders faced the dilemma of being both a reliable ally within NATO and a *Zivilmacht* (civilian power). Germany was torn between its commitment to multilateralism (and therefore its support for the NATO-led military operation against Serbia) and its domestic culture of antimilitarism.[63]

Similarly, Germans thought that multilateral international institutions would enable Germany to pursue its national interests without raising negative reactions from other states. In particular, they believed that NATO would be a useful institutional framework through which Germany could influence powerful member states like the United States and France.[64] From their experience in the Kosovo War, however, it became increasingly clear to German political leaders that it was difficult to control the United States through NATO. To be sure, US military officers were very much frustrated by political interference from European states in their operational decisions over the selection of bombing targets during the war.[65] The US forces had to carry out the operation according to a list of bombing targets approved by European officials without a coherent plan based on systematic effects-based target analysis.[66] So the lesson that the US forces learned from OAF, according to General Michael Short, was, "coalitions aren't good ways to fight wars."[67]

Nevertheless, the US forces virtually dominated the operation against Serbia. Not only did they carry out 80 percent of all airstrike sorties, but they also selected nearly every target because they provided almost all the aerial intelligence in the operation.[68] In the later stage of operation, target selection was increasingly carried out by the United States alone, although target approval was still made by the "Quints"—the United States, Britain, France, Germany, and Italy.[69] From the American point of view, it was natural to dominate the operation because American military capabilities were far superior to those of its European allies, and the United States made the largest contribution to the operation.

Such US dominance over the operation, however, raised concerns among German political leaders and officials. As the United States was increasingly dominating the operation, Germany was becoming a blind follower of the US leadership, thereby losing its influence over the operation. Throughout OAF, German officials felt that the United States failed to consult them. Although they were kept informed by the United States about the operation, they felt that the information provided by Americans was not "full" information, and that their American counterparts did not really trust them. Because of the lack of information, the Germans were unsure about what the United States' ultimate goal in the operation was.[70] This, in turn, increased Germany's fears of future participation in US-led operations. While participating in OAF, German political leaders began to realize that the United States was not willing to constrain itself through multilateral structures, and they began to see such US behavior as an expression of its "arrogance of power."[71] In the end, the Kosovo War ended successfully with Milosevic's acceptance of NATO's settlement in June 1999. Yet this experience had a profound effect on Germany's fear of entrapment in future US-led military operations.

To make matters worse, the United States' commitment to European security affairs began to decline with the end of the Cold War, thereby increasing Germany's fear of abandonment. As many American analysts claimed, the reason that OAF was prolonged had less to do with the European allies' interference in bombing selections, and more to do with the Clinton administration's reluctance to commit ground troops to Kosovo at the beginning of the operation.[72] For the United States, Europe was no longer as strategically important as it had been during the Cold War, and therefore, the Clinton administration determined that it was not worth making a commitment of ground troops to Kosovo. From the American point of view, European affairs should be handled by Europeans themselves, with NATO shifting focus to pursue (American) global interests.[73] After the Kosovo War, therefore, European countries tried to develop the European Security and Defense Policy (ESDP) in order to decrease their dependence on the United States.[74] But this effort has proven rather feckless, as European countries are unwilling to increase defense spending and contribute more to the ESDP. As a result, they are still incapable of handling intense conflicts and continue to need the US security commitment to the region.

If Germany's fear of entrapment began to emerge during the conflict in Kosovo, it was confirmed by its involvement in NATO-led operations in Afghanistan beginning in 2001. From the start, Germany had no control over how the United States initiated the war against al-Qaeda. Despite the fact that the NATO Secretary General invoked Article 5 immediately after the attacks on the United States on September 11, 2001, the United States ignored NATO and initiated war against al-Qaeda virtually alone. Still, early on, Germany decided to send 3,900 troops to Afghanistan in order to show its pledge of solidarity with the United States,[75] and these troops later came under NATO-led International Security Assistance Forces (ISAF) in Afghanistan. Yet, as the conflict between the Taliban and NATO forces intensified in southern Afghanistan, the United States demanded Germany send troops to the south. The demand frustrated Germans who felt they had already contributed enough troops to a war that the United States started and controlled largely without consulting Germany. German leaders recognized that securing stability in Afghanistan was in their country's interest and therefore took part in the NATO-led ISAF. However, the strong discontent with the way in which the United States started and carried out the war on terrorism has continued to exist among Germans.[76]

What is more, the characteristics of both NATO and the Bundeswehr further increased Germany's fear of entrapment in US-led overseas wars, while those of the US-Japan Security Treaty and the Self Defense Forces (SDF) kept the likelihood of Japan's entrapment low. The reason that German political leaders were so concerned about the lack of consultation from the United States, whereas their Japanese counterparts have never expressed such concerns, is that NATO requires Germany much more contributions and risks than does the US-Japan Security Treaty. Under the Security Treaty, Japan is not obliged to exercise the right of collective self-defense should the United States be attacked by a third country (though the United States is expected to do so in the event of an attack on Japan). Although the 1996 US-Japan Revised Defense Guidelines expanded Japan's role in bilateral cooperation in the event of regional contingencies, its role was still limited to noncombat, rear-area functions, and the revised guidelines still do not require Japan to exercise the right of collective self-defense.[77] The lopsided nature of the Security Treaty has therefore effectively shielded Japan from the danger of entrapment in a US-led war abroad.

Moreover, Japanese political leaders have skillfully used Article 9 (the "no-war clause") of the Japanese Constitution, which prohibits Japan from exercising the right of collective self-defense, to protect Japan from being dragged to US-led overseas military affairs since the US occupation authority wrote a new constitution and introduced it to Japan in 1946. Not only does Article 9 prohibit the government from sending the SDF abroad for the purpose of use of force (*buryoku kōshi*), but it also prohibits SDF activities from being integrated into (*ittaika*) combat operations of other countries. SDF activities should be taken place in a noncombat zone, so that they will not take part in a combat operation.[78] Although Article 9 and the absence of the alliance obligation to exercise the right of collective self-defense on the part of Japan do not completely protect Japan from being dragged into US-led wars abroad, they have substantially made it easier for Japan (especially compared to the case of Germany) to make as small a concession as possible to US demand, and to withdraw their forces from overseas missions once security conditions became unfavorable, thereby lessening the likelihood of entrapment.

In contrast, all NATO member states are, in principle, supposed to exercise collective self-defense should one member state be attacked by a third country. NATO's Article 5 (the collective self-defense clause) does not, however, automatically compel the member states to take military action. Article 5 is written vaguely enough to give member states the freedom to maneuver in deciding how to enact collective defense. Nonetheless, the collective security guarantee is important for the member states for several reasons. Even after the end of the Cold War, countries neighboring Russia (countries such as Norway) still see NATO's collective security guarantee as vital for their national security.[79] Many East European countries are also seeking to become members of NATO because they wish to benefit from its collective security guarantee.[80] Even a country like Germany, which was surrounded by friendly nations after the collapse of the Soviet Union, still considers Article 5 important because of future uncertainties. For Germans, the collective security guarantee is important not only for territorial defense but also for reassurance.[81] Moreover, Article 5 has prevented potential conflicts between the member states (such as that between Turkey and Greece). As such, Article 5 has worked as an important mechanism for promoting peace and stability in the region. In sum, Article 5 is crucial for the credibility of NATO, and it is difficult for member states not to exercise collective self-defense when one of their fellow member states is attacked, even though Article 5 does not necessarily compel them to do so. For this reason, the likelihood of Germany's entrapment is high, and Germany has to be more concerned about what its American ally is going to do than does Japan.

Additionally, a more fundamental consequence of no legal constraints on Germany to exercise the right of collective self-defense is that, as oppose to the case of Japan's SDF, the German Bundeswehr can not only work closely with NATO troops but also participate in NATO's combat operations abroad. To be sure, the Bundestag (German parliament) can place limitations (caveats) on Bundeswehr activities in NATO-led overseas operations in order to avoid causalities;

however, it has become increasingly difficult for Germany to use caveats since such an action is seen as unfair by other NATO allies, and thereby destroying NATO's solidarity.

Furthermore, while the primary purpose of the US-Japan Security Treaty has remained the defense of Japan, the purpose of NATO has been transformed from territorial defense of the member states to out-of-area overseas PKOs. To be sure, the United States has used the Security Treaty to maintain its military bases in Japan, from which it has projected its forces, from East Asia to the Middle East since the Cold War period. However, regardless of how the United States has used its military bases in Japan, Japan has regarded the sole purpose of the Security Treaty as the defense of its territorial integrity. Japan's 1999 Defense Guidelines bill (*shūhen jitaihō*), along with the revisions to the SDF Law, introduced by the Japanese government as a result of the 1996 Joint Declaration, expanded the scope of SDF's support for US forces to the entire Asia-Pacific region in case of regional contingencies that impact the security of Japan. However, the Guidelines deliberately defined the term *shūhen*—the area surrounding Japan that would presumably impact Japanese security—in vague terms so that the Japan can choose not to support the United States if Japan judged that the matter would not impact its own security.[82]

Because Japan has limited the purpose of the Security Treaty to the defense of Japan, Japan has never sent the SDF overseas under the Security Treaty. Japan, for example, began to dispatch the SDF to overseas UN peacekeeping (noncombat) operations under the PKO law passed in 1992, but not under the Security Treaty. Japan also sent the SDF to the Indian Ocean in 2001 and to Iraq in 2004, not under the Security Treaty, but under the Anti-Terror Special Measures Law and the Iraq Special Measures Law, respectively, both of which were effective for only a limited time and had to receive Diet approval for their renewal. As such, Japan is able to limit its participation in overseas PKOs and can place conditions on troop deployment to prevent entrapment.

In contrast, because the purpose of NATO has been transformed from territorial defense of the member states to out-of-area PKOs since the new Strategic Concept was adopted in 1991,[83] Germany virtually has no choice but to go anywhere NATO goes in the world. Such a "global NATO," however, increases the likelihood of Germany's entrapment because, as I previously discussed, the United States tends to dominate NATO's operations, and Germany can have little or no input in the operations. In addition, although Germany can place caveats, there are virtually no legal constraints to prevent the Bundeswehr from participating in combat operations. It is hard for Germany to withdraw its forces once it sends them out to overseas missions for the sake of NATO's solidarity.

Lastly, the characteristics of Japan's and Germany's military institutions had a significant impact on the likelihood of their entrapment in US-led wars abroad. The German Bundeswehr is much more willing to deploy troops outside of the country and to participate in overseas operations than are the Japanese SDF. This is primarily a result of the Bundeswehr's long-term socialization with foreign forces since the Cold War era. The Bundeswehr has been called the "alliance army" because it was put under NATO command when it was established in 1955. During the Cold War, massive numbers of troops from various NATO countries—such as the United States, Britain, Belgium, and the Netherlands—were stationed in West Germany in order to provide a counterweight to the Warsaw Pact troops. Bundeswehr officers and servicemen had numerous formal and informal interactions with the NATO troops through a number of military activities both during and after the Cold War. As a result, they have developed a strong sense of camaraderie with their NATO counterparts.

Quite to the contrary, since its founding in 1954, the SDF's interactions with foreign troops have been limited almost exclusively to interactions with US forces. Yet even the SDF's relations with US forces have been more limited than those of the Bundeswehr, as Article 9 of the constitution (which again prohibits Japan from exercising the right of collective self-defense) places restrictions on the SDF's activities with the United States. There are, however, differences among the three SDF forces—Air, Ground, and Maritime—regarding the regularity and character of their interactions with their US counterparts. While the MSDF has strong ties with the US Navy because it has been incorporated into the strategic structure of the US Seventh Fleet (the relationship between the two actually closely resembles that of NATO allies), the Ground Self-Defense Force (GSDF) has been quite distant from the US Army since it was established in the early 1950s. And the nature of the relationship between the ASDF and the US Air Force rests somewhere in between.

The GSDF's distant relationship with the US Army and the lack of camaraderie, in particular, is strikingly different from the case of the German Army. The difference between the GSDF and the German Army has important implications for the two countries' actual contributions to US-led overseas operations. To be sure, both Germany and Japan are democratic countries, and both militaries are under civilian control. Nevertheless, the attitudes and policy preferences of military officers—shaped by long-term socialization processes with their ally/allies—play an important role in military policymaking and implementation. German Army officers are willing to work with their NATO allies and do not hesitate to take risks in overseas operations, whereas GSDF officers tend to be reluctant to work with foreign troops (including the US Army) and are very conservative about the risk of casualties.[84] For example, right after 9/11 German Army officers were willing to send their troops to Afghanistan in order help their US counterparts, whereas GSDF officers were reluctant to send troops to Afghanistan. The GSDF in fact rejected LDP politicians' proposals to send troops to Afghanistan and Pakistan twice.[85] The German Army, therefore, is much more willing to participate in multilateral overseas PKOs, even to fight in combat operations, than is the GSDF. This difference is so important because ground operations tend to produce more casualties than air or maritime operations, thereby increasing the likelihood of the two countries' entrapment.

In sum, Japan supported the US war on Iraq, whereas the FRG opposed it, because Japan's fear of entrapment in the war was lower than that of the FRG during the critical period of 2001–2003. This was true for three reasons. First, while Europe witnessed a series of civil wars in former Yugoslavia, there were no military conflicts in East Asia in the 1990s. Consequently, Japan did not have any negative experiences working with the United States in an actual military operation, whereas Germany did. Second, Japan's alliance obligation was much lower than that of Germany because Japan does not have to exercise the right of collective self-defense under the US-Japan Security Treaty; plus, the purpose of the Security Treaty has remained primarily the defense of Japan. Finally, the German Bundeswehr was more ready to participate in multilateral overseas operations (including combat operations) than the SDF because of its long-term socialization with NATO allies. In particular, the difference between the German Army and the GSDF is significant because ground operations entail high risks of casualties, and thereby increase the likelihood of entrapment.

III. Methods and Hypotheses

This study is based on the "most similar nations" design,[86] in which researchers choose two cases that appear to be very similar but experience different outcomes. By choosing two similar nations, researchers can "exclude certain types of explanations or certain confounding variables categorically."[87] As with Germany, other advanced industrialized democratic countries—such as France and Norway—opposed the US invasion of Iraq. However, those countries were excluded from this study because they do not share the similar historical background with Japan. To be sure, Germany is different from Japan in many aspects. For example, the war did not really end for Germany after 1945 because it was divided into West and East and was the most likely battlefield during the Cold War. Japan remained undivided and was also the greatest beneficiary of US protection during the Cold War. (See chapter 3 for detailed discussions about the two countries during the Cold War.) Yet Germany is the most similar to Japan among other industrialized democracies in the sense that both countries experienced hypernationalism and militarism in the 1930s, invaded their neighboring countries, and started the world war that ultimately led to their own devastation. As a result of this historical experience, both Germany and Japan have developed cultures of antimilitarism and been skeptical about the efficacy of use of force to solve international conflicts. In addition, the two countries are similar in terms of the size of their economies, exercising similar degrees of economic influence over other nations, as well as international institutions.

Although the aim of this study is to explain why Germany and Japan pursued different policies toward the US invasion of Iraq in 2003, it does not intend to present exact explanatory variables for the specific decision-making processes of the two countries' leaders. I point to the three factors that increase or decrease the likelihood of the two countries' entrapment in US-led overseas wars in order to explain their different responses to the US invasion of Iraq. The influence of the three factors is rather comprehensive and may not be directly related to the decision making of the two countries' leaders with regard to the US invasion of Iraq. Prime Minister Koizumi Jun'ichiro, for example, may not have thought over each of the three factors per se when he decided to support the US attack on Iraq in March 2003. Still, I argue, these three factors provided the overall background when he assessed his support for the United States might endanger Japanese troops and find the country entrapped in the US war.

On the path to reaching the conclusions just introduced, I first set up hypotheses based on possible explanatory variables for the two countries' responses to the US invasion of Iraq. I conducted

Table 1.2 List of Interviews in Germany

Political Parties	Social Democratic Party (SPD)	8
	Christian Democratic Union (CDU)	3
	Christian Social Union (CSU)	2
	Free Democratic Party (FDP)	3
	Leftist Party (Die Linke)	2
Federal Ministries	Foreign Office	5
	Bundeswehr (German Armed Forces)	2
	Navy	2
	Air force	2
	Army	3
	Ministry of Economics and Technology	1
Others	Association of German Chambers, Commerce and Industry	1
	American Jewish Committee, Berlin Office	1
	TOTAL	**35**

my research keeping these variables and hypotheses in mind, but I also kept my eyes open to other unidentified variables throughout the course of my research. For my research, I employed the process-tracing method—one of the qualitative case studies methods. With this method, I tried to identify causal relationships by tracing step-by-step the events that provide links between possible causes based on hypotheses and observed outcomes.[88] This method allowed me to test hypothesized explanatory variables for state behavior, as well as to search for other, potential, yet still unidentified explanatory variables. The method of process tracing requires the intricate description of complex phenomena and thereby creates the risk that the researcher will get buried in the details of the case and will fail to make a valid theoretical contribution. This risk, however, is minimized by developing hypotheses, prior to beginning process tracing itself, that allow the researcher to look for specific evidence that tests major theoretical propositions in a broader field.

I used both primary and secondary sources to carry out this project. Given that the project covers recent events, the primary source materials include an extensive examination of newspaper accounts, surveys of public opinion, the public speeches of key political actors, and parliamentary records. I also conducted interviews with key political actors in both countries in order to fill the gaps in the written record and establish direct links between my hypotheses and state behavior (tables 1.2 and 1.3).

Table 1.3 List of Interviews in Japan

Political Parties	Liberal Democratic Party (LDP)	4
	Democratic Party of Japan (DPJ)	5
	Japan Communist Party (JCP)	1
Ministries	Ministry of Foreign Affairs (MOFA)	7
	Ministry of Defense/Defense Agency (civilian officials)	2
	Self-Defense Forces (uniformed officers)	
	Maritime	4
	Air	4
	Ground	5
	Ministry of Finance	1
	Ministry of Economy, Technology, and Industry (METI)	6
	Cabinet Legislation Bureau	1
Others	Energy Researcher	1
	Defense Expert	2
	TOTAL	**37**

The possible explanatory variables and hypotheses are as follows.

1. Realism

(a) *Presence of External Threats*: Japan needed (or would need in the future) US help to cope with external threats more than did the FRG.
(b) *Dependence on the US Market*: Japan's economy was more dependent on the US market than was the economy of the FRG.
(c) *Dependence on the Middle Eastern Oil*: Japan was more dependent on Middle Eastern oil than was the FRG.

These hypotheses test the neorealist theory of state behavior. Neorealists contend that states act in the international system to ensure both their present and future security. For that purpose, states strive to maximize their power and to prevent others from increasing their capabilities in a way that might alter the balance of international power in an unfavorable way.[89] There are three security concerns that might explain the differences between the foreign policies of Japan and Germany during the Iraq crisis. One security concern is the likelihood that each country might require US support to cope with external threats in the near future. According to this hypothesis, Japan supported the Iraq War because it needed (or would need) US help to cope with external threats, whereas the FRG did not because it did not have such threats. The second and third security concerns would be the two countries' relative degrees of dependence on the US market as well as on Middle Eastern oil, and the anticipated negative reaction of the United States and the oil-producing states to the two countries' policies toward the US-led attack on Iraq. According to the second hypothesis, Japan supported the US decision to attack Iraq, whereas Germany did not, because the Japanese economy was much more dependent on the US market than was the German economy. Regarding the third hypothesis, Japan could go to either direction. Japan might hesitate to support the US decision to attack Iraq for the possible negative reaction from the oil-producing countries in the Middle East. Or, Japan might support the US attack on Iraq because the United States is the country that has maintained security and stability in the Persian Gulf region.

2. Domestic Institutions

(a) *Formal Institutions*: Article 9 of the Japanese Constitution prohibits Japan from exercising the right of collective self-defense; whereas the FRG does not have such a law.
(b) *Bureaucratic Politics*: The notion that Japan should always closely follow US leadership is a long-established institutional norm within Japan's Ministry of Foreign Affairs (MOFA); whereas the German Federal Foreign Office lacks such a norm.
(c) *Partisan Differences*: The parties controlling the German government during the Iraq crisis were the progressive SPD and the Greens; whereas those controlling the Japanese government were the conservative LDP and its small coalition partner, the Kōmeito.

Many studies have argued that domestic decision-making processes may outweigh external security concerns in shaping foreign policy. Domestic determinants of foreign policy include formal and informal institutions, while key policy actors include governmental and non-governmental organizations. Policymaking occurs within an institutional framework of long-standing laws and policies. With regard to the Japanese case, formal institutions are those such as Article 9 (renunciation of war) of the postwar peace constitution. Informal institutions include the policy to keep defense spending under one percent of GNP; the so-called Yoshida Doctrine that Japan should concentrate on economic activities, rely on the United States for its national territorial defense, and avoid participating in international strategic affairs; and the "three non-nuclear principles," which prescribe that Japan will not produce, use, or introduce nuclear weapons. None of these policies are the subject of formal law, but they have significantly constrained the government's behavior.

Much research on policymaking processes has focused on governmental organizations, such as bureaucratic agencies and political parties. Following Graham Allison, who stresses the impact of bureaucratic politics on foreign policymaking, William Grimes argues that the explanation for Japan's foreign policy lies in the "institutionalized inertia" of its domestic political actors.[90] Recent studies of Japan's MOFA have elaborated upon this point. Yakushiji Katsuyuki of Asahi Shinbun, for example, suggests that the MOFA is unable to change its policy orientation institutionalized over time since the early 1950s, which is to blindly follow US leadership, even though the international environment changed substantially after the end of the Cold War.[91]

Some scholars have also argued that the type of parties controlling the government—the Left or the Right—is the most important explanatory variable for foreign policy outcomes. Brian C. Rathbun, for example, contends that if the conservative Christian Democratic Union (CDU) and the Christian Social Union (CSU) had won the September 2002 German Bundestag (parliamentary) election and controlled the government, the CDU/CSU government would have supported the US action and might even have participated in the Iraq War.[92]

3. Liberalism

Timing of Election: There was a parliamentary election in the summer of 2002 in the FRG, whereas there was no parliamentary election in Japan in 2002.

The liberal school of thinkers in international relations contends that a commitment to democratic institutions changes the preferences and actions of states operating in the anarchical international system. The liberal theory of democratic peace asserts that democratic states are more reluctant than nondemocratic states to go to war, especially against each other. Oneal and Russett, for example, argue that democratic states are less inclined to make war because the domestic political costs associated with the use of force are much higher in democracies than in nondemocracies.[93] Likewise, Immanuel Kant writes that citizens in democratic states can influence governmental policy through public opinion and their representatives.[94] Elections are obviously an important mechanism that forces a government to consider the will of the people. Political leaders in democracies, therefore, often experience high political costs from fighting wars, and because of these domestic costs of war, leaders in democracies tend to refrain from using force to solve international conflicts. According to this logic, Germany opposed the US attack on Iraq because there was a parliamentary election in September 2002 (before the US attack on Iraq in March 2003), in which candidates had to consider the "will of the people" regarding the possible US attack on Iraq; whereas Japan did not oppose the US decision to attack Iraq because there was no national election in 2002.

4. Constructivism

Differences between the Two Countries' Antimilitarist Cultures: There might have been differences between the two countries in terms of the ideas and principles of their political-military cultures.

The Constructivists focus on the impact of cultural norms on a state's definition of its security interests and the determination of its policies.[95] Thomas Berger and Peter Katzenstein, for example, claim that the German and Japanese reluctance to become actively involved in international military affairs since the end of World War II has stemmed from their domestic cultures of antimilitarism. In their view, the domestic political culture, not the international balance of power, has shaped the two states' security policies.[96] Thomas Berger defines political-military culture as the "subset of the larger historical-political culture that encompasses orientations related to defense, security, the military as an institution, and the use of force in international affairs."[97] It influences a nation's defense and security policy by: (1) supplying the fundamental goals and norms of political actors, (2) determining how political actors perceive the existing domestic political environment, (3) influencing actors' assessment of the international situations, and (4) strongly conditioning actors' ability to mobilize national resources for military purposes. Thus, while the structural realists assume that the national interests of all states are fundamentally similar, Berger argues that national interests are constructs "emerging out of contingent historical, social, and rational processes that can vary considerably across different states at different points in time."[98]

Although Berger discusses the cultures of antimilitarism in the FRG and Japan, he also points out the differences between the characteristics of the two countries' political-military culture. He explains that the differences in the two countries' cultures of antimilitarism stem from the differences in "the conditions under which the two countries surrendered; the way in which denazification and issues of war guilt were handled; and the process through which their new political institutions were established."[99] He thus acknowledges the significant role of history and political institutions in forming the different political cultures in the respective countries. Accordingly, the differences in the two countries' political cultures might have led to the two countries' different responses to the Iraq War.

IV. Procedures

The book proceeds as follows. In chapter 2, I provide a basic account of events from September 2001 to the end of December 2003. Chapters 3 through 5 present detailed analyses of the three explanatory variables discussed above. The regional security environment in Europe and East Asia is addressed in chapter 3. Chapter 4 examines the differences in alliance institutions (NATO versus the US-Japan Security Treaty), and chapter 5 discusses the characteristics of the two countries' military institutions (Japanese SDF versus German Bundeswehr). In chapter 6, I carefully examine the hypotheses listed above and highlight the theoretical and empirical contributions of my research in relation to the other possible explanations. Chapter 7 offers concluding remarks.

2

Background

In this chapter, I will describe the backgrounds of the Federal Republic of Germany (FRG) and Japan and their responses to 9/11 and the Iraq War in order to enable readers to follow the discussion in subsequent chapters.

I. The FRG and Japan, 1945–2000

The total defeat of Nazi Germany and Imperial Japan in World War II brought about enormous material and psychological damages to both countries. The major cities of the two countries were reduced to rubble as a result of the Allied bombings during the war. Although Japan was attacked with two atomic bombs, the number of German casualties was in fact much higher than that of Japan. Six and a half million Germans (including civilians) died, while three million Japanese died during the war.[1] Moreover, Germany was divided into the Federal Republic of Germany (FRG: West Germany) and the German Democratic Republic (GDR: East Germany) after the war, while Japan was kept almost intact (the Soviet Union took the northern islands). As a result of these historical pasts, both Japan and the FRG have been reserved in using military force in order to solve international conflicts since 1945. Instead, they have used their energy for attaining economic prosperity and welfare and have continued to maintain the position of the second (Japan) and third (the FRG) largest economies in the world (as of year 2000),[2] even though both of them suffered from serious economic recessions in the 1990s.

Although the two countries shunned getting involved in overseas military strategic affairs throughout the Cold War period, the end of the Cold War and the Persian Gulf War of 1990–1991 brought changes to the two countries' reticent policies concerning overseas dispatch of troops. During the Persian Gulf War, the two countries made huge financial contributions to the US-led Allied forces;

however, they did not send any troops to the Gulf (though the FRG sent its air force to Turkey to protect it from Iraq's attack, and Japan sent mine sweepers to the Persian Gulf after the war ended). Lacking consensus among both politicians and the public more broadly, neither country was ready in the early 1990s to contribute troops.

Throughout the Cold War period (1945–1989), FRG leaders determined that it was unconstitutional to dispatch the Bundeswehr (German armed forces) outside the NATO arena. In addition to the question of constitutionality, they rejected the possibility of sending the Bundeswehr outside of NATO territory for two practical reasons. First, German political leaders were concerned that the dispatch of German troops would generate negative reactions, not only among its Western allies, but also among the Warsaw pact countries because they still possessed a high degree of resentment and mistrust toward Germany as a result of the atrocities it committed during the war. Hence dispatching its troops outside of the NATO arena would only make it more difficult for the FRG to attain its primary foreign policy goal: to unite divided Germany. Second, the threat from the Soviet Union was so imminent that FRG leaders were concerned that any Bundeswehr dispatch outside of NATO territory would weaken the FRG's defense against a Soviet invasion.[3]

Similarly, for decades, Japanese political leaders determined that Article 9 (the no-war clause) of the Japanese Constitution prohibited Japan from dispatching its Self-Defense Forces (SDF) overseas, even under UN-authorized peacekeeping operations. They used Article 9 to dodge the American demand of rearmament and to keep Japan out of US-led regional wars, such as the Korean War and the Vietnam War. This strategy enabled Japanese political leaders to concentrate national resources on economic recovery and assure the public at home and in other Asian countries that there would be no resurgence of Japanese militarism.

After the Gulf War, however, the two countries' political leaders realized that their reticent foreign policies were no longer acceptable to their allies and that they had to make their countries "normal nations" that were willing to make both financial and "human" contributions to peacekeeping operations around the world. They resolved, in short, to transform their countries from security consumers to security producers. The Gulf War was an especially "traumatic" experience for Japanese political leaders, since neither the United States nor Kuwait expressed any thanks to Japan, despite the enormous amount of money (13 billion US dollars) it contributed to the Allied war efforts.[4] (The FRG contributed 11.5 billion US dollars.) While the FRG could justify not sending its troops to the Gulf by stressing its preoccupation with the unification process following the breakdown of the Berlin Wall in November 1989, Japan had no room to excuse itself in light of its tremendous economic success in the late 1980s. Thus, in 1992 Japan passed the UN Peacekeeping Operations Cooperation Bill (PKO Bill), which ended the ban on dispatching SDF troops abroad. Then in 1994, the FRG Constitutional Court ruled that it was constitutional for the government to dispatch the Bundeswehr outside of NATO territory with a UN or NATO mandate, so long as it secured a majority of support in the German Bundestag (parliament).

Although both the FRG and Japan have gradually expanded the scope of their activities in overseas PKOs since the early 1990s, their experiences with overseas activities have been very different. While the FRG made great commitments to operations to stop the civil wars in former Yugoslavia, Japan's participation in overseas PKOs has remained modest. In 1996, the FRG government—then controlled by the conservative Christian Democratic Union (CDU) and Christian Social Union (CSU) with their small coalition partner, the Free Democratic Party (FDP)—sent some 3,000 ground troops (including combat troops) to the Stabilization Force in Bosnia-Herzegovina (SFOR), and after defeating the CDU/CSU–FDP in the Bundestag elections of September 1998, the new Social Democratic Party (SPD)/Green Party government coalition committed even more German troops. In the 1999 Kosovo War, both German Air Force Tornadoes and hundreds of Bundeswehr support troops actively participated in NATO's Operation Allied Force. Approximately 8,000 Bundeswehr troops served in the NATO-led Kosovo Force (KFOR).[5]

In contrast, Japan's SDF has never participated in combat operations abroad. Although the SDF has been dispatched to approximately 20 different countries in Africa, the Middle East, and Southeast Asia, most of their activities have been limited to transportation services and disaster relief. Moreover, while 41 Bundeswehr soldiers died in both combat and noncombat operations overseas between 1993 and 2004,[6] no SDF personnel have died in overseas PKOs to date. As such, while both the FRG and Japan changed their cautious policies and gradually expanded their overseas activities following the 1990–1991 Gulf War, the nature of their involvement in overseas peacekeeping and enforcement activities has been quite different.

II. The FRG and Japan, 2001–2004

1. 9/11 and US Attack on Afghanistan (Fall 2001)

On September 11, 2001, German chancellor Gerhard Schröder was stunned by the terrorist attacks in the United States. He wrote in his memoirs:

> I turned on the television. The images that I saw deeply upset me... I remember seeing desperate people jumping out of the windows of the Twin Towers. I remember people who were running for their lives on the streets, and I remember my own tears, cried out of sympathy for those innocent people who were exposed to the inferno. Helplessness and rage at those who did this were my first reactions.[7]

At 5 p.m. on the same day, Chancellor Schröder quickly declared the "unlimited solidarity" of his government with the United States and supported the invocation of Article 5 (the collective self-defense clause of the NATO treaty) by NATO secretary general George Robertson. Moreover, he risked his chancellorship by linking a vote of confidence to the parliamentary ratification of the Bundeswehr's participation in Operation Enduring Freedom (OEF) in Afghanistan on November 16, 2001, leaving no choice for all the Bundestag members of his SPD and coalition partner Greens but to vote for the dispatch of Bundeswehr troops to Afghanistan.

Interestingly, Japanese prime minister Jun'ichiro Koizumi's initial reaction to the 9/11 terrorist attacks was not emotional at all. Koizumi first heard of the terrorist attacks around 10 p.m. on 9/11 (Tokyo is 13 hours ahead of US Eastern/Standard Time), when he came back to his prime minister's residence after having dinner outside. When asked by a group of reporters about his reaction to the terrorist attack in the United States, he made only a short remark: "It's scary, because it's unpredictable."[8] More than 12 hours had passed since the terrorist attacks when he finally made an official statement to express his condolences and support for the United States in the next morning at 10 a.m. After Koizumi and other leading officials in the Cabinet Secretariat realized the seriousness of the attacks on the United States, they quickly gathered information from other ministries (mainly from the Ministry of Foreign Affairs [MOFA] and the Maritime Self-Defense Force [MSDF]) and announced a support plan on September 19, 2001. They also drafted the Anti-Terrorism Special Measures Law (ATSML), which authorized the dispatch of MSDF ships to the Indian Ocean to support OEF, and passed that bill in parliament on October 29, 2001. It is important to note, however, that the level of Japan's involvement in OEF was much less than that of the FRG. While the FRG began to send its ground troops to Afghanistan in late December 2001 and further increased its commitment under the NATO-led International Security Assistance Forces (ISAF) (Germany's number of troops in Afghanistan has increased from 3,000 to approximately 4,200 since 2001 [as of October 2009]),[9] Japan has not sent any ground troops, limiting its contribution to fuel support supplied by the MSDF in the Indian Ocean.[10]

Although Chancellor Schröder and Prime Minister Koizumi both expressed their support for the United States after 9/11—and for its subsequent military attack on Afghanistan—public opinion in the two countries revealed skepticism about the ability of the US military strikes to solve the problem of terrorism, as well as misgivings about their countries' involvement in the operations in Afghanistan. According to a poll taken in October 2001, 44 percent of German respondents felt that Schröder's expression of "unlimited solidarity" with the United States was proper, whereas 47 percent answered that he should have been more careful about his statement.[11] A poll taken on September 12, 2001, also revealed that 47 percent of the respondents believed it appropriate for SPD parliamentary leader Peter Struck to say, "Now we are all American," right after 9/11; 42 percent disagreed.[12] Moreover, according to a poll taken by Institute für Demoskopie (IfD) in November and December 2001, 69 percent of Germans believed either that Germany should avoid getting involved if at all possible or that Germany should not take part in the US-led military operations in Afghanistan at all. Only 23 percent responded that Germany should take part without placing any conditions on its participation.[13]

Likewise, a poll taken by the progressive newspaper *Asahi Shinbun* on September 28–29, 2001, revealed that 46 percent of the respondents opposed Prime Minister Koizumi's decision to establish a new bill authorizing a SDF dispatch to support US forces, while 42 percent supported the decision. Another poll taken by *Asahi Shinbun* on October 13–14, 2001, found that 46 percent of respondents would support the U.S. attack on Afghanistan, while 43 percent would not. In the same poll, 36 percent of respondents felt that the U.S. military strike on Afghanistan would be "effective" in countering terrorism; 49 percent believed that it would not be effective. Similarly, a poll taken by the conservative newspaper *Yomiuri Shinbun* on November 2–5, 2001, found that 33.3 percent of respondents felt that the US military operation in Afghanistan would "not be very effective" in countering international terrorism, and 24.1 percent felt it would "not be effective at all"; only 9.5 percent responded that it would "be very effective," and 21.1 percent chose "somewhat effective." As we can see then, there was already a substantial gap between the stance taken by the two countries' political leaders and the attitude of their respective publics toward the US military strike on Afghanistan, as well as their countries' possible involvement in the US-led war on terrorism in fall 2001.

2. The Iraq Crisis (2002–2003)

Political leaders around the world began to realize the likelihood of a US attack on Iraq when President George W. Bush gave his State of the Union address in January 2002, in which he denounced Iraq, Iran, and North Korea as the "axis of evil." President G.W. Bush stated:

> Our second goal is to prevent regimes that sponsor terror from threatening America or our friends and allies with weapons of mass destruction. Some of these regimes have been pretty quiet since September the 11th, but we know their true nature.
>
> North Korea is a regime arming with missiles and weapons of mass destruction, while starving its citizens.
>
> Iran aggressively pursues these weapons and exports terror, while an unelected few repress the Iranian people's hope for freedom.
>
> Iraq continues to flaunt its hostility toward America and to support terror. The Iraqi regime has plotted to develop anthrax and nerve gas and nuclear weapons for over a decade. This is a regime that has already used poison gas to murder thousands of its own citizens, leaving the bodies of mothers huddled over their dead children. This is a regime that agreed to international inspections, then kicked out the inspectors. This is a regime that has something to hide from the civilized world.
>
> States like these and their terrorist allies constitute an axis of evil, arming to threaten the peace of the world. By seeking weapons of mass destruction, these regimes pose a grave and growing danger. They could provide these arms to terrorists, giving them the means to match their hatred. They could attack our allies or attempt to blackmail the United States. In any of these cases, the price of indifference would be catastrophic...
>
> The last time I spoke here, I expressed the hope that life would return to normal. In some ways, it has. In others, it never will. Those of us

who have lived through these challenging times have been changed by them. We've come to know truths that we will never question: Evil is real, and it must be opposed. Beyond all differences of race or creed, we are one country, mourning together and facing danger together. Deep in the American character, there is honor, and it is stronger than cynicism. And many have discovered again that even in tragedy—especially in tragedy—God is near.[14]

Although the French and Germans genuinely felt sympathy for the Americans after 9/11, they thought that attacking Iraq was not a good idea. Philipp H. Gordon and Jeremy Shapiro provide an excellent summary of the reasons for this skepticism. To begin, European leaders thought that it would be extremely difficult to maintain stability in Iraq after an invasion because of the country's ethnic divisions, a resentful Shiite majority, artificial borders, and unequally allocated natural resources. They feared that instability created by a US invasion would spill over to the entire Middle East, which would be worse than the current dictatorship of Saddam Hussein. Second, the Europeans did not see any link between Saddam Hussein and al-Qaeda. They were concerned that a US military invasion in Iraq would actually provide an opportunity for al-Qaeda to recruit young Muslims with anti-American (or anti-Western) sentiment and thereby create, in French president Jacque Chirac's words, "a large number of little bin Ladens." Third, Europeans differed fundamentally from the Americans in their views on the best way to address Saddam Hussein, as well as the threat of terrorism in general. While US policymakers sought regime change in Iraq and a complete eradication of terrorism, Europeans did not think that such goals were realistic. Whereas the United States had, until 9/11, been relatively insulated from international terrorism, Europe had experienced and lived with terrorism for decades. From their long-term experience with terrorism, they concluded that it was impossible to completely eradicate the phenomenon. Instead, they felt, containment was the best strategy.[15]

A dramatic break occurred between Germany and the United States when Chancellor Schröder stated in an election campaign speech on August 5, 2002, that he would not provide any troops or money for a US attack on Iraq. Several months earlier, in May 2002, Schröder met US president George W. Bush in Berlin, where (according to Schröder's account) Bush told Schröder that he had no war plan on his desk and that he would consult Germany on the decision to go to war. (According to US officials' accounts, Schröder told Bush that he would not make opposition to the invasion of Iraq part of his election campaign.) However, in the face of the growing Washington debate over Iraq in summer 2002, Schröder felt that he had been betrayed by Bush, and Vice President Dick Cheney's speech at the Veterans of Foreign Wars in Nashville, Tennessee, on August 26, 2002, seemed to validate this sense of betrayal. Cheney stated:

> As we face this prospect, old doctrines of security do not apply. In the days of the Cold War, we were able to manage the threat with strategies of deterrence and containment. But it's a lot tougher to deter enemies who have no country to defend. And containment is not possible when dictators obtain weapons of mass destruction, and are prepared to share them with terrorists who intend to inflict catastrophic casualties on the United States.
>
> Simply stated, there is no doubt that Saddam Hussein now has weapons of mass destruction. There is no doubt he is amassing them to use against our friends, against our allies, and against us. And there is no doubt that his aggressive regional ambitions will lead him into future confrontations with his neighbors—confrontations that will involve both the weapons he has today, and the ones he will continue to develop with his oil wealth.
>
> In other times the world saw how the United States defeated fierce enemies, then helped rebuild their countries, forming strong bonds between our peoples and our governments. Today in Afghanistan, the world is seeing that America acts not to conquer but to liberate, and remains in friendship to help the people build a future of stability, self-determination, and peace.
>
> We would act in that same spirit after a regime change in Iraq. With our help, a liberated Iraq can be a great nation once again.[16]

Not only did Cheney stress that Saddam Hussein had weapons of mass destruction and would use them against the United States and its allies, but he also rejected a strategy of containment to deal with the Iraq problem and emphasized the importance of regime change in Iraq. From the German chancellor's point of view, Cheney's speech was proof that Bush had broken his promise to consult with Schröder (although from Bush's point of view, Schröder was a "liar" who broke his promise not to make Iraq an issue during the election campaign).[17] In the end, Schröder's campaign pledge not to send any troops to Iraq should the United States decide to invade appealed to German voters and shifted their attention from economic issues to Iraq, ultimately ensuring the victory of the SPD.[18]

After the SPD's victory over the conservative, pro-US CDU and the CSU in September 2002 Bundestag elections, however, France took Germany's place as the most critical opponent to the Iraq invasion. As a member of the UN Security Council (UNSC), France held the right to veto any proposals for military action that the United States brought before the UNSC. Moreover, once its bilateral relations with the United States became strained, Germany was no longer able to play its traditional role as a mediator between the United States and France and had no choice but to rely on France.

A fight started within the UNSC between the United States and France over what to do with Iraq in September 2002 and lasted for eight weeks. France, backed by Russia and China, fought the United Sates over how to draft (what would become) UN Resolution 1441 on Iraq. The United States essentially wanted to craft a new resolution that would authorize the United States to automatically launch an attack on Iraq should Iraq fall anywhere short of full compliance with UN weapons inspections. France, on the other hand, tried to eliminate the possibility of automatic triggers for military action and to keep control over any decision to act in the hands of the Security Council. Resolution 1441 was finally passed by the UN in November. However, it was written in such a way that both sides could interpret it to suit their own ends. The Americans determined that the resolution allowed the United States to automatically use force against Iraq in the event of noncompliance, whereas the French determined that in the case of Iraq's noncompliance, the Security Council as a whole would make a final decision concerning military force. Such a decision would require a second resolution, France believed, while the Unites States held firm in its stance that Resolution 1441 was all that was needed to authorize an attack on Iraq.[19]

In the months that followed, the fight between the two camps—the United States and Britain versus France, backed by Russia—over the second resolution became intense. The United States' leaders, who ultimately agreed to seek a second resolution, fiercely competed with France's leaders to win votes from the so-called undecided six—Angola, Cameroon, Chile, Guinea, Pakistan, and Mexico—among the nonpermanent members of the Security Council. In the end, French president Jacques Chirac shut down this competition with the decisive statement, made on March 10, 2003, that France would veto any new ultimatum to Iraq "whatever the circumstances, because France believes this evening that there is no reason to make war to reach the objective we have given ourselves, the disarmament of Iraq."[20] Thus, the United States gave up pursuing a second UN resolution and went to war against Iraq unilaterally on March 20, 2003.[21]

* * *

Although Japanese political leaders consistently advised their American counterparts to act within the UN framework throughout the Iraq crisis of 2002–2003, their attitude toward the United States over the Iraq issue was never confrontational. Their advice regarding Iraq remained just that—advice—and they never attempted to work with France or Germany to push this policy preference. Furthermore, as 2003 drew near, Japanese leaders helped the United States win votes from the "undecided six." And when the United States eventually decided to attack Iraq without a second resolution in March 2003, Japanese political leaders lined up in support of the US decision.

According to accounts in the *Asahi Shinbun* newspaper, Japanese political leaders first became concerned about a possible US military attack on Iraq in December 2001. In his conversation with Defense Secretary Donald Rumsfeld in the Pentagon on December 10, 2001, Defense Agency director general Nakatani Gen stated that, in the event that the United States decided to expand its military operations beyond Afghanistan to a certain country (that is Iraq), Japan could support US forces if: (1) there was a causal relationship between the 9/11 terrorist attacks and the country, (2) other countries also cooperated in the military operation, and (3) the military operation was in accord with the UN Charter. Nakatani wanted to prevent the SDF from being used by the United States for an unlimited military operation abroad, and therefore tried to make the conditions under which Japan could support US forces clear to Secretary Rumsfeld.[22]

Officials of the MOFA also began to consider how Japan should respond if the United States decided to use force against Iraq in December 2001. If the United States decided to attack Iraq on the grounds that Iraq is one among several terrorist nations, Japan would not "support" but would "understand" the US decision. If the United States decided to attack Iraq because Iraq refused UN weapons inspections, however, Japan would be likely to support the US decision.[23] At the earliest stage, MOFA officials already regarded the UN as a key variable in Japan's policy regarding the Iraq invasion, and they continued to publicly express their desire that the United States would act within the UN framework from then forward.

On August 2002, for example, Vice Minister for Foreign Affairs Takeuchi Yukio told US assistant secretary of state Richard Armitage,

"We don't want American unilateralism, although American leadership in the international society is necessary."[24] He proposed "three basic principles" to Armitage: (1) The United States should make efforts to pursue diplomatic solutions to the Iraq problem as much as it can. (2) The United States should frame the Iraq problem not as "the US vs. Iraq" but as "the international society vs. Iraq," and, as such, the United States should bring the problem of weapons of mass destruction (WMD) to the UN Security Council and solve that problem with the international society. (3) If Saddam Hussein's regime collapsed as a result of the US attack, the Middle East might become unstable. Thus, the United States should consider a blue print to construct a democratic regime in postwar Iraq.[25]

In the Upper House session on September 26, 2002, the director general of the North American Affairs Bureau, Ebihara Shin, also stated, "If the United States attacks Iraq, it is reasonable that it will act according to international law."[26] Even as the Bush administration became increasingly impatient with the progress in UN weapons inspections at the end of 2002, MOFA officials continued to tell their American counterparts that nothing good would come of a US decision to attack Iraq without a new UN resolution. Such a decision would not only put the United States, Britain, and Japan in a difficult position, but would also make postwar reconstruction of Iraq difficult. On February 10, 2003, Takeuchi again told Armitage, "In the event that a US attack on Iraq is imminent, a new UN resolution is desirable. A picture of the international society vs. Iraq is very important."[27]

Unlike the French or Germans, however, MOFA officials did not fundamentally oppose a US attack on Iraq. They knew that there was nothing to prevent the Americans from pursuing whatever action they wanted to take. MOFA officials also knew that whatever action the United States did take, they would support the United States. However, in order to support a US action, they needed legal justification to do so. Thus, MOFA officials wanted the United States to work within the UN framework and pursue a second resolution. For this reason, Foreign Minister Kawaguchi Yoriko approached the "undecided six" among the UNSC nonpermanent members and tried to convince them to vote for the second resolution.[28]

Likewise, Prime Minister Koizumi Jun'ichiro tried to persuade US president George W. Bush to be cautious about unilaterally launching a war against Iraq. However, his attempts to persuade Bush were somewhat indirect. In his meeting with Bush in February 2002, Koizumi told the US president, "Power without cause is 'violence.'

Cause without power is 'impotent.' The United States has both power and cause now. That's why the United States should pursue international cooperation [to deal with Iraq]."[29] Similarly, in the September 2002 meeting, Koizumi told Bush, "There is a champion called 'Yokozuna' in Japan's sumo wrestling. Yokozuna never starts fighting from his side. He starts fighting when the other side starts. The United States should be like Yokozuna."[30] Using these indirect statements, Koizumi tried to convince Bush to refrain from taking unilateral action against Iraq.

Overall, however, Koizumi tried to avoid confrontation with Bush. Contrary to his European counterparts, who became seriously uneasy about the negative impacts of a US attack on Iraq after Bush's "axis of evil" statement, Koizumi's attitude toward Bush was very supportive. Even when Bush came to Japan in February 2002, right after his State of the Union address, Koizumi optimistically said to Bush, "Japan's role is important in eradicating terrorism, and we will continue to support the United States."[31] Koizumi expressed his support for Bush, because his position in his Liberal Democratic Party (LDP) was weak. He was facing difficulties pulling Japan out of its long-term economic recession at that time, and he needed Bush in order to boost his leadership. High-ranking US officials—as well as the Japanese public—were expressing their irritation over Koizumi's inability to implement economic reforms. In exchange for his support for Bush, Koizumi succeeded in drawing strong support from Bush for his plan to combat deflation and speed up structural reform, and Bush agreed not to put pressure on Koizumi over economic issues at their summit meeting.[32]

Throughout the Iraq crisis of 2002–2003, Koizumi dodged questions from the opposition parties about what he would do if the United States decided to pursue a unilateral military strike on Iraq. When Koizumi was asked during a parliamentary session on March 13, 2003, about his response should the United States fail to obtain the second UN resolution, he answered, "I will decide based on the atmosphere at that time."[33] Once US President George W. Bush issued an ultimatum to Iraq on March 17, 2003, however, Koizumi quickly announced his support for the US decision.

Similarly, although politicians of the ruling LDP expressed negative views about the possible US military attack on Iraq during 2002, they changed their attitudes and had become supportive of the United States by 2003. LDP secretary general Yamazaki Taku, for example, stated in September 2002:

I understand the American argument that if the rogue states and terrorist organizations obtain WMD, that will be a serious threat to the whole world. It is problematic, however, if the United States behaves like the world's policeman in response to that threat. There is the U.N. to deal with world security. Japan, as an ally of the United States, should advise the United States to act under the UN.[34]

In May 2002, chairman of the LDP Policy Research Council Kyuma Fumio also told US assistant secretary of state Richard Armitage that "Japan has heavily depended on oil in the Middle East, so it cannot follow a forceful action of the United States. If the United States acts against the UN, Japan cannot support it."[35] In August 2002, former prime ministers Miyazawa Kiichi and Nakasone Yasuhiro also advised Koizumi that Japan should put a brake on any US radical action against Iraq. Nakasone stated, "Prime Minister Koizumi has a good friendship with President Bush. So he can give advice to him."[36] Most LDP politicians, therefore, wanted the United States to act within the UN framework. They worried about the negative impact of US action on Japan's relations with the Middle East, primarily because Japan was so heavily dependent on the region for oil.

Nevertheless, the LDP politicians began to change their attitudes as the invasion of Iraq became inevitable in 2003. In February 2003, Yamazaki, for example, stated that, having considered "national interests, peace and security, and the problem of North Korea," he would support a new UN resolution drafted by the United States and Britain.[37] When asked by *Asahi Shinbun* whether he would choose the US-Japan alliance rather than the UN, Yamazaki answered, "Japan has no choice but to support the United States."[38] Upon Bush's ultimatum to Iraq on March 17, 2003, Miyazawa and Nakasone also backed Koizumi's decision to support the United States. Nakasone stated, "It is right behavior as a politician to support the [Japanese] government's decision [to support the US attack on Iraq]."[39] Likewise, Miyazawa said that he would "ultimately support Koizumi's decision." He argued that if political leaders wanted to continue to fend off right-wing politicians who were calling for Japan to acquire nuclear weapons, maintaining a healthy US-Japan alliance was critical.[40] The only LDP politician who opposed the US action was Kono Yohei. He directly told Koizumi that Japan should not support the United States. He asked, "Does Japan have to support the U.S. preventive attack just because Japan is an ally of the United States? Japan sometimes has to give advice to the United States."[41] Other LDP politicians, however, did not follow Kono's protest. And it seems that even

Kono himself just wanted to share his personal views with Koizumi, since there is no evidence that he tried to organize a group within the LDP or across different parties in order to change the government's decision.

After Bush's "mission accomplished" announcement in April 2003, the LDP/Kōmeito coalition government submitted the SDF-Iraq Bill to the Diet. The bill, which authorized the deployment of SDF troops for postwar reconstruction efforts, was passed in the Diet on July 26, 2003. Although the government was initially planning to send the SDF sometime in the fall of 2003, it postponed the dispatch as a result of the bombing of the UN headquarters in Baghdad on August 19, 2003. The postponement was revoked in late August, however, after US assistant secretary of atate Richard Armitage demanded that Japan not "walk away" from the task of reconstructing Iraq.[42] As a result, the Cabinet Secretariat told the Japan Defense Agency (JDA) to consider deploying the SDF within the year. Although there was a Lower House election in November 2003, the LDP succeeded in playing down the issue of the SDF dispatch to Iraq during the election campaign and was able to win the election. Subsequently, 600 Ground SDF (GSDF) and 200 Air SDF (ASDF) personnel were dispatched to Iraq in January 2004, solely for humanitarian reconstruction purposes. None of the SDF personnel in Iraq participated in any combat operations. In the end, all the GSDF and ASDF personnel returned home safely, without any casualties, in July 2006 and in December 2008, respectively.

3

REGIONAL SECURITY ENVIRONMENTS AND US SECURITY COMMITMENT

EAST ASIA VERSUS EUROPE

I. INTRODUCTION

Chapters 3 through 5 provide detailed explanations about how the three variables—(1) the regional security environments (Europe versus East Asia) and the US security commitment to the two countries, (2) the type of alliance institutions (NATO versus the US-Japan Security Treaty), and (3) the characteristics of military institutions (the Bundeswehr versus the Self-Defense Forces [SDF])—influenced Germany's and Japan's alliance security dilemma with the United States. In short, these three variables increased the likelihood of Germany's fear of entrapment into US-led overseas military affairs during the critical period of 2001–2003, while keeping that of Japan low. Because of the differences in their alliance security dilemmas with the United States, Japan supported the US unilateral decision to attack Iraq, whereas Germany rejected it.

In this chapter, I first go over the impact that the regional security environments along with the US security commitment to the two countries had on their alliance security dilemmas with the United States in both the Cold War and post–Cold War periods in order to provide readers with the important information about the nature of the two countries' alliance security dilemma with the United States over time up until 9/11. Then, I explain how the two countries' alliance security dilemmas in 2001–2003 influenced their responses to the US invasion of Iraq. As I show in detail in this chapter, the two countries' alliance security dilemma with the United States is not a mere product of the presence or absence of external threats. But it is also greatly influenced by how the United State acted in the region and how much security commitment it showed to the two countries.

Although the regional environment surrounding Germany became significantly improved after the end of the Cold War, it became difficult for Germany not only to ensure US commitment to the regional security affairs in Europe, but also to control the US behavior through NATO. German political leaders had already experienced the lack of its influence over the operation (thereby the fear of entrapment) during the 1999 Kosovo War as a result of US dominance over the operation. In addition, although the German leaders supported the US-led war on terror following 9/11 and sent troops to Afghanistan to help the US forces, they were in fact deeply dissatisfied with the way in which the United States launched the war against al-Qaeda in fall 2001. The United States started the war on terror almost alone outside of the NATO's framework, leaving no room for Germany to influence how to wage war or carry out the operation. The US unilateral action over Afghanistan inevitably increased the likelihood of Germany's entrapment. It was thus difficult for German political leaders to support a potential US attack on Iraq during 2002–2003.

On the other hand, the regional environment in post–Cold War East Asia was relatively stable. Although there were a series of crises in East Asia in the 1990s, none of them developed into actual military conflicts. The United States—a de facto hegemon in East Asia at least 1990s[1]—well restrained its military power and used it only for defense and deterrence.[2] Its policy toward East Asia was to maintain the status quo and uneasy stalemate rather than pursuing a drastic strategy to resolve security problems.[3] As a result, Japan did not experience serious fear of entrapment into US-led regional conflicts or suffer from US unilateralism. For this reason, Japanese political leaders were more tolerant of the US attack on Iraq than were their German counterparts.

II. The Federal Republic of Germany (FRG)
1. Cold War Period, 1949–1989

Many German and American intellectuals have talked about the decline of the US "benign hegemon" since the late 1990s, implying that there were once "good old days" between the FRG and the United States that are now gone. Yet the relationship between the two countries was not perfectly amicable, even during the Cold War. Throughout the Cold War period, not only was the FRG (West Germany 1949–1990, unified Germany 1990-present) constantly under threat from the Soviet Union, but it also had hard times to ensure the US security commitment. Although FRG leaders were very skeptical about the American commitment to defend the FRG in the event of a Soviet invasion, they had virtually no alliance alternative to the United States. In spite of his strong conviction that reconciliation with France was indispensable for the FRG's integration into the European community and for the future formation of a European federation, and in spite of his good relationship with French president Charles de Gaulle, first FRG chancellor Konrad Adenauer (Christian Democratic Union [CDU], in office 1949–1963) thought that the United States—not France—was the only country with great enough military capability to guarantee the security of the FRG.[4] NATO was an important alliance institution for the FRG, because it permanently coupled the security of the FRG to that of the United States.[5]

Following Nazi Germany's surrender to the Allied Forces in 1945, Germany was occupied by the four powers (the United States, the Soviet Union, France, and the United Kingdom) and subsequently divided into two states in 1949—the Federal Republic of Germany (FRG) (West Germany) and the German Democratic Republic (GDR) (East Germany). Because the border between the FRG and the GDR was the demarcation line separating the Western and Soviet blocs (leaving West Berlin in the middle of the GDR), Germany was the most likely battlefield should a war between the Western and the Soviet blocs ever break out. As a result, the FRG's fear of abandonment by the United States was very high.

During the Cold War period, FRG political leaders agonized over how to ensure the United States' commitment to defend their country against a Soviet invasion. After the Soviet Union caught up with US nuclear power and obtained the capability to launch nuclear attacks on the continental United States in the 1960s, FRG leaders came to doubt whether the Americans would really use nuclear weapons in response to a Soviet invasion of the FRG, since this would inevitably result in the destruction of American territory and the deaths of many American people.[6] They were extremely worried that the United States (and France) might make a deal with the Soviet Union at the expense of the FRG.

FRG leaders, for example, were unhappy with the way in which the new US president John F. Kennedy responded to the 1961 Berlin Crisis. They doubted the strength of United States resolve to defend West Berlin (and the FRG as a whole) and the effectiveness of its nuclear deterrence against the Soviet Union, because Kennedy did not do anything to stop the Soviets from building the Berlin Wall.[7] Moreover, John F. Kennedy's new strategic doctrine of "flexible response" was "anathema"[8] to the FRG leaders, because it was intended to decouple the United States from Western Europe. The basic idea of flexible response was to save the United States from a nuclear war that was most likely to start as a result of a Soviet invasion of the FRG. The specific plan was for the United States to respond to a Soviet attack on the FRG (or anywhere else in Western Europe) with conventional forces rather than massive nuclear weapons. By permitting the possibility of conventional war in Europe, US policymakers tried to avoid becoming entrapped into a nuclear war in Europe.

This strategy, however, made FRG leaders extremely nervous. If the United States declared that it would not respond to a Soviet assault on Western Europe with nuclear weapons, how could the Soviet Union be deterred? If the United States publicly stated that it would limit itself to conventional troops, the Soviets might be tempted to invade the FRG. Above all, FRG leaders did not want war on their soil—regardless of whether it was nuclear or conventional. From their point of view, the only way to prevent a Soviet invasion was to deter the Soviet Union by threatening early use of nuclear weapons.[9]

The concern among FRG leaders about weak US resolve to use nuclear weapons against the Soviet Union was unlikely to be addressed, given the decline of US nuclear superiority and the FRG's consistent dependence on US nuclear protection. No matter how skeptical FRG leaders were about US nuclear credibility or its resolve to defend the FRG, they had no choice but to continue to turn to the US for protection. Neither the United States nor any other Western country would permit the FRG to possess its own nuclear weapons. Nor did the FRG desire nuclear weapons since obtaining them would surely result in the country's international isolation. FRG ambassador to Washington, DC, Wilhelm Grewe (in office 1958–1962), for example, writes:

> German and American security interests are in part coterminous—but only in part. Important differences existed, which could not be removed through discussions or compromise. It followed that the interests (and the strategic plans and dispositions which implemented them) of the stronger prevailed, and that the weaker had to accept them and try to live with them. Nor could we afford reactions of spiteful defiance (Trotzreaktionen) as did the French.[10]

The FRG's structural dependence on US nuclear protection did not fundamentally change, even after the development of *Ostpolitik* and the economic miracle of the 1970s. In 1969, Chancellor Willy Brandt

(Social Democratic Party [SPD], in office 1969–1974) initiated *Ostpolitik*—a policy to normalize the FRG's relations with the Soviet Union, the GDR, and other East European countries in order to reduce the level of political and military tensions between the East and West. Although the previous German chancellors from the CDU continued to refuse to recognize the GDR, Brandt acknowledged the GDR as a legitimate state and accepted the general status quo in Europe. In spite of his *Ostpolitik*, however, Brandt had no intention of changing the FRG's western orientation or giving up its commitment to NATO.[11] He and other FRG leaders fully understood that the success of *Ostpolitik* ultimately depended on support from the United States. Without strong US backing, the Soviet Union would not have been willing to deal with the FRG.[12] Moreover, in order to resolve the dispute over the status of West Berlin, the formal involvement of the United States, France, and Britain was necessary. FRG leaders were well aware that their attempt to improve the FRG's relationship with the GDR would raise suspicions among their Western allies. They therefore made it clear that *Ostpolitik* would not result in neutrality and that they had no intention of pursuing a new German *Sonderweg* (special way).

In addition, although the FRG was able to improve its relations with the GDR and other Communist countries in the Eastern Bloc through trade and economic assistance, it could not change the fundamental nature of its dependence on US nuclear protection. In the late 1970s, for example, Chancellor Helmut Schmidt bitterly expressed his dissatisfaction with the United States' failure to address the problem of the SS-20 medium-range missiles that the Soviet Union was pointing at Western Europe. The United States instead worked toward removing the Soviet's long-range intercontinental missiles, which were aimed at the United States itself.[13] Throughout the Cold War, therefore, the FRG continued to be under the Soviet threat and to fear US abandonment.

2. After the Cold War, 1990–2003

(i) In the 1990s

Not only did the end of the Cold War make it possible for the FRG to obtain its long-term dream of reunification, but it also freed the FRG from the imminent threat of a Soviet invasion. In 1995, Bundeswehr chief of staff General Klaus Naumann stated, "For the first time in 300 years, Germans are no longer the object of external pressure but have the chance to prevent conflicts and make peace more secure."[14]

The 2003 Defense Policy Guidelines authored by Federal defense minister Peter Struck (SPD, in office 2002–2005) also stated, "At present, and in the foreseeable future, there is no conventional threat to the German territory."[15] The end of the Cold War thus greatly improved the FRG's international security environment and decreased the FRG's fear of abandonment by the United States. Still, the fall of the Berlin Wall did not bring the FRG's structural dependency on the United States to an end. NATO continued to be an important alliance institution for Germany; it would maintain the US military presence in Europe and ensure US involvement in European security affairs.[16]

There were several reasons why it was necessary for the FRG to keep its alliance with the United States through NATO, even after the end of the Cold War. First of all, the FRG needed US military presence in Europe in order to solve regional crises and conflicts, especially to stop the civil wars in the former Yugoslavia. The Socialist Federal Republic of Yugoslavia (FRY) was once composed of six republics (Bosnia-Herzegovina, Croatia, Macedonia, Montenegro, Serbia, and Slovenia) and two autonomous provinces (Kosovo and Vojvodina, both within Serbia) that contained multiethnic and mixed religious populations. When both Slovenia and Croatia declared independence in 1991, Yugoslavia quickly descended into chaos, with a series of civil wars and ethnic cleansings, eventually resulting in the breakup of the FRY.[17]

The events in Yugoslavia raised great concern among German political leaders. Not only were they afraid that the regional conflicts might spill over into neighboring countries, but they were also concerned about the massive refugee flows into Germany. Germany was geographically close to former Yugoslavia and, during the first half of the 1990s, took some 400,000 war refugees from Croatia and Bosnia—more than any other West European country.[18] German leaders were afraid that the massive influx of refugees would bring about a revival of German nationalism and xenophobia and, consequently, social instability in their own country.[19]

Second, Germany needed to maintain NATO because of the uncertainty of the threat posed by Russia and, in the face of that uncertainty, the continued need for nuclear protection from the United States. Although Russia withdrew its forces from Eastern Europe, ending the possibility of a massive conventional offensive attack on Germany, it was still unclear whether Russia would become a stable democracy in the near future.[20] Under these circumstances, Russian nuclear weapons remained threats to Germany. And as long as Germany was unable to possess its own nuclear weapons, it had to make the US nuclear guarantee credible through NATO.[21]

Third, Germany needed to keep its alliance with the United States through NATO in order to reassure its neighbors that there was no possibility of a resurgence of German militarism. The presence of US military forces in Europe could work as an important counterweight to Germany's power and military potential and remove the fear among other European countries that they might have to face an overly powerful and aggressive Germany again. In addition, because the FRG government had placed the Bundeswehr (German armed forces) under NATO command since it was first established in 1955, NATO worked as a vehicle for denationalization of the Bundeswehr, helping to prevent the resurgence of German nationalism.[22]

Finally, maintaining the NATO alliance allowed Germany to keep its defense costs low. The unification process was a heavy, long-term financial burden for the FRG, and the country desperately needed to find areas where it could cut expenditures. Through NATO, Germany was able to maintain highly sophisticated US military forces in Europe and use them for deterrence, as well as for regional crises and conflict management, at relatively small cost. Ultimately then, while the end of the Cold War released the FRG from the intense fear of Soviet invasion, Germany still needed the US military presence in Europe.

The end of the Cold War, moreover, generated another element of the alliance security dilemma for Germany: the fear of overseas entrapment. Especially, the 1999 Kosovo War revealed that it became difficult for Germany to control the United States through NATO as a result of the disparity between the United States and Europe in their military capabilities, thereby increasing the likelihood of Germany's entrapment.

The Kosovo War began when US-led NATO forces started bombing Serbia on March 24, 1999, in order to stop Serbian aggression in Kosovo. Kosovo was an autonomous province within the Republic of Serbia, and 90 percent of the population was ethnic Albanian practicing Islam ("Kosovars"). (The Serbs adhered to Orthodox Christianity, which gave them close ties to the Russians.) Although the Kosovars had enjoyed autonomy in their province since 1974, the president of Serbia, Slobodan Milosevic, amended the Serbian constitution to limit Kosovo's autonomy in 1989, resulting in Kosovar riots and protests. The events in Kosovo began drawing serious attention from Western leaders in the early 1990s. The Western leaders were concerned that a conflict in Kosovo could become more serious than the wars in Slovenia, Croatia, or Bosnia, because it might bring neighboring countries (such as Bulgaria, Turkey, and Greece) into the conflict. In December 1992, US president George Bush sent Milosevic a secret "Christmas Warning" saying, "In the event of conflict in Kosovo caused by Serbian action, the United States will be prepared to employ military force against Serbians in Kosovo and Serbia proper."[23] The Clinton administration and the leaders of other NATO member countries sent similar warnings to Milosevic on several occasions through 1998. In spite of these warnings, violence between the Kosovo Liberation Army (KLA) and Serbian authorities in Kosovo escalated. In March 1998, for example, the Serbian security forces massacred over 50 members of the Jashari family in the village of Prekaz in response to KLA attacks on Serbian police. In the following summer, the Serbian forces intensified their attacks on the KLA and Kosovo Albanian villages, driving out thousands of Albanians from key areas. The most shocking incident, which became a catalyst for NATO action, was the Racak massacre of January 1999, in which Serb security forces killed 45 unarmed villagers (Kosovo Albanians) in retaliation for a KLA attack on four Serb policemen.[24]

Not only was it morally impossible for German political leaders to ignore the humanitarian suffering in Kosovo, but they were also concerned about the flow of refugees from Kosovo.[25] In addition, they worried that if NATO did not act to stop the Serb aggression in Kosovo, NATO's credibility would be called into serious question.[26] Moreover, Kosovo presented an opportunity for Germany to raise its international profile—to promote its democratic credentials on the world stage, as well as demonstrate that it was a normal, reliable, and responsible alliance partner.[27] For these reasons, Chancellor Gerhard Schröder and Foreign Minister Joschka Fischer convinced their parties and the public that the use of force was necessary to solve the civil conflict in Kosovo by using the logic of "never again Auschwitz."[28] In the end, they succeeded in dispatching 14 Tornado aircraft to participate in NATO-led Operation Allied Force (OAF).[29]

German political leaders were convinced that an intense civil conflict like Kosovo could not be solved without the US forces, and Germany had to be a reliable ally to support the NATO's bombing campaign against Serbia.[30] However, from the beginning, neither Schröder nor Fischer was enthusiastic about the use of force to solve the problem. They basically remained as "quiet observers" throughout the operation. In order to show that Germany was a reliable ally, they decided to keep quiet throughout the war unless the conditions became really unacceptable for Germans.[31]

Although German political leaders and officials quietly followed the US leadership, they constantly felt uneasiness about the way in which the United States was conducting the military operation throughout the war because they had a sense that they were not fully consulted by their American counterparts. Although they were kept informed by the United States about the war operation, they knew that the information provided by Americans were not "full" information.[32]

To be sure, the US forces were frustrated by political interference from European civilian officials to their operational decisions over selections of bombing targets during the war.[33] The US forces had to carry out the operation according to an "ad hoc" list of bombing targets approved by European officials without a coherent plan based on systematic effects-based target analysis.[34] So the lesson that the US forces learned from OAF, according to US Air Force general Michael Short, was, "Coalitions aren't good ways to fight wars."[35]

Nevertheless, the US forces virtually dominated the operation against Serbia. Not only did the US forces carry out 80 percent of all air strike sorties, but they also selected nearly every target because it provided almost all the aerial intelligence in the operation.[36] In the later stage of operation, target selection was increasingly carried out by the United States alone, although target approval was still made by the "Quints"—the United State, Britain, France, Germany, and Italy.[37] Americans might have thought that there was nothing wrong with the US dominance over the operation since American military capabilities were far superior to those of its European allies, and the United States made the largest contribution to the operation.

German political leaders and officials, however, were concerned about such US dominance over the operation. As the United States increasingly dominated the operation, Germany fell into a blind follower of the United States. Because of the lack of consultation and "full" information from Americans, Germans were not very sure about what the US forces were actually doing in the operation, or, more importantly, to where the United States was ultimately leading its NATO allies in the operation or how the United States was planning to end the war.[38]

Especially, the question of sending ground troops to Kosovo in the later stage of the operation put German political leaders in a difficult position because it was impossible for them to dispatch ground troops to Kosovo. Although the majority of the German public constantly supported the NATO-led air campaign against Serbia, it opposed Germany's sending ground troops to Kosovo throughout the war.[39] Thus, when the United States and the United Kingdom began, after six weeks of the bombing campaign, to discuss plans to deploy ground troops, German chancellor Schröder publicly denied that Bundeswehr troops would be deployed in Kosovo.[40]

Fortunately, Germany did not have to come to a showdown with the United States over the deployment of ground troops in Kosovo because Milosevic accepted the allies' demands in June 1999. But the Kosovo War revealed that it became increasingly difficult for Germany to control the US behavior through NATO, and the US dominance over NATO would increase the likelihood of Germany's entrapment into US-led overseas wars because Germany was unable to influence over them.

At the same time, Germany was not able to free from its dependence on the United States for the maintenance of stability and peace in Europe. Although Germans were uneasy about the US leadership in OAF, NATO was in fact the only credible alliance institution that was capable of ending the Kosovo conflict. Germany had tried to resolve international problems through various European security institutions, such as the Conference on Security and Cooperation in Europe (CSCE) and the European Security and Defense Identity (ESDI). However, these institutions were simply not equipped to address the type of conflicts occurring in former Yugoslavia.[41]

German leaders succeeded in ending the Kosovo War by bringing Russia to NATO's side and thereby increasing the pressure on Milosevic to accept NATO's demands. In this way, they were able to avoid sending ground troops to the combat operations in Yugoslavia.[42] Although many Germans questioned the efficacy of the allied bombings in Serbia, it is clear that Russia never would have intervened without the United States' show of formidable air power and without NATO solidarity. At first, Russian president Boris Yeltsin did not believe that NATO would strike Serbia. Once NATO took action, however, Yeltsin worked to put an end to the conflict as quickly as possible.[43] Indeed, Chancellor Schröder wrote in his memoir that conflicts like the Kosovo War could not be solved by EU countries alone; they needed the help of the United States.[44]

Since the end of the Kosovo War, Germany and other EU countries have tried to develop the European Security and Defense Policy (ESDP)[45] in order to lessen their dependence on and increase their leverage vis-à-vis the United States.[46] The EU has assumed a greater role in peacekeeping, not just in Southeastern Europe, but in other parts of the world as well.[47] However, the ESDP is not yet capable of dealing with intense regional military conflicts like the Kosovo War, because the EU countries remain reluctant to spend more on defense, and the United States is unwilling to share its NATO assets with them.[48]

What is more, Germans leaders are ambivalent about the future of the ESDP. They want to have an independent European security institution in order to avoid getting entangled in a US-dominated war. The ESDP would also be useful should the United States elect to rescue itself from European affairs. However, if the ESDP improved its capabilities, US politicians might conclude that there was no reason to keep American forces in Europe any longer. It is unclear whether Germany and other EU countries really desire this outcome. The United States has played an important role as "pacifier" in the region—"containing Germany" and reassuring the rest of Europe.[49] Furthermore, as long as Germany cannot possess its own nuclear weapons, it has to rely on the US nuclear protection. Since the late 1990s, therefore, German political leaders have been vexed by their alliance security dilemma with the United States—between the desire to preserve the US commitment in Europe through NATO and the desire to avoid getting entrapped into US-dominated overseas military operations in which Germany has little or no input.

(ii) After 9/11 and the Iraq War: 2001–2003

After the terrorist attacks on September 11, 2001, this dilemma grew even greater and placed the SPD-Green government in a very difficult position. The Iraq question eventually led German political leaders to confront the United States, because their fear of entrapment into the US-led preventive war on Iraq—which was legally and morally questionable from the German point of view—overwhelmed that of abandonment by the United States. German political leaders were especially frustrated with US unilateralism.

Right after 9/11, German leaders expressed strong support for the United States. They hoped that they could keep US action within the NATO framework and thereby exercise some degree of influence over the US action. The United States, however, did not act with NATO when it launched the attack on Afghanistan in fall 2001, and the US leaders' propensity to act alone seemed to grow even stronger in 2002. German leaders felt extremely uneasy about George W. Bush's "axis of evil" statement in January 2002, and most members of the Bundestag—within all parties—were skeptical about the justifications the US was providing for a war against Iraq. They did not believe there was convincing evidence that Iraq possessed weapons of mass destruction (WMD).

Immediately after 9/11, Schröder declared Germany's "unlimited solidarity" with the United States and showed he was determined to support the United States by linking a vote of confidence in his chancellorship to the Bundestag approval of Bundeswehr participation in Operation Enduring Freedom (OEF) in Afghanistan in November 2001. However, many members of Schröder's own SPD party—as well as its coalition partner, the Greens—opposed the dispatch of Bundeswehr troops to OEF. One SPD Bundestag member, who abstained from voting for the bill authorizing the Bundeswehr's participation in the NATO operation in Kosovo in November 1998, for example, told me that he was also against the November 2001 OEF bill. According to his estimate, there were approximately 30–40 SPD Bundestag members who were opposed to the measure. However, the SPD placed enough pressure on its members to force them to vote for deployment to OEF. When the member with whom I spoke was first elected to the Bundestag in September 1998 and abstained from voting for German participation in Kosovo two months later, there was no pressure or punishment from the party. Instead, because of his abstention, SPD parliamentary group leader Peter Struck came to learn his name. In November 2001, however, Struck came to him and bluntly told him that if he voted against or abstained from voting, he would be kicked out of the party the very next day.[50] Similarly, Green Party managers "bullied the dissidents" in order to ensure that all members voted for the OEF bill. One Green official said, "We have offered the carrots, waved the stick—now we're on to the electric cattle prod."[51] Head of the Green Party and foreign minister, Joschka Fischer, also threatened to resign if his party voted against the OEF bill.[52] In the end, the SPD had only one defector, the Greens four. As a result, the SPD-Green government succeeded in passing the OEF bill on November 16, 2001, and authorized 3,900 troops to deploy to Afghanistan.

Although Schröder's determination to support the United States was strong in the fall of 2001, this "unlimited solidarity" did not necessarily mean that Germany would blindly follow the United States under any conditions. Schröder supported the US attack on Afghanistan, not just because he felt strong sympathy for the victims of the terrorist attacks, but also because he hoped to keep the United States within the NATO framework so that Germany would be consulted and have a chance to influence US policy.[53] As early as September 19, 2001, Schröder stated:

> Naturally: Every right corresponds with a duty. But this, of course, also applies the other way around, which means information and

consultation. What do we want to achieve as Germans and Europeans: unlimited solidarity with the United States in all necessary measures. Risk, including military, will be shared by Germany but she is not prepared for adventures. These are not asked for by the American administration, because of its considerate position after the attacks, and they will certainly not be asked for in the future.[54]

By ruling out "adventures," Schröder tried to prevent Germany from becoming entrapped in dangerous US operations.

Schröder did not get his way, however. Instead of working within the NATO framework, in October 2001 American political leaders decided to go to war against al-Qaeda essentially alone. The Americans learned a different lesson from the Kosovo War than did its European allies: The United States possesses the best military forces in the world in terms of both quality and quantity. US military forces are far superior to those of its European allies—not just in terms of the number of troops, but also in the level of technology. The Kosovo War particularly highlighted the "unacceptable" technology gap between the United States and Europe.[55]

American political elites therefore came to think that working with their European allies through a multilateral framework would reduce US readiness and capabilities. In order to pursue its own national interests, they concluded that it would be more efficient for the United States to conduct military operations alone than to work with its European allies.[56] In the wake of 9/11, the members of the Bush administration—especially Secretary of Defense Donald Rumsfeld—opposed including European forces in the military operation to attack al-Qaeda. Rumsfeld stated that he was afraid that "some German battalion or French frigate could get in the way of his operation."[57] The American leaders feared that they would have to give up command-and-control authority in exchange for nothing "more than a token contribution from their European allies."[58]

German political elites still feel bitter about the fact that the United States did not start the war against al-Qaeda within the NATO framework. Even a well-known pro-US senior SPD member of the Bundestag, who did not support his party's decision to oppose a possible US attack on Iraq in summer 2002, told me that it was a "mistake" for the United States to start the war against al-Qaeda without NATO.[59] In addition, Bundeswehr officers are usually regarded as pro-American, because they have been had a lot of contact with their American counterparts under NATO command.[60] However, even these officers think that the war in Afghanistan should have been carried out within the NATO framework. One of the Bundeswehr officers with whom I spoke in summer 2008, for example, expressed his extreme dissatisfaction with the way in which the United States started the war in Afghanistan. I asked him about the recent disputes between Germany and the United States regarding the peacekeeping operation in Afghanistan. Since 2006, the United States has been accusing the Bundeswehr of limiting its operations to the relatively peaceful northern part of Afghanistan, while the United States, Canada, and the United Kingdom are engaged in heavy fighting against the Taliban in the south.[61] When I brought up this issue, he immediately became upset and replied with visible contempt that US forces first went to Afghanistan without NATO. Germany sent the Bundeswehr to Afghanistan in late 2001 just to help the United States. The Bundeswehr went to Afghanistan, even before the International Security Assistance Force (ISAF) was established under NATO authority in 2002, in order to maintain security. Moreover, when the Bundeswehr first went to Afghanistan, nobody wanted to take responsibility for security in the north of the country. Yet the United States now blames Germany for taking this assignment.[62]

Echoing this respondent's sentiments, the majority of German political leaders think that the maintenance of security in and peaceful development of Afghanistan are in Germany's national interests, and Germany is willing to do whatever it can to prevent Afghanistan from becoming a sanctuary for terrorists again. However, if the United States wanted Germany to take part in peacekeeping operations in Afghanistan as its "partner," the Americans should have consulted with the Germans about how to carry out the operations before launching an attack. There are some things that Germany can and cannot do. For example, the government must obtain parliamentary approval to send the Bundeswehr to overseas military operations, which is often very difficult. Moreover, the majority of the German public has a much more conservative attitude toward the use of military force than does the American public.[63] German minister of defense Franz Josef Jung (CDU, in office 2005–2009), for example, stresses the need for "integrated security" and civilian-military reconstruction in Afghanistan, whereas US secretary of defense Robert Gates places his priority on counterinsurgency combat operations.[64] Many Germans feel uncomfortable with the American way of fighting the Taliban, since the ruthless US military campaign in the south has resulted in many civilian casualties. German political leaders have been concerned that such an uncompromising US approach in the south will alienate local Afghan residents and negatively affect peaceful regions in the north.[65]

By January 2002, German political leaders had grown alarmed about the possibility of a US attack on Iraq. Just days after President George W. Bush made his "axis of evil" statement (which declared Iran, Iraq, and North Korea to be part of an "axis of evil"), Schröder raised four points of concern in a meeting with Bush in Washington, DC. He stressed that before an attack on Iraq were launched: (1) they must ensure that the war on terrorism in Afghanistan would not be undermined, (2) the solid link between al-Qaeda and Iraq had to be proved, (3) there must be an exit strategy, and (4) a UN mandate must be in place.[66]

Schröder was not the only German political actor who was concerned about Bush's "axis of evil" statement at that time. To be sure, there were some people in the opposition parties, as well as in the Bundeswehr, who agreed, to a certain extent, with Bush's characterization. One CDU member of the Bundestag told me that the statement contained some basis in reality. Saddam Hussein had, after all, used poison gas against the Kurds.[67] Another high-ranking Bundeswehr officer said that he understood Bush's use of the statement at that time, since the President had to use provocative words in order to appeal to the public about the necessity of fighting rogue states.[68] However, there were many German political actors, even in the opposition parties, who questioned Bush's turn of phrase. The source of their uneasiness seemed to come from the subjective judgment of the threat made by George W. Bush and his administration. One CDU member of the Bundestag Defense Committee, for example, told me that he thought that Bush's statement was dangerous and problematic, because he believed that all conflicts should be solved by political means, not by military means. He argued that Bush should handle each country differently. Iran, Iraq, and North Korea were very different cases.[69] Similarly, one high-ranking Free Democratic Party (FDP) Bundestag member (the FDP was a likely coalition partner for the CDU/CSU if they won the 2002 election) bluntly said that the "axis of evil" statement was "totally wrong (*grottenfalsch*)."[70] Although the three countries were not democratic, there were no rational reasons to demonize them.

Some of the high-ranking Bundeswehr officers whom I interviewed were also critical of Bush's statement. One of them thought that the "axis of evil" was a "moral category," not a "political category." According to this officer, "the moral category" expresses a feeling, and "the political category" represents interests, threats, and power. He wondered why there were only three countries in the "axis of evil."[71] Other high-ranking Bundeswehr officers raised similar questions: Are only three countries "evil"?[72] Countries such as Syria and Libya are also "rogue states."[73] Bush's "axis of evil" designation seemed subjective and arbitrary to them.

The question of subjective judgments went to the heart of the debate over a "preemptive" or "preventive" war in Iraq. The SPD-Green government had regarded Germany's participation in the 1999 Kosovo War as morally justified, even though there was no UN mandate, since its aim was to end ongoing ethnic cleansing. Even in such a clearly justified intervention, however, Chancellor Schröder refused to send ground troops to Kosovo. German political leaders simply could not express support for a preemptive attack on a country based on subjective and dubious assertions. Their support for the Iraq War could not remain just lip service. Once the German government expressed its support for the US attack on Iraq, it would become very difficult to refuse the US demand to send Bundeswehr troops there in the future.

Robert Worley defines preemptive and preventive wars as follows:

preemptive wars: initiation of war because an adversary's attack—using *existing* capability—is believed to be imminent.

preventive wars: fighting a winnable war now to avoid risk of war later under less favorable conditions.[74]

The US attack on Iraq was in fact preventive, though President Bush justified it as preemptive, saying that Iraq possessed WMD and an attack from Iraq was imminent.[75] However, as long as the United States was unable to present solid evidence of Iraq's possession of WMD, it was hard to justify the assertion that the threat from Iraq was imminent and that the US action was therefore self-defense.

Most Bundestag members, regardless of their party affiliation, rejected the possibility of Germany's participation in the war without convincing evidence that Iraq posed an immediate threat. During the 2002 election campaign, Chancellor Schröder stated:

We hear unsettling news from the Middle East regarding a new danger of war. I think that we demonstrated after September 11 that we will react decisively but prudently, that we will show solidarity with our partner, but that we are not available for adventure, and we stand by that." (August 1, 2002) [76]

Even Schröder's CDU/CSU competitor for the chancellorship, Edmund Stoiber, offered his support for an attack on Iraq only if there was a UN mandate. During the election campaign, CSU party leader Michael Glos also stated, "There is no intention on our part to participate anywhere in the world in a military adventure."[77]

In addition, while all three of the FDP politicians with whom I spoke bitterly criticized Schröder for exploiting the Iraq issue during the 2002 election campaign, when asked whether a CDU/CSU–FDP government would have sent the Bundeswehr to Iraq if they had won the election, all adamantly maintained they would not.[78] One of them bluntly stated that the US attack on Iraq was one-sided, and US unilateralism was unacceptable for everyone.[79] Another pro-US FDP member of the Bundestag Foreign Relations Committee answered that it would be difficult to send the Bundeswehr to Iraq, because there was no substantial proof that Saddam Hussein had WMD. He mentioned that the Bundestag Foreign Relations Committee met about two weeks before US secretary of state Collin Powell's presentation at the UN Security Council (on February 5, 2003) concerning Iraq's possession of WMD. In that meeting, according to him, August Hanning, president of the Federal Intelligence Service (Bundesnachrichtendienst [BND]), told the committee members that there was very little evidence that Iraq had WMD, and, as a result, most German politicians were not convinced by Powell's claims.[80]

CDU politicians whom I had interviewed also claimed that their party never would have sent the Bundeswehr to Iraq. One CDU member of the Bundestag Defense Committee stated that it was totally "out of the question."[81] Another CDU Bundestag member, who used to serve as a parliamentary secretary in the Ministry of Defense, contended that if a CDU-led government had supported the US attack on Iraq, Germany surely would have faced a "revolutionary situation."[82] Most opposition party politicians were well aware that the majority of their constituencies opposed a US attack on Iraq, and most politicians, across Germany's various political parties, opposed Germany's involvement in a US-led assault.

It should be noted, however, that although the fear of entrapment into a US war eventually led the SPD-Green government to oppose an attack on Iraq in summer 2002, members of the government did everything they could do to prevent abandonment by the United States. The government, for example, granted US forces the right to transit German territory and air space, as well as the right to use US military installations in Germany, should the United States choose to go forward with an attack on Iraq. Had the SPD-Green government wanted to show truly strong opposition to the Iraq War, it could have closed Germany's airspace to the US Air Force. But it did not do that.[83] The Bundeswehr also aided US forces as much as it could. The Federal Ministry of Defense sent 8,000 Bundeswehr soldiers to protect US bases in Germany and sent NBC tanks to Kuwait.[84]

What is more, despite their general opposition to a US attack on Iraq, in fall 2002, high-ranking members of Germany's governing parties were wavering over whether the Bundeswehr should be deployed to the Iraq-Kuwait border regions in order to help US forces. They disagreed over whether the Bundeswehr's Fuchs tanks (reconnaissance vehicles) stationed in Kuwait could be deployed to aid US forces if US bases were attacked by Iraq. On November 23, 2002, Hans-Ulrich Klose, a pro-US SPD Bundestag member and chairman of the Bundestag Foreign Relations Committee, stated, "If biological or chemical weapons are used in the Iraqi-Kuwait border regions, German armored cars will come to their aid."[85] Hans Georg Wagner (SPD), parliamentary state secretary of the Federal Ministry of Defense, made a similar remark: "Our forces would of course be deployed [if Iraq attacked US bases in Kuwait]."[86] Defense Minister Peter Struck (SPD), however, rejected Klose's statement and denied that Bundeswehr troops stationed in Kuwait would take any part in a conflict in Iraq. He stated that the government, on principle, would not support the new US doctrine of launching preventive strikes against Iraq: "This is not allowed according to our constitution, and no one intends to change the constitution."[87] Similarly, Kerstin Müller, (Green) minister of state in the Federal Foreign Office, expressed her opposition to the deployment of the Fuchs tanks, arguing that there was no link between Iraq and al-Qaeda. Ultimately, the Bundestag did not approve the use of the Fuchs tanks in Iraq.[88]

Disagreements between high-ranking members of the ruling parties over the deployment of the Bundeswehr in Iraq resurfaced in October 2004. This time, Defense Minister Peter Struck started a controversy. At the NATO meeting in Romania, he told German reporters, "It is certainly thinkable that there could be a time—perhaps in years—when Germany will become engaged [in Iraq]."[89] The Chancellor's Office, however, quickly denied that the government had changed its opposition to the US-led invasion of Iraq. Chancellor's Office spokesman Thomas Steg stated, "I want to say clearly and unmistakably what the Chancellor told the Cabinet in agreement with the defense minister: The position of the German government as far as Iraq is concerned is clear—it will not be changed."[90] Other members of the ruling parties followed Steg's statement. Gernot Erler, deputy chairman of the SPD parliamentary group, remarked, "I can say definitely that there will be no deployment of German soldiers in Iraq with the approval of the Social Democrats, and Peter Struck knows that."[91] Rainer Arnold (defense speaker of the SPD parliamentary group and a member of the Bundestag Defense Committee) also rejected any possibility that the Bundeswehr would be deployed in Iraq, even in the long term. Likewise, Guenter Nachtwei (Green member of the Bundestag Defense Committee) made a strong statement: "We do not want and must not be drawn into this disaster [the Iraq War]."[92] Therefore, even though the SPD-Green government formally opposed a US attack on Iraq in summer 2002, ruling-party politicians continued to disagree about the possibility of deploying the Bundeswehr both before and after the United States launched its attack in March 2003.

Further evidence of Germany's conflicted position emerged when the German media began revealing in 2006 that Germany had provided US forces with significant assistance to carry out its military operations in Iraq.[93] The German Navy, for instance, escorted US and British warships at the Horn of Africa during the Iraq War by using the framework of OEF. Accusing the German Navy of providing support for the preparation and implementation of the Iraq War, Left Party Defense Policy spokesman Paul Schäfer blasted, "This form of support for aggressive wars violating international law is not covered by a Bundestag mandate."[94]

Even more remarkably, it seems the SPD-Green government allowed the BND to cooperate with the United States, helping the Bush administration to both justify their war, and to directly implement military operations in Iraq. The SPD-Green government, for example, gave the CIA permission to use questionable information that the BND obtained from an Iraqi asylum seeker known as "Curveball." Curveball told a BND agent that the UN inspectors were unable to find WMD in Iraq because the biological weapons program was mobile. US secretary of state Colin Powell used this story at the UN in February 2003 in order to convince the world that it was necessary to attack Iraq. The story later proved to be fabricated.[95]

In February 2003, the SPD-Green government also authorized the BND to send two German agents to Iraq in order to "obtain a perspective independent from that provided by the Americans" and to share the information with the US military. The two agents were professional soldiers. One was a lieutenant colonel who had served in the German Air Force and another was a paratrooper.[96] The information from the two BND agents proved "invaluable" for the US military as it sought to make critical decisions about how to carry out the ground invasion in March 2003. US Army general James Marks, a senior intelligence officer working at Camp Doha in Kuwait in spring 2003, claimed in an interview with German magazine *Spiegel*:

> The German information was of extreme importance and value for us...We trusted the information from the Germans more than we trusted the CIA because we knew that the Germans tend to be anal retentive and would only report on things they had seen, felt or smelled or that they were very sure of...We owe the two courageous Germans who were in Baghdad during the war who risked their lives our deepest and heartfelt thanks. With their intelligence they saved American lives; there is no doubt about that.[97]

US general Tommy Franks, who led Operation Iraq Freedom, also stated, "It would be a huge mistake to underestimate the value of the information provided by the Germans. These guys were invaluable."[98]

The more the US generals praised the German contribution to the US invasion of Iraq, the more difficult and awkward the position of SPD and Green leaders became. Foreign Minister Frank-Walter Steinmeier (SPD, in office 2005–2009)—a chief of staff in the Chancellor's Office during the Iraq crisis of 2002–2003—has long insisted that the agents in Baghdad had been instructed to preclude active support for combat operations and that their mission was to ensure that civilian facilities in Baghdad would not be targeted. In December 2008, however, Steinmeier was finally summoned by the Bundestag committee investigating the extent to which the German intelligence agents assisted the US military during the invasion. Grilled by the Bundestag committee, Steinmeier lost his temper and pounded loudly on the table.[99]

Such stories show how difficult it was for the SPD-Green government to deal with its alliance security dilemma—to avoid entrapment into the US-led war on Iraq while simultaneously maintaining its alliance relations with the United States. An analysis of the spy mission scandal by conservative German newspaper *Die Welt* illustrates the dilemma:

> The government was realistic enough not to break entirely with the United States. And of course the government would have been informed enough to know that information gathered by BND agents would find its way into the international spy community, and that the Americans might find it useful. In a networked world, both positions can be true: Germany against the war, but also slightly involved.[100]

In sum, German political leaders opposed a US attack on Iraq in 2002–2003 not only because US unilateralism had precluded Germany from influencing US-led military operations since the late 1990s, thereby increasing the likelihood of Germany's entrapment, but also because they did not see any justifiable reasons for the United States to go to war against Iraq. German political leaders had already had bitter experiences of US unilateralism in the 1999 Kosovo War, as well as in the ongoing war on terrorism in Afghanistan. They, therefore, did not want to send Bundeswehr soldiers to another war in which Germany would have little or no input. In spite of its opposition to the possible US attack on Iraq in 2002–2003, however, the SPD-Green government tried to do everything possible to maintain Germany's alliance relationship with the United States, as there was no alternative to NATO. NATO was still the only credible alliance institution capable of dealing with intense regional military conflicts in Europe. In the end, the German government did as much as it could do to help the US military in Iraq without actually deploying Bundeswehr troops.

III. Japan

While the FRG suffered from the intense fear of abandonment by the United States during the Cold War and from that of entrapment into US-led wars (and of abandonment as well) after the Cold War ended, Japan did not experience a comparable alliance security dilemma in its relationship with the United States. Although Japan did face the fear of both entrapment and abandonment, the level of their alliance security dilemma with the United States was much lower than that of the FRG. During the Cold War, the Soviet Union's military capabilities in the Far East were substantially weaker than in Europe. At the same time, the international environment had raised the strategic value of Japan for US policymakers. As such, the fear of abandonment by the United States was not particularly strong for Japanese political leaders, which allowed them to focus on ensuring that Japan would not be drawn into any US-led wars overseas.

After the Cold War, however, Japan's fear of abandonment by the United States increased. The Persian Gulf War of 1990–1991 was especially difficult for Japanese politicians and government officials and made them realize that they could no longer take US military protection for granted. Still, the Japanese fear of abandonment was relatively minor, as the United States continued to have a strong interest in maintaining military bases in Japan. Moreover, the regional environment in post–Cold War East Asia was much more stable than that in Europe. This is not to say, of course, that East Asia has been completely secure. To be sure, North Korea has developed nuclear weapons and, since 1993, has repeatedly test-launched missiles capable of striking Japan. China also created a crisis in 1996 when it launched a series of missile tests across the Taiwan Straits in order to intimidate proindependence politicians and activists ahead of Taiwan's national election.

Yet these crises did not result in all-out military operations, as did the crises in former Yugoslavia. Not only was the stability in East Asia resulted from growing economic interdependence among Asian states,[101] continuing consolidation of Asian countries as modern-nation states, and the development of a normative structure that disputes should be settled without recourse to war in Asia.[102] But it also stemmed from the United States' well-restrained behavior. The US military power was overwhelmingly preponderant in East Asia at least in the 1990s,[103] and the United States used its power only for defense and deterrence.[104] The United States had never pursued a drastic strategy to resolve security problems in East Asia. Rather, it tried to maintain the status quo and uneasy stalemate because that enables the presence of US forces in the region. If the regional security problems were completely solved, there will be no justification for the United States to maintain its forces in East Asia.[105] China's and North Korea's possession of nuclear weapons also discouraged the United States to pursue drastic measures to solve regional problems.[106] For these reasons, Japanese political leaders had never had to face a difficult question about whether to send troops to support US-led combat operations within the region. Nor had they had to deal with the consequences of US unilateralism in a manner similar to Germany. Japanese political leaders were thus more tolerant of the possibility of a US attack on Iraq in 2002–2003 than were their German counterparts.

In addition, while the United States was increasingly losing its interest in European security affairs after the end of the Cold War, thereby increasing Germany's fear of abandonment, it has never lost its security interest in East Asia or contemplating giving up its military presence in the region. In fact, the United States and Japan announced the revision of the US-Japan guidelines for Defense Cooperation in April 1996 in order to strengthen their alliance and cope with regional contingencies in the future. Moreover, the United States would never give up its security commitment to Japan because such a move would result in Japan's arming with nuclear weapons. The nuclearization of Japan will not only escalate tensions and arms racing in East Asia but also make it difficult for the United States to maintain its military bases in Japan.[107] In short, because Japan lacks a negative experience of working with the United States in an actual military operation in the region, and because Japan had little fear of outright abandonment by the United States, the Japanese government was able to announce its support for the US attack on Iraq in March 2003, though it sent a minimum number of troops to Iraq and limited their mission to humanitarian reconstruction efforts.

1. Cold War Period, 1949–1989

In contrast to the German political leaders, who were desperate to maintain the United States' commitment to defend the FRG against a Soviet invasion, during the Cold War, Japanese political leaders were most concerned with avoiding becoming entrapped in US-led overseas conflicts. Prime Minister Yoshida Shigeru (Liberal Party; in office 1946–1947, 1948–1954) laid out principles for Japan's postwar foreign policy. He concluded: (1) Japan's economic recovery should be the first priority; (2) In order to defend its territory, Japan should allow US military forces to stay on its soil; and (3) Japan should avoid involvement in overseas military affairs.[108] These principles were later called the "Yoshida Doctrine," and they became firmly ensconced in the government's policies throughout the Cold War.

While West Germany was forced to stare down the massive ground forces stationed in the Warsaw Pact countries along its borders, the regional environment surrounding Japan during the Cold War was relatively peaceful. Yoshida and subsequent Japanese political leaders did not believe that either the Soviet Union or China posed a serious threat. They considered Communism a threat, and thus were quite hostile toward the Soviet Union. However, they thought that a full-scale Soviet invasion was unlikely, because the size of Soviet forces in the Far East was fairly small, and their only supply line was the highly vulnerable, one-track Siberian railway, which did not have the capacity to transport even the 12 divisions that would minimally be necessary to take Hokkaido.[109]

As for China, Yoshida did not seem to care whether this neighbor was "red or green," because he saw China as a natural market for Japanese goods.[110] In addition, Yoshida—who lived in China for many years as a diplomat in the prewar period and called himself a China expert—was not disturbed by the growing strength of the Communists in China in the late 1940s. He believed that the Chinese people could not become "real Communists," because they were pragmatic, materialistic, and highly individualistic.[111]

Given this regional environment, Yoshida concluded that allowing US military forces to stay on its soil was sufficient for Japan to protect its territory. Although US secretary of state John Foster Dulles refused to provide an explicit protection guarantee in the 1951 US-Japan Security Treaty (as a result of Yoshida's firm resistance to US demands for rearmament), Yoshida was not particularly concerned. He remained convinced that if Japan were invaded by foreign forces, US military forces stationed in Japan would have no choice but to defend the country.[112]

The greatest danger for Japan, Yoshida felt, was the possibility of being drawn into US overseas military affairs. He worried that involvement in such affairs would jeopardize Japan's autonomy and hinder its economic recovery. Yoshida reasoned that once Japan built up a large army, the United States would surely press Japan to dispatch it for overseas wars.[113] He was afraid that new military forces would become a "Trojan horse" within the structure of the Japanese state and transform Japan into an American military colony.[114] Yoshida, therefore, resisted the US demand for large-scale rearmament and tried to keep the country's new military forces as small as possible.

One of the most striking differences between the FRG and Japan during the Cold War—one that clearly illustrates the contrasting nature of the two countries' alliance security dilemmas—was the way in which they related to regional collective security organizations. The FRG firmly committed itself to NATO, whereas Japanese political leaders steadfastly refused to involve Japan in any kind of regional collective security organization. Japan remained steadfast in this refusal out of the fear that such an organization would force Japan to play a military role in US efforts to fight the Cold War in the region. In 1950, US secretary of state Dulles attempted to establish a regional security organization like NATO in the Asia Pacific. The proposed organization was to comprise Japan, South Korea, and Taiwan (and potentially several other Western Pacific countries). Yoshida firmly refused, however.[115] While the FRG pursued a strategy of "never alone" and "never again," Japan pursued an isolationist strategy of "one-country pacifism" (*ikkoku heiwa shugi*).[116] The FRG was willing to give up its autonomy to become a member of NATO and tied itself to the United States and other West European countries in an effort to defend its territory and to prevent the resurgence of its own militarism, whereas Japan tried to maintain its autonomy by isolating itself from all overseas military commitments whatsoever and sought to defend its territory almost exclusively by allowing US forces to stay on its soil.

The FRG and Japan also reacted very differently to changes in US military strategy. FRG leaders grew nervous every time a new US president took office and announced a new strategic doctrine. They were also worried that the United States would make a deal with the Soviet Union at the expense of the FRG. New US presidents—and the subsequent changes in US military strategy they brought with them—did not, however, substantially disturb Japanese political leaders, and they were never worried about the possibility that the United States would make a deal with the Soviet Union to the detriment of Japan. The only time that the United States upset Japanese political leaders during the Cold War was in 1971, when US president Richard Nixon suddenly announced the normalization of relations with China. Known as the "Nixon Shock," the announcement caused Prime Mister Sato Eisaku to lose some face, as the United States did not inform him of the new policy until a few minutes before the announcement was made. Nevertheless, the overall impact of the "Nixon Shock" on the US-Japan Security Treaty was minimal.

Another instructive difference between Japan and the FRG is the way in which they relied on US nuclear protection. Although both countries depended on the US nuclear umbrella, the degree of the FRG's dependence was much higher than that of Japan. While the German political leaders cursed the new US strategy of flexible response in the 1960s, pro-LDP conservative intellectual Kosaka Masataka wrote in the magazine *Chūō kōron* in 1964 that nuclear weapons had undermined the effectiveness of military power.[117] By the 1970s, most Japanese political elites had come to believe that, as a result of the nuclear stalemate between the superpowers, struggles for power in the international system had shifted from the military to the economic realm.[118] In 1967, Prime Minister Sato Eisaku pronounced Japan's three nonnuclear principles: Japan would not produce, possess, or permit the introduction of nuclear weapons on its soil.[119] (Sato received the Nobel Peace Prize in 1974 for establishing the three principles.) Former US ambassador Edwin Reischauer, however, revealed in a 1980 interview with *Mainichi Shinbun* that the Japanese government had acquiesced in US Navy's bringing nuclear weapons to Japanese ports for the two previous decades.[120] As we can seen then, in contrast to the FRG, which desperately (but not very successfully) tried to ensure strong US resolve in early use of nuclear weapons to deter a Soviet attack, Japan's dependence on US nuclear protection was subdued. Its essentially silent dependence on the US nuclear umbrella was sufficient for Japan to protect its security during the Cold War.

2. After the End of the Cold War

(i) In the 1990s

Although Japan's fear of abandonment by the United States increased after the end of the Cold War, its alliance security dilemma with the United States has been limited by the relatively stable regional environment in East Asia. Japan needed US forces to maintain their presence in the country, even after the end of the Cold War for the same reasons as Germany. To begin, Japan needed the United States in order to defend its territory and maintain stability in the region. North Korea and China in particular have become great concerns for Japan. In December 1993, a US National Intelligence Estimate revealed that North Korea had already developed one or two nuclear weapons and that it was possible for North Korea to attack Japan with Nodong missiles loaded with nuclear bombs. Since then, North Korea has taken numerous provocative actions against Japan. In August 1998, for example, North Korea launched a ballistic missile called Taepo-dong directly over Japan's airspace, and in March 1999, the Japan Maritime Self Defense Force (MSDF) fired warning shots against a North Korean spy ship that was within Japanese waters. The most dramatic event to cause resentment among the Japanese public toward North Korea occurred during the summit meeting between Japanese prime minister Junichiro Koizumi and North Korean leader Kim Jong Il in Pyongyang in September 2002. In that meeting, after decades of denial, Kim Jong Il finally acknowledged that North Korea had kidnapped Japanese citizens in the 1970s and 1980s.[121] Although Kim Jong Il apologized for the kidnappings (because he wanted to pave the way for better Japan–North Korea relations), the fact that eight of the Japanese abductees (including a then-middle-school-aged girl) had died under mysterious circumstances raised tremendous emotional resentment among the Japanese media and public. This made the normalization of the two countries' relations impossible.

Of course, not all Japanese officials wanted to rely on the United States to provide security. A new generation of officials emerged within the Ministry of Foreign Affairs (MOFA) after the end of the Cold War claiming that Japan should pursue its own national interests (*kokueki*), rather than solely depending on US leadership. These "Young Turks" contended that the US-Japan Security Treaty should be used as a tool to achieve Japan's national interests, and Japan's national interests should be placed above the security treaty.[122] Tanaka Hitoshi, for example, stated in one informal meeting among colleagues, "We don't have to ask for US approval every time that we come up with a foreign policy initiative. Japan is not a protectorate of the United States."[123] Tanaka and his like-minded colleagues believed that Japan was capable of making its own foreign policy, especially toward East Asia, and implementing it by itself.[124]

The problem with the Young Turks' position, however, is that the US-Japan Security Treaty is actually one of the most useful tools available for achieving their national security goals. Put simply, it is not clear that the Young Turks' goals can be obtained without using the United States. For example, though around 2001 Tanaka secretly (and without consulting with the United States) began negotiating with a North Korean agent called "Mr. X" to normalize relations between the two countries, the September 2002 summit between North Korea and Japan came about only because of the strong stance the United States took against North Korea at the time. A high-ranking MOFA official told me in an interview that North Korean leaders became very nervous after US president Bush's "axis of evil" speech in January 2002, worried that North Korea would become the next target of a US attack after Iraq. The North Koreans agreed to meet with the Japanese simply because the United States refused to talk with them.[125] Indeed, it was North Korea, not Japan, that took the initiative to bring about the 2002 summit.[126] Tanaka even remarked later, "Dialogue and negotiations [between Japan and North Korea] are inconceivable without some sort of pressure mechanism in the background...The tough US stance on North Korea made the Pyongyang Declaration possible."[127]

China also became a concern for Japan after the end of the Cold War. Although Japan had provided China with a large amount of Official Development Aid (ODA) since the 1970s, China's nuclear test in May 1995 made Japanese political leaders realize that there was a limit to how much economic assistance and investment could influence Chinese behavior. The territorial dispute between Japan and China over the Senkaku Islands (small islands off Okinawa) also escalated in the mid-1990s, when Chinese oil exploration vessels began to arrive at the islands. The Japanese government then used the US-Japan Security Treaty to demand a strong commitment from the United States to defend Japan's right over the Senkaku Islands. In 1996, moreover, China test-fired a series of missiles across the Taiwan Straits, which was designed to discourage those supporting Taiwanese independence from China ahead of Taiwan's national elections.[128] During the crisis, Prime Minister Hashimoto Ryutaro said he was unable to sleep for two nights, afraid that China might really invade Taiwan in the guise of military exercise. Japan was simply not prepared for this worst case scenario.[129]

But it was not until 2000 that Japanese political elites became seriously concerned about the future of China. Until then, China was considered a "small, backwoods country," reliant on Japan for economic aid. After the turn of the century, however, Japanese elites began recognizing that China was becoming a "big country"—both economically and militarily. China's economic growth rate was very high. This, in combination with the decline in Japanese birthrates, meant that China was likely to replace Japan as the largest economy in East Asia within 10 to 15 years. On top of this, China's military spending was not transparent.

Tensions between Japan and China are likely to remain high for the foreseeable future. Beyond military and economic considerations, social and cultural issues continue to undermine the possibility of building constructive relations between the two countries. LDP right-wing conservative politicians, for example, continue to visit the Yasukuni Shrine, where World War II war criminals are buried, and the Chinese government has long capitalized on anti-Japanese sentiment among the Chinese public in order to distract from social, political, and economic problems at home.[130] In order to cope with the uncertainty generated by its tense relationship with China, Japan needs to maintain its alliance with the United States.

Japan also needs the US nuclear umbrella, since—as with Germany—it is impossible for Japan to develop and possess nuclear weapons. Tanaka Hitoshi has explained the limits of what Japan can do to defend itself. He notes that three of Japan's neighbors—Russia, China, and North Korea—possess nuclear weapons, and although it is unlikely that either Russia or China will attack Japan, the future is always uncertain. Yet if Japan decides to build up its own nuclear defense, under the terms of the Nuclear Non-Proliferation Treaty (NPT), Japan will find itself isolated by the international community and will be formally tried at the UN. Japan therefore has no choice but to depend on US nuclear protection.[131] In addition, Takemi Keizo, an LDP member of the Upper House who specializes in foreign policy, suggests that the US-Japan Security Treaty is important because it prevents the Japanese from adopting the simplistic and dangerous argument that the only way to defend the country is to possess nuclear weapons. Japan's acquisition of nuclear weapons, Takemi argues, would surely lead to military competition among East Asian countries and would destabilize the region.[132]

Finally, Japan needs the US-Japan Security Treaty to contain the resurgence of its own militarism and to keep the cost of defense low— again, just as with Germany. By allowing US forces on its soil, Japan can not only keep the size of the SDF small but also limit the power of right-wing elements within politics. That was precisely why Prime Minister Yoshida Shigeru resisted the United States' demand that Japan undertake large-scale rearmament in the early 1950s. Although public support for SDF dispatches to overseas peacekeeping operations under UN authority has gradually increased since the UN Peacekeeping Operations Cooperation Bill (PKO bill) was passed in 1992, the public still seems to fear the resurgence of militarism, and Japanese politicians' reluctance to discuss revising the constitution reflects that public fear.

At the time of the Persian Gulf Crisis of 1990–1991, senior LDP politicians such as Gotōda Masaharu and Miyazawa Kiichi strongly opposed the overseas dispatch of the SDF, fearing that such an attempt would bring Japan back to the militarism of the prewar period. Gotōda remarked that if the restraints on overseas SDF dispatch disappeared, "a great economic power would become a great military power."[133] Miyazawa also argued, "We must clearly state that we cannot change the Japanese Constitution [which prohibits Japan from sending the SDF abroad] at this time. Even if other countries say that having such a constitution is outrageous we must maintain the position that we decided on this and it's not for others to interfere."[134] By 2001, this older generation of LDP politicians who opposed dispatching the SDF overseas had disappeared from the political arena, and the public attitude toward overseas SDF dispatch to UNPKO has gradually turned to favor overtime in the 1990s.[135]

Nevertheless, the majority of the Japanese public still opposes revising Article 9 (the "no-war clause") of the constitution, as well as any changes in the current interpretation of the right of collective self-defense.[136] (The Japanese government has interpreted that Article 9 prohibits Japan from exercising the right of collective self-defense, even though the UN Charter says that all states have that right and therefore Japan also has that right.) In an interview, a young Diet member of the Democratic Party of Japan (DPJ) said that he did not see any problem with discussing dispatch of the SDF to overseas peacekeeping missions during election campaigns. However, he noted, it was still difficult to discuss constitutional revision; once he talked about it, he contended, people tended to label him as being on either the "right" or "left."[137] Although most German politicians do not have a problem being labeled as either "right" or "left," many

Japanese politicians in the catchall, middle-of-the-road parties—namely, the LDP and DPJ—have a strong tendency to avoid discussing "touchy" issues like constitutional revision, because they do not want to alienate either side. This reluctance on the part of middle-of-the-road politicians to talk about revising Article 9 of the constitution seems to indicate that there are still a number of constituencies who feel anxiety about the resurgence of militarism.

Right-wing LDP conservatives have criticized the Cabinet Legislation Bureau (CLB) for its narrow interpretation of the constitution, which hinders the government from exercising the right of collective self-defense.[138] However, a retired high-ranking CLB official contended that the CLB's interpretation of the constitution must be convincing to the public. The right-wing conservatives have criticized the CLB; yet none of them has developed a new argument that has convinced the public of the need for a different interpretation of the constitution or the need for Japan to exercise the right of collective self-defense. The best way to make the exercise of the right of collective self-defense constitutional, the CLB official argued, is not to expand the interpretation of constitution, but to put the issue to a national vote and then seek two-thirds votes in both the Lower and Upper Houses to revise the constitution.[139] The fact that the right-wing LDP and DPJ conservatives have not yet succeeded in revising the constitution indicates that the majority of the public still believe that Article 9 is necessary to contain the resurgence of militarism, as well as to keep defense expenditures low.

So far, I have explained the reasons why Japan needed the United States, even after the Cold War. The relationship between the two countries was not one-sided, however. The United States (and other Asian countries) also wanted Japan to maintain the US-Japan Security Treaty. The balance of the strategic dilemma that Japan faced was not, therefore, overwhelming tipped by the fear of abandonment.

One high-ranking civilian official in Japan's Ministry of Defense (MOD), for example, told me that US forces remain in Japan not because of its strategic location, but because of the generous support ("sympathy budget": *omoiyari yosan*) the host nation provides. If the United States considered only strategic location, he argued, the Philippines would be much better than Japan, because they are closer to China. Yet US forces left the Philippines and stayed in Japan. US forces would remain in Japan, he contended, as long as Japan proves economically useful.[140]

There is, however, a limit to Japan's financial support for US bases. The Ministry of Finance (MOF), for example, reduced the host nation's support in 2000. According to one high-ranking MOF official whom I interviewed, in the late 1990s, the MOF determined that the amount of Japan's support was unreasonably high compared to other countries—such as South Korea, Germany, and Saudi Arabia—hosting US bases. Moreover, while the United States was enjoying an economic boom in the late 1990s, Japan was suffering its "lost decade" (*ushinawareta jūnen*) of deep economic recession. In addition, because the SDF had begun to contribute to PKO activities around the world, the MOF questioned whether Japan should continue to pay for luxurious recreational facilities—such as golf courses and bowling alleys—as well as for the (overused) utilities (water and electricity) on US bases.[141] Therefore, although Japan depended on the United States for its defense, its financial support for the US bases was not unlimited.

In addition, neither the United States nor other Asian countries want Japan to arm itself with nuclear weapons. When asked what would have happened if Japan had not sent the SDF to Iraq in January 2004, one DPJ member of the Lower House specializing in foreign affairs replied that Japan's relations with the United States might have cooled down temporarily, but because the United States does not want Japan to pursue its own independent defense policy with its own nuclear weapons, the relationship between the two countries would have recovered quickly.[142]

Similarly, the United States and other Asian countries share an interest in containing the resurgence of Japanese militarism. Although US policymakers have urged Japan to assume more responsibilities in the US-Japan alliance system, they have mixed feelings about the future consequences of their demands. They want Japan to play a major role in US security strategy, but they do not want Japan to become independent from the United States. They are concerned that should Japan obtain sufficient military capabilities to defend itself without US protection, there would be no reason for Japan to follow US leadership.[143] Chinese political leaders also think that the US military presence in Japan is crucial for their national security, as it prevents Japanese military buildup. They want US forces to stay in Japan in order to keep Japan down indefinitely. The Chinese see any attempt by the United States to encourage Japan to take on more of the alliance burden or to play a significant military role in the region as problematic.[144] Either the withdrawal of the US forces from Japan or too much pressure from the United States placed on Japan to share alliance responsibilities, therefore, could lead to destabilization in the region.[145] As we see, then, Japan's fear of abandonment by the United

States is offset by the US desire to stay in Japan, where the financial support for its operations is substantial, as well as by the United States' (and other Asian countries') concerns about the potential for the resurgence of Japanese militarism.

Japan's fear of entrapment into US-led overseas wars was also less significant than that of the FRG because East Asia was much more stable than Europe in the 1990s. As discussed above, there have been a series of crises in East Asia since the end of the Cold War, and Japan has faced problems with North Korea and China. Nevertheless, unlike the 1999 Kosovo War in Europe, these crises in East Asia did not develop into a full-scale war. Moreover, the United States enjoyed de facto hegemon in East Asia at least in the 1990s and well restrained its forces in the region. Therefore, unlike their German counterparts, when the United States began threatening to attack Iraq, Japanese political leaders had not already experienced the drawbacks of US unilateralism in an actual combat operation. Nor had they directly experienced entrapment into US-led overseas military operations in their region. As a result, the Japanese were much more tolerant of the United States' actions in Iraq than were the Germans.

This is not to say that Japanese political elites were fully satisfied with US policy toward East Asia after the Cold War. They were particularly displeased with the United States' handling of the Korean Peninsula Energy Development Organization (KEDO). KEDO was established as a result of the 1994 US-North Korea Agreed Framework. KEDO's main mission was to construct a light water reactor nuclear power plant in North Korea in order to stop North Korean nuclear weapons development. Tokyo, however, was dissatisfied with the way in which the United States set up the KEDO project—in part because Japan was not invited to the talks that established KEDO, in part because it was forced to finance the expensive project by the United States. In the end, KEDO did not prevent North Korea from developing nuclear weapons or from carrying out provocative actions against Japan. What is more, after George W. Bush became US president in 2001, he renounced the Clinton administration's policies toward North Korea, including the KEDO project (on which Japan had already spent a great deal of money).[146] One of the MOFA officials who worked for KEDO in the 1990s told me he felt that the United States was not serious about solving problems in the Korean peninsula. North Korea is far away from the United States, and therefore, he argued, the United States does not feel as threatened by North Korean nuclear development as does Japan. In spring 2008, when I conducted the interview, he also complained that the United

States had virtually abandoned the Six-Party Talks, which had begun in 2003 to try to prevent North Korea from developing any more nuclear weapons.[147]

Nevertheless, the significance of the alliance security dilemma with the United States seems to have been much lower for Germany, because the North Korean nuclear crisis did not develop into full-scale war. Although Japan had to pay for the expensive KEDO project, which the United States essentially established unilaterally, the United States did not launch a military attack against North Korea. Had the United States launched an attack on North Korea, it is clear that financial and human costs would have been enormous for Japan. Not only would the United States have forced Japan to provide financial support for such a measure (which would surely have been much more expensive than was the KEDO project), but it might also have urged Japan to send troops to the Korean peninsula. Japan also would have faced a massive influx of refugees from the Korean peninsula. Fortunately, however, the United States did not take any unilateral military action against North Korea. While it was problematic that a terrorist country like North Korea had developed its own nuclear weapons, in a way, this development may have actually contributed to regional stability, since the very fact that North Korea possessed nuclear weapons made it difficult for the United States to carry out a military attack. Just as the mutual possession of nuclear weapons kept the United States and Soviet Union from attacking one another during the Cold War, North Korea's own nuclear weapons created an intense standoff, but no worse, in post–Cold War East Asia.

Some MOFA officials whom I interviewed felt that the North Korean threat was real and that the United States was the only country capable of protecting against that threat. Some stressed that, considering the security environment in East Asia, Japan had no choice but to support the US attack against Iraq in March 2003.[148] One who had worked at the UN told me that the only country that can defend Japan is the United States. Some people argue that the UN can protect Japan; however, this MOFA official argued, those people do not understand how the UN works. The UN might be able to deal with problems such as HIV and carry out humanitarian operations around the world, but it can in no way guarantee Japan's security. The UN is a huge bureaucratic organization, he maintained, and is not suitable for coping with an imminent security crisis.[149]

Nevertheless, the threat from North Korea does not seem to be as imminent as these MOFA officials have stressed. One senior LDP member of the Lower House, who twice served as minister of defense, told me that North Korea was unlikely to attack Japan with nuclear missiles, because such an action would surely lead to North Korea's quick demise. It is inconceivable, he contended, that North Korea would take such suicidal action.[150] Moreover, the MOF has questioned the claim forwarded by the Ground Self Defense Force (GSDF) that 2,500 North Korean special commandos could invade Japan from the sea. Katayama Satsuki, a high-ranking official in the MOF Budget Bureau, argued that it was impossible for such a large number of North Korean commandos to approach the Japanese coast without being detected, because both the United States and Japan have satellite surveillance systems. These North Korean commandos would undoubtedly be captured by the Japan Coast Guard, the MSDF, or the US Navy before reaching the Japanese coast. According to Katayama, the GSDF made this claim simply to justify its budget for tanks and artilleries and to resist the MOF's demand that the GSDF reduce the number of its personnel.[151] Tensions may run high between Japan and North Korea, but they have never resulted, and likely will never result, in full-scale war.

Likewise, although relations between Japan and China have long been extremely strained in the post–Cold War period, they are unlikely to lead to armed conflict. Even the 1996 Taiwan Strait Crisis remained relatively calm. Immediately after China test-fired its missiles across the Taiwan Straits, the United States sent two carrier battle ships to the Straits. That proved enough to deter further Chinese aggression. No countries—including the United States, China, Taiwan, and Japan—wanted the crisis to develop into an actual military conflict.[152] Moreover, although relations between Japan and China have deteriorated as a result of Prime Minister Koizumi's visit to the Yasukuni Shrine and the anti-Japanese demonstrations in China after 2001, it is unlikely that such frictions will develop into full-scale war. The two countries are economically interdependent. Indeed, China has replaced the United States as Japan's number one trading partner since 2004. Japanese business leaders (such as Kobayashi Yōtarō, president of the Fuji Xrox Company, and Okuda Hiroshi, president of the Toyota Motor Company) even called on Prime Minister Koizumi and asked him to stop visiting the Yasukuni Shrine.[153] For the Japanese, therefore, China has never posed a concrete military threat, per se. Instead, China has generated a vague concern about its potential to pose a threat in the future.

Officials in the MOD also think that Japan is unlikely to be attacked by any other countries. One high-ranking civilian official in the MOD told me that one day soon, Japan would have no enemies.

As a result, he expected the SDF's main activities to involve PKOs.[154] Similarly, a high-ranking MSDF officer told me that although the US-Japan Security Treaty was set up to defend Japan during the Cold War (at least from the Japanese point of view), the likelihood of an attack on Japan decreased after the end of the Cold War. As such, the purpose of the US-Japan Security Treaty should be expanded to include fighting terrorism together in the world.[155]

In sum, at the time of the 9/11 terrorist attacks in 2001, Japan had not faced a significant alliance security dilemma in its relations with the United States, because the regional environment in East Asia was relatively stable. Although there were a series of crises in post–Cold War East Asia, there was no major war. Consequently, Japan had no direct experience with the fear of entrapment into US-led military operations. The Japanese did not have to consider difficult questions about whether to send ground troops to overseas military operations, as did the Germans in the 1999 Kosovo War. Nor did the Japanese have experience with the negative consequences of US unilateralism in an actual military operation. Because of the low degree of the alliance security dilemma in its relations with the United States, Japan did not have to search for an alliance alternative either. While the Kosovo War prompted Germany to develop the European Security and Defense Policy (ESDP) in an attempt to lessen its alliance security dilemma, there was virtually nothing to compel Japan to search for an alternative to the US-Japan Security Treaty. Instead, Japan reaffirmed its alliance relationship through the 1996 Japan-US Joint Declaration on Security, followed by the 1997 Revision of the US Japan Guidelines for Defense Cooperation, which upgraded bilateral cooperation to deal with regional contingencies. In 1999, the Diet passed legislation (*shūhen jitaihō*), including revisions to the SDF Law, that provided a legal framework to mobilize the SDF and provide other support for the United States and implemented the 1997 Revised Guidelines. As we see, then, while German political leaders were already concerned about entrapment into overseas US-led military operations by fall 2001, and therefore strongly rejected the United States' call for a military attack on Iraq in 2002, Japan was more supportive of the United States' actions in Iraq.

(ii) After 9/11 and the Iraq War: 2001–2003

The difference in the two countries' alliance security dilemma with the United States seems to have influenced the countries' political leaders' intentions, attitudes, and reactions to the issues surrounding the war on terrorism following 9/11 and the Iraq crisis of 2002–2003.

Although both German and Japanese political leaders expressed their strong support for the United States in the wake of 9/11, the intensions and motivations behind Japanese leaders' support for the United States were quite different from those of their German counterparts. While German political leaders expressed their "unlimited solidarity" with the United States following 9/11—with the intention of keeping the United States tied to the NATO framework and thereby exercising some degree of influence over US action—Japanese leaders had no such intention. They never thought that they could constrain US action by using the US-Japan Security Treaty. Nor had they any reason to try, since they had never dealt with US unilateral action in combat. Instead, in fall 2001, Japanese political leaders were considering how they could maintain good relations with the United States by providing modest support as quickly as possible.

MOFA officials were particularly anxious about not repeating the fiasco in the 1990–1991 Persian Gulf Crisis. During the crisis, Japan provided the United States with 13 billion dollars; however, this came begrudgingly, piece-by-piece, and only after the United States applied intense pressure.[156] At the time, trade friction between the United States and Japan was at its highest point. Japanese money was flowing into the US market, and Japanese companies were buying American assets, while foreign companies and products were unable to access the Japanese market because of protectionist practices in Japan. The Americans, therefore, saw Japan (rather than the Soviet Union) as their primary threat, fearing that Japan could replace the United States as the world hegemonic power. One high-ranking MOFA official, who was working in the Japanese embassy in Washington, DC during the Persian Gulf Crisis, provided an interesting illustration of how Japan was seen in the United States at that time. He told me about the picture on the front cover of Paul M. Kennedy's famous book *The Rise and Fall of the Great Power*, published in 1988. In the picture, a sumo wrestler was competing with other Western powers to reach the globe above them. In the late 1980s and early 1990s, Americans feared that US power was in decline, and Japan would likely be the next great power to influence the world. So when the Persian Gulf War broke out, Americans regarded Japan as "selfish" for simply writing checks rather than making human contributions to the war. MOFA officials were the primary targets of "Japan bashing" by the Americans at the time. With the Persian Gulf Crisis in mind, then, in the wake of 9/11, MOFA officials determined to make both financial and human contributions to the United States as quickly as possible.[157]

Although Japan swiftly provided financial and human support for US-led OEF in fall 2001, satisfying the Americans, Japanese support was actually rather modest. Immediately after 9/11, the Cabinet Secretariat announced a support plan, and the Diet passed the Anti-Terrorism Special Measures Law (ATSML) in November 2001, allowing the government to send MSDF ships to the Indian Ocean to participate in OEF. However, unlike Germany, Japan did not send ground forces to Afghanistan. I will discuss why Japan did not dispatch the GSDF in greater detail in chapter 5. But suffice it to say that leaders within the GSDF itself resisted deployment, and, because the United States was satisfied with the MSDF deployment alone, the Japanese government did not feel the need to dispatch the GSDF against its leaders' will. Unlike Germany, therefore, Japan has not had bitter disputes with the United States over burden sharing in Afghanistan.

But the most striking difference between Germany and Japan, which stemmed from the differences in the two countries' alliance security dilemmas with the United States, is the overall attitudes and reactions of political elites toward the issues surrounding 9/11 and the Iraq War. When I conducted interviews with important political actors in the two countries in 2007–2008, these differences were immediately apparent. While German elites were very talkative, sometimes very emotional, and had clear opinions and memories about these events and issues, their Japanese counterparts were very quiet and indifferent—even apathetic. Diet members seemed to be particularly uninterested in either 9/11 or the Iraq War. Not only were these events physically and emotionally distant for them, but they did not feel they had serious stakes in these events, since it was less likely that the events would greatly affect either Japan's security or its alliance security dilemma with the United States. For this reason, Japanese politicians were more likely to acquiesce to the US attack on Iraq in March 2003, even though many of them did not fully agree with the US action.

When I conducted interviews with the Germans, many of them told me emotional stories about their reactions to the 9/11 terrorist attacks. They had clear memories of the day, and their narratives were usually quite similar. In the afternoon of 9/11, they were suddenly told by someone (most likely their secretary or assistant) to turn on the television. They were shocked by the scene of the twin towers in New York. Some of them began crying, and others simply did not know what to do. They shared their vivid memories of 9/11, as if the tragedy happened only yesterday.

None of the Japanese elites with whom I spoke, on the other hand, shared stories of their reactions to 9/11. One DPJ member of the Lower House who opposed the ATSML in fall 2001 and who wrote an article opposing the revision of Article 9 in the well-known leftist magazine *Sekai* in 2006, told me that he did not actually remember much about the events of fall of 2001, including 9/11, the antiterrorism law, and how he felt about them at that time (!).[158] And he was not the only Japanese politician who suffered from apparent amnesia. When I interviewed a high-ranking senior LDP politician who was chairman of the LDP General Council in July 2003 (when the Diet passed the SDF-Iraq bill), he told me that he did not remember what happened during that time, in spite of the fact that he published a book in 2006 that discussed the SDF-Iraq bill (!). He actually spent the first half of the interview reading the minutes of the LDP General Council on the bill in order to refresh his memory and throughout the interview, he continued looking at the record of minutes and even read portions of it aloud in front of me.[159]

When I asked my German respondents about their reactions to President Bush's "axis of evil" statement in January 2002, they openly expressed opinions. Again, they were happy to share their thoughts with me regardless of whether their opinions were positive or negative, and it was very interesting for me to listen to their explanations about why they held those opinions. The Japanese elites, on the other hand, had little to say on this matter either. When I interviewed a young LDP member of the Lower House who had opposed the Iraq War, he expressed general apathy toward the subject. Although he did answer all the questions I asked (without any apparent memory loss), it seemed he felt it was no longer worth talking about the issues related to 9/11 or the Iraq War.[160] He could not change the LDP's policy toward the Iraq War in 2003, and all the GSDF personnel dispatched to Iraq came back home safely in summer 2006. So by spring 2008 (the time of my interviews), Iraq was already the past. This past was not so pleasant for Japanese politicians and, therefore, should be forgotten as quickly as possible. Another high-ranking senior LDP politician (and former defense minister), was not at all interested in talking about the LDP's decision to support the Iraq War. In fact, he became quite angry in the middle of the interview, growing upset because it was difficult and unpleasant for him to discuss why he and his LDP party supported the Iraq War.[161]

All the MOFA officials with whom I spoke expressed their support for the US attack on Iraq. But even their support seemed reluctant. One high-ranking MOFA official (who used to be a close advisor to Prime Minister Koizumi), told me that in 2002 he believed that no matter what Japan said to the United States, the United States would attack Iraq. So Japan would be best off just supporting the United States.[162] Likewise, one high-ranking official in the Ministry of Economy, Trade, and Industry (METI) told me that even if Japan asked the United States not to go to war against Iraq, it would have no effect. All Japan could do, therefore, was accept the inevitable.[163]

It seems that by 2002, most Japanese political elites had already given up thinking about whether Japan should support a US attack on Iraq, because they believed opposition to an attack would have no impact on the US decision. For Japanese politicians and high-ranking officials, the questions of whether the US attack on Iraq was preemptive or preventive, whether Iraq really had WMD, and whether there was a link between Saddam Hussein and al-Qaeda were meaningless. It was not worth considering whether the US action was legal or not, nor whether it was morally justified. Whatever conclusion they reached, the outcome would be the same. The United States would attack Iraq. They could do nothing about it. What is more, Japanese politicians felt no overwhelming need to oppose the attack, since the question of Iraq would not greatly affect either Japan's security or its alliance security dilemma with the United States. An attack on Iraq would not have serious consequences for the regional security environment in East Asia. Nor would it drastically increase the possibility of Japan's entrapment into a war. Not only does Japan's constitution prohibit Japan from directly participating in the war, but also Japanese political elites mistakenly believed that the conflict in Iraq would be settled very quickly. (At least they believed that way through July 2003, when the Diet passed the SDF-Iraq bill.)[164]

It is unclear exactly when and how Prime Minister Koizumi made up his mind to support a US attack on Iraq. Some sources say that the prime minister had already promised US president Bush that Japan would support the United States in the summit talk in February 2002.[165] Other sources say that he made up his mind in the summit meeting in September 2002.[166] But it is certain that Koizumi had already decided to support the United States and to dispatch the SDF to postwar Iraq by September 2002 because the Cabinet Secretariat started calling MOFA and MOD officials to draft a new SDF-Iraq bill at that time.[167] Prime Minister Koizumi's exact reasons for supporting the United States on this matter are also not completely clear. He may have reached his decision on the advice of others (most likely MOFA officials). Even so, he was the one who ultimately chose to follow that advice. And on March 20, 2003, he publicly stated the reasons for his choice to support the US attack on Iraq as follows:

> It is uncertain when Japan would be threatened from outside. I think that Japan has to rely on the US-Japan Security Treaty and the US-alliance relations in order to protect the security of Japanese citizens in case Japan cannot deal with the threat by itself. The United States clearly states that it will regard an attack on Japan as that on the United States... Japanese citizens should not forget that that was a great deterrence against any country that tries to attack Japan.[168]

Although Prime Minister Koizumi emphasized the importance of the US-Japan Security Treaty in dealing with threats from outside, as discussed above, the regional environment in East Asia was rather stable and no threat was imminent. Koizumi's support for the US attack on Iraq more likely stemmed from the fact that such support would not drastically increase the chances of Japan being entrapped into US-led military operations. He could therefore keep the United States happy without incurring too much risk.

Although Prime Minister Koizumi expressed his support for the US attack on Iraq in March 2003, his commitment to supporting the US efforts to stabilize Iraq did not seem to be quite as strong, despite his public intimacy with US president Bush. The Cabinet Secretariat did everything it could do to keep the risk of SDF's entrapment into Iraq as low as possible, as well as to keep the issue out of the realm of public discussion. The friction between the Cabinet Secretariat and the GSDF in the fall of 2003 shows how reluctant the Cabinet Secretariat and Prime Minister Koizumi were about dispatching the GSDF to Iraq. While the GSDF was not exactly enthusiastic about going to Iraq, if they had to go and risk their lives, it wanted to have full support from the government and clear public understanding about their mission. Instead, the Cabinet Secretariat was rather cold toward and unsupportive of the GSDF. When the Japan Defense Agency director, Ishiba Shigeru, asked the Cabinet Secretariat to issue a formal order to prepare for the dispatch in fall 2003, the Secretariat refused. It did not want the SDF's dispatch to become a contentious issue during the November 2003 Lower House election campaign. So the Japan Defense Agency and the GSDF had to prepare for the mission without a formal order from the Cabinet Secretariat, even though that seemed to violate the principle of civilian control over the military.[169]

A high-ranking GSDF officer who actually drafted a plan for the GSDF dispatch to Iraq in fall 2003 complained to me about the then chief cabinet secretary Fukuda Yasuo. He told me that the Cabinet Secretariat was not capable of acting as commander in chief. Because the Cabinet Secretariat did not give the GSDF any direction about what was to be achieved in the mission, it was very difficult for him to draw up plans for the operation. Yet he still took the time to write up a plan and bring it to the Cabinet Secretariat. He told Fukuda that 700 GSDF personnel were necessary to carry out that plan. Fukuda rejected this and reduced the number to 600. In January 2004, Fukuda also suddenly changed the GSDF departure date, which forced the families of the GSDF personnel to change their schedules to see the troops off. According to the high-ranking GSDF officer, Fukuda disliked the military. He was not interested in the SDF and so did not try to understand how difficult it was for the GSDF to draw up and implement the Iraq dispatch plan.[170] Although this GSDF officer told me that Prime Minister Koizumi was more sympathetic toward the GSDF than was Fukuda, Koizumi was the one who appointed Fukuda. If Koizumi really felt that the SDF dispatch to Iraq was so important, he would have told Fukuda to treat the GSDF well. Fukuda's cold attitude toward the GSDF thus seems to have reflected Koizumi's general disinterest in the GSDF dispatch to Iraq.

Koizumi's low commitment to Japan's support for the US effort to stabilize Iraq was also evident in what the GSDF actually did in Iraq. At first, the purpose of the GSDF dispatch was to aid in US efforts to maintain security in postwar Iraq. However, it proved impossible for the GSDF to work with US forces, because the risk of GSDF personnel becoming entrapped in combat situations was very high. Accordingly, the GSDF's mission was changed, and Japanese troops began supporting humanitarian reconstruction efforts in Iraq. In the end, the GSDF chose to settle in Samawah, a remote town in southern Iraq, because it was far from Baghdad where US forces were stationed.[171] The GSDF's main activities in Samawah were to provide local residents with water and to repair public buildings and roads.[172] The GSDF and MOFA decided to bring the troops back home in summer 2006, when local security maintenance authority was transferred from British and Dutch forces to the Iraqi police. Neither the GSDF nor MOFA believed that Iraqi police would be able to guarantee the security of GSDF personnel, and they felt that the GSDF would be unable to maintain local security or defend itself from outside attacks.[173]

In sum, Japan supported the US decision to attack Iraq in March 2003 and sent the GSDF to postwar Iraq for humanitarian reconstruction purposes in January 2004, because, unlike Germany, Japan lacked negative experiences of working with the United States in actual military operations as a result of the relative stability in East Asia in the 1990s. German political leaders had bitter experiences of emerging US unilateralism in the 1999 Kosovo War as well as in the way in which the United States started the war on terrorism following 9/11, thereby suffering from the fear of entrapment into US-led wars that Germany had little or no influence over. On the other hand, their Japanese counterparts did not have significant negative experiences of US unilateralism, or suffer from the fear of entrapment into US-led military operations because of the absence of military conflicts in East Asia, the well-restrained behavior of the United States in the region, and the US security commitment to Japan. They were thus essentially content with its alliance relationship with the United States, and thereby tolerant of the US attack on Iraq, even though they did not fully agree with it.

VI. Conclusion

Two conclusions can be drawn from this chapter. To begin with, the decision made by the SPD-Green government to oppose a possible US attack on Iraq in summer 2002 was not a mere result of the ad hoc election strategy of the SPD leaders who sought to win the September 2002 Bundestag election. The SPD-Green government had already known how difficult it was to work with the United States from its experience of the 1999 Kosovo War, and saw US unilateralism as problematic, even before the 9/11 terrorist attacks took place. German political leaders and officials were also dissatisfied with the way in which the United States started the war on terror in fall 2001 without NATO. It was thus extremely difficult for the SPD to support a US attack on Iraq, especially one that was legally and morally questionable. No matter what time the election would have taken place, the SPD would have opposed a US attack. Moreover, even if the CDU/CSU–FDP had won the 2002 Bundestag election, it would have been very difficult for them to dispatch ground troops to Iraq unless there was concrete evidence that Iraq possessed WMDs. Germany's opposition to the US invasion of Iraq, therefore, was not a result of a temporary calculation by SPD leaders during the election campaign, the personal characteristics of Chancellor Schröder, or the partisan differences between the SPD and the CDU/CSU.

Second, this comparative study of the impact of regional environments on alliance security dilemmas shows that although it is widely believed that Japan supported the US attack on Iraq because of the threat from North Korea, the post–Cold War regional environment in East Asia was in fact much more stable than that of Europe. During the Iraq crisis of 2002–2003, Japanese conservatives often emphasized that Japan must support the US attack on Iraq because the US-Japan Security Treaty was necessary for Japan to cope with the threat from North Korea. Asakura Toshio, chairman of *Yomiuri Shinbun*'s editorial committee, for example, wrote in November 2003:

> If a crisis occurs on the Korean Peninsula, countries that can deal with the crisis are not the European countries, China, Russia, or the U.N. but the United States. The European countries might oppose North Korea's nuclear armament. But France, Germany, and even Britain will not or cannot do more than express verbal opposition. Both China and Russia have special relations with North Korea. They also possess massive nuclear arsenals, thus they do not feel particularly threatened by North Korea, even though North Korea is a neighboring country…
>
> I wonder whether North Korea—that has carried out kidnappings, drug trafficking, and counterfeiting as a national enterprise—will concede without being threatened by force. It is better if we can solve the problem without using force. However, North Korea will not change its attitude unless there is a possibility that force will be used against it.
>
> The *Yomiuri Shinbun* does not think that the [US-Japan Security] treaty will be enforced simply because it is written on a piece of paper. There have been many cases of treaties being broken in the past. We thus have to make continuous efforts in order to get the treaty enforced.[174]

As I explained, however, the reason Japanese political leaders were tolerant of or acquiesced to the US attack on Iraq was not so much the threat from North Korea, but the low level of Japan's alliance security dilemma with the United States. As a result of the relative stable regional security environment in post–Cold War East Asia and the well-restrained behavior of the United States in the region, Japan did not suffer from serious fear of entrapment into a regional military conflict or have a negative experience with US unilateralism in an actual military operation.

4

ALLIANCE INSTITUTIONS

NATO versus US-Japan Security Treaty

I. Introduction

In addition to the differences in the regional security environments and the US security commitment to the two countries, the characteristics of the alliance institutions to which Germany and Japan belong (NATO in the German case and the U.S.-Japan Security Treaty in the Japanese case) had a significant influence on the two countries' alliance security dilemmas in their relations with the United States and, in turn, on their respective responses to the US attack on Iraq. The reason that German political leaders and officials were so concerned about the lack of consultation and information from the United States, whereas their Japanese counterparts have never expressed such concerns is that NATO requires Germany much more commitment and risks than does the US-Japan Security Treaty. German Chancellor Schröder, for example, became angry when US president Bush did not consult him regarding the decision to attack Iraq in summer 2002 because such a decision would bring about potentially far-reaching political and economic ramifications for the interests of Germany.[1] Compared to such a strong reaction of Chancellor Schröder to the growing likelihood of US attack on Iraq in summer 2002, a reaction of Prime Minister Koizumi seems to be rather nonchalant. In his September 2002 meeting with US president Bush, Koizumi indirectly suggested Bush to refrain from taking a unilateral action against Iraq by using a story of Japan's sumo wrestling. However, he never tried to seriously attempt to stop Bush from taking a unilateral action or complained about the lack of consultation or information from the United States (see chapter 2 for a detail story).

In this chapter, I will discuss the two important characteristics that increased the level of the FRG's security dilemma with the United States but kept that of Japan low: the alliance obligation to exercise the right of collective self-defense and the purpose of the alliance institutions. The fact that Japan has no obligation to exercise the right of collective self-defense under the US-Japan Security Treaty whereas the FRG has such an obligation under NATO has a great effect on their respective alliance security dilemmas with the United States. For the absence of an obligation to exercise the right of collective self-defense under the security treaty, Japan has been able to remain aloof from US-led overseas military affairs during both the Cold War and post–Cold War periods. Even if the United States is attacked by a third country, the Security Treaty does not oblige Japan to fight against that country with the United States. Moreover, because the purpose of the Security Treaty remains defense of Japan (at least from Japan's point of view), Japan's Self-Defense Forces (SDF) does not have to follow US forces wherever they go in the world. US unilateralism, therefore, is not very much problematic for Japan, as long as it directly affects the regional security of East Asia.

On the other hand, the collective security obligation under NATO and the transformation in NATO's purpose from territorial defense to out-of-area peacekeeping operations made it difficult for Germany to be indifferent to US unilateralism. With growing US unilateralism in the 1990s, the two characteristics of NATO increased the likelihood of Germany's entrapment into US-led NATO operations abroad, while eliminating the benefits that Germany could enjoy from NATO. Under the Cold War bipolar structure, Germany was able to satisfy its domestic culture of antimilitarism (well-resented by phrases such as "never alone"' and "never again") and practical national interests through NATO. By tying itself to NATO, Germany was able to prevent it from pursuing *Sonderweg* (special way) in order to avoid repeating the same mistake that it had made before 1945. NATO was also a useful framework through which Germany could control powerful member states like the United States and France. However, the two characteristics of NATO along with emerging US unilateralism made it difficult for Germany to influence NATO operations since they were increasingly dominated by the United States. These differences in their respective alliance security dilemma caused by the characteristics of alliance institutions affected the two countries' different views toward the US attack on Iraq in 2003.

II. The Alliance Obligation to Exercise the Right of Collective Self-Defense

1. Japan

Japanese political leaders have used Article 9 (the "no-war clause") of the Japanese Peace Constitution, which prohibits Japan from exercising the right of collective self-defense, to protect Japan from being drawn into US-led overseas military affairs since the US occupation authority wrote a new constitution and introduced it to Japan in 1946. Although the Japanese government dispatched some minesweepers to Korean waters during the Korean War (1950–1953), it began to interpret that Article 9 did not allow Japan to exercise the right of collective self-defense after the end of the Korean War.[2] This decision was reflected in Prime Minister Yoshida Shigeru's strong determination to prevent Japan from getting entangled in American overseas wars. As I discussed in chapter 3, Yoshida felt that economic recovery should be the top priority for postwar Japan. Considering the Cold War international environment surrounding Japan, he concluded that Japan could sufficiently defend its territory by allowing US military forces to stay on its soil. He also concluded that the American demand for Japan's large-scale rearmament should be rejected, because it would both hinder Japan's economic recovery and make Japan a mere satellite of the American military. He was also afraid that the American demand for rearmament would strengthen the power of the military, leading to the resurgence of prewar militarism. Yoshida thus skillfully used Article 9 to evade the American rearmament demand and assume as little alliance obligation as possible.

Consequently, the US-Japan alliance system became rather unequal. Under the US-Japan Security Treaty, the United States is obliged to defend Japan from attack by a third country, whereas Japan has no obligation to defend the United States in the event of an attack on the United States. Indeed, it is unconstitutional for the SDF to fight alongside US forces against a third country, even though the United States is Japan's ally. Even if a third country attacked Japan, the SDF is prohibited from leaving Japan's territory to launch offensive assaults on the aggressor country with US forces, as Article 9 prohibits the SDF from carrying out offense attacks against any country. The SDF's role should remain defensive, not offensive. Thus, US forces would have to launch any offensive strikes against a third country that attacked Japan while the SDF provides the United States with logistical support.

One of the reasons why Japanese politicians were not as interested in the Iraq crisis of 2002–2003 as were the Germans was that the likelihood of Japan's being entrapped into overseas military conflicts (not just in East Asia but in other parts of the world as well) was low due to the fact that Japan could not exercise the right of collective self-defense. To be sure, the power of Article 9 to limit Japan from exercising the right of collective self-defense is not absolute. Indeed, there are allegations that the SDF activities in the Indian Ocean and Iraq had already violated Article 9 of the constitution. The Japanese government officially specified conditions that SDF's overseas activities have to satisfy in order to be constitutional. As long as their activities satisfied those conditions, they are constitutional. The first condition is that the purpose of SDF's overseas dispatch must not be use of force (*buryoku kōshi*). In other words, an SDF dispatch for the purpose of using force is unconstitutional. The second one is that SDF's overseas activities must not be integrated into (*ittaika*) combat operations of other countries. Criteria for judging whether SDF's overseas activities are integrated into the combat operations of other countries would be: (1) whether SDF's activities are taken place in a noncombat zone; (2) concrete contents of their activities; (3) how close the relations between the SDF's activities and foreign troops that are going to use force in combat operations are; and (4) the current conditions of the combat operations.[3]

Handa Shigeru of Tokyo Shinbun, for example, points out that the Maritime Self-Defense Force's (MSDF) activity in the Indian Ocean under the Anti-Terrorism Special Measures Law (ATSML) did not satisfy these conditions, thereby violating the constitution. Not only was the area where the MSDF's activity took place specified as "combat zone" by the United States, but also the MSDF's activity was logistics (*heitan*) for US Navy—the most important part of modern warfare. Therefore, the MSDF's activity in the Indian Ocean, according to Handa, was nothing more than exercising the right of collective self-defense.[4]

A Japanese peace group called Peace Depot also claimed that the MSDF's activity in the Indian Ocean was closely related to US Navy, which participated in the combat operation against Iraq in the Persian Gulf in 2003. In September 2007, Peace Depot, which obtained internal US Navy documents, accused the MSDF of violating both the ATSML and Article 9 of the constitution, not only because the ATSML was designed to allow Japan to provide support for antiterrorism operations in and around Afghanistan only, not in Iraq; but also because one of its fuel supply ships operating in the

Indian Ocean was indirectly involved in US offensive operations in Iraq. Peace Depot revealed that the same amount of fuel (18,704 barrels) that the US Navy oiler *Pecos* received from an MSDF fuel supply ship called *Tokiwa* on February 25, 2003, was transferred to USS *Kitty Hawk* on the same day and that the *Kitty Hawk* later moved into the Persian Gulf and took part in the offensive operations against Iraq.[5]

Similarly, although the Ground SDF (GSDF) was sent to a relatively safe local city in southern Iraq called Samawah far away from Baghdad, the GSDF's camp was in fact attacked by local tribes (who were unable to get a job from the GSDF) with bombs for 13 times.[6] Thus, it is hard to call Samawah a "noncombat" zone. More importantly, the Nagoya High Court judged that the SDF dispatch to Iraq was unconstitutional in April 2008, although it rejected an appeal from a group of lawyers who demand the court (legally) verify that the SDF dispatch to Iraq was unconstitutional, the government pay 10,000 yen (about 80 US dollars) for each lawyer as a compensation for violating their right of citizens to live in peace, and the government stop the ongoing Air SDF's (ASDF) activity in Iraq. (At that time, all GSDF troops had already retuned to Japan.) The lawyers in fact lost their suit since the court turned down their appeal, and the court's judgment on the SDF dispatch as unconstitutional did not have any legal power to change the government's decision since the law suit was a civil procedure (*minji soshō*).

Nevertheless, it was still significant in the sense that the court publicly recognized that the SDF dispatch to Iraq was violating the constitution based on what US forces and the ASDF had actually done in Iraq. The court recognized the US air raids on Fallujah and Baghdad were against humanity since many civilians, including children, were killed. In the US air raids on Fallujah in 2004, for example, US forces used weapons internationally regarded as inhumane, such as cluster bombs, napalm bombs, mustard gas, and white phosphorus. The court stated that the ASDF's transportation activity between Kuwait and Baghdad (2006–2008) violated the constitution not only because Baghdad was not a noncombat zone (ASDF's C130 transport aircrafts had to use flare in order to avoid missiles attacks in Baghdad), but also because ASDF's C130 aircrafts were transporting (allegedly) American soldiers who were going to carry out air raid on Baghdad or counterinsurgency operations, which injured or killed many Iraqi civilians.[7] For these reasons, the SDF's activities in the Indian Ocean and Iraq violated Article 9 prohibiting Japan from exercising the right of collective self-defense. Not only were the SDF's activities taking place de facto combat zones, but also their activities were closely related to US combat operations, which often injured or killed civilians.

Moreover, even though Japan did not have an obligation to exercise the right of collective self-defense under the US-Japan Security Treaty, and even though Article 9 of the constitution put restriction on Japan's exercising that right, it was difficult for Japan to withdraw its forces from Iraq without a (tacit) US consent once Japan sent the SDF to Iraq. For example, from 2004 to 2006, the ASDF was transporting goods necessary for the GSDF's humanitarian activities in Samawah. In exchange for GSDF's withdrawal from Iraq in 2006, however, the United States demanded the ASDF provide regular transportation service between Kuwait and Baghdad for US forces.[8] One retired, high-ranking ASDF officer told me that there was a tacit consent from the United States about the GSDF's withdrawal from Iraq in 2006. The ASDF also wanted to withdraw from Iraq at that time; however, it was difficult for the ASDF to find a timing to withdraw.[9] Thus, once Japan sent the SDF to Iraq, it was difficult to refuse the US demand that Japan make more contributions to US combat operations.

Nevertheless, Japan's Article 9 still has power to limit what the SDF can do in their overseas activities. Although it is difficult for Japan to refuse US demand, Article 9 still makes it possible for Japan to excuse and make as small concession as possible. Especially compare to Germany—more than 4,000 Bundeswehr troops are still in Afghanistan—Article 9 along with no obligation on the part of Japan to exercise the right of collective self-defense under the Security Treaty makes it easier for Japan to withdraw its forces from overseas operations without seriously impairing the credibility of the Security Treaty. For example, as a result of the scandal that the MSDF's fuel supply was used for the offensive operation against Iraq in the Persian Gulf by USS *Kitty Hawk* in 2007, along with the opposition parties' success in controlling the upper house after the July 2007 election, the government failed to renew the ATSML in November 2007, and subsequently, all MSDF ships operating in the Indian Ocean were ordered to return to Japan.[10] Although the government later succeeded in passing a new antiterrorism law in January 2008, and the MSDF resumed the fueling mission in the Indian Ocean, the MSDF activity—a free gas station for foreign navies participating in OEF—was unpopular among the Japanese public, thereby under constant attack from the opposition parties. In the end, as soon as the Democratic Party of Japan (DPJ) took over the government in September 2009, the DPJ put an end to the MSDF activity in the

Indian Ocean. Likewise, the ASDF's transportation activity from Kuwait to Baghdad was also ended in December 2008—eight months later, the Nagoya High Court judged that the SDF dispatch to Iraq was unconstitutional. Therefore, neither Article 9 nor the absence of alliance obligation on the part of Japan to exercise the right of collective self-defense under the Security Treaty might completely eliminate the risk of Japan's entrapment into US-led overseas war. But compare to that of Germany (see the next section for detail), the likelihood of Japan's entrapment is much lower. For these reasons, it was possible for Japanese political leaders to react with relative indifference to 9/11 and the Iraq War and to acquiesce to the US attack on Iraq. Even though Japan gave verbal support for the US attack on Iraq and subsequently dispatched the SDF to Iraq under US pressure, the range of actual actions that could be taken by the SDF was fairly limited.

2. The FRG

German political leaders, on the other hand, were unable to remain indifferent to 9/11 and the Iraq War, because, as opposed to the "unequal" US-Japan Security Treaty, all the member states of NATO are supposed to exercise the right of collective self-defense should one member state be attacked by a third party. Article 5 of the NATO Charter stipulates that an armed attack against one member state will be considered an attack against all member states and, consequently, all member states will come to the aid of the injured party. Because Article 5 requires such high commitment from member states to defend one another, the likelihood of entrapment into a military conflict started by a third party's attack on a single member state is high. NATO member states thus show reasonable concern about other member states' present and future actions, since their behavior could ultimately affect every single member of the alliance system.

It has to be noted, however, that Article 5 does not require an automatic response from the member states in the event of an attack by a third party. In the process of drafting the NATO Charter in 1948, the United States, with an eye toward its traditional isolationism, tried to dilute its commitment to defend Europe. To avoid entrapment into a conflict in Europe, George Kennan—an American diplomat and the father of containment policy—carefully drafted Article 5 as follows:

> The Parties agree that an armed attack against one or more of them in Europe or North America shall be considered an attack against them

all and consequently they agree that, if such an armed attack occurs, each of them, in exercise of the right of individual or collective self-defense recognized by Article 51 of the Charter of the United Nations, will assist the Party or Parties so attacked by taking forthwith, individually and in concert with the other Parties, *such action as it deems necessary, including the use of armed force*, to restore and maintain the security of the North Atlantic area [emphasis added].

Because of the wording "such action as it deems necessary, including the use of armed force," the member states can use their own discretion to decide not only whether it is necessary for them to exercise the right of collective self-defense in the first place, but also whether armed force or other means should be used in response to an attack.[11]

In addition, Article 24 of the Basic Law of the FRG provided it with a way to evade its alliance obligation to NATO and thereby protect itself from being entrapped into overseas military affairs. The second paragraph of Article 24 (international organizations) says:

For the maintenance of peace, the Federation *may* enter a system of mutual collective security; in doing so it shall consent to such limitations upon its rights of sovereignty as will bring about and secure a peaceful and lasting order in Europe and among the nations of the world [emphasis added].

The FRG, therefore, may or may not exercise the right of collective self-defense within the NATO framework. That is ultimately its own decision. And the Bundestag (parliament) has the right to make such decisions. A 1994 constitutional court ruling stated that a Bundeswehr deployment outside of the NATO area that could involve fighting did not violate the Basic Law, since that was a part of a mandate within an international alliance and in accordance with international law. However, the court also stipulated that the government has to obtain majority approval from the Bundestag for such overseas Bundeswehr deployments.[12]

Although NATO's collective security guarantee is not automatic, Article 5 is still important for various reasons. First, it has worked as an important deterrence against outside threats for the European allies. During the Cold War, the European allies felt psychologically secure in the face of communist threats, because Article 5 gave the strong impression that the United States would come to defend its European allies in case of an emergency.[13] Although the significance of Article 5 declined for the FRG after the end of the Cold War, it has been still important for Germany and other European members as well not only for deterrence but also for reassurance because of future uncertainty.[14] Especially, countries neighboring Russia (countries such as Norway) still see NATO's collective security guarantee as vital for their national security.[15] Many East European countries are also seeking to become members of NATO because they wish to benefit from its collective security guarantee.[16] Moreover, NATO's collective security based on Article 5 has continued to be important to maintain the US commitment to European security for the reasons discussed in chapter 3.

The significance of Article 5 is not just that it provides the member states with the practical collective security guarantee, but also that it facilitates the solidarity among the member states. One retired German diplomat told me that the advantage of Article 5 comes from its flexible interpretation. European states have joined (or want to join in the future) NATO for various reasons. Some states might seriously look for the collective security guarantee, whereas others not. The flexible interpretation of Article 5 can bring many European states into NATO.[17] In addition, Article 5 has prevented potential conflicts between the member states (such as that between Turkey and Greece) by guaranteeing their national territorial integrity. Article 5, therefore, has worked as important mechanism for promoting peace and stability in the region. In sum, although Article 5 does not necessarily compel the member states to automatically exercise the right of collective self-defense, it is difficult for member states not to do so when one of their fellow members is attacked, because it is important to keep its credibility in order to maintain and produce the benefits discussed above. As a result, the likelihood of Germany's entrapment into overseas operations under NATO—which tend to be dominated by the United States—is high.

However, the more fundamental consequence of NATO's Article 5—especially compared to Japan's case regarding the likelihood of entrapment into US-led overseas wars—is that there is virtually no legal constraints that prevent Germany from exercising the right of collective self-defense. As oppose to the case of Japan's SDF, not only can the German Bundeswehr be dispatched to an overseas mission for the purpose of use of force (*buryoku kōshi*), but also there is nothing wrong even if the Bundswehr closely works with other NATO's troops, or their activities are integrated into (*ittaika*) NATO's combat operations. In fact, since it was established in 1955, the Bundewsehr has been placed under NATO's command, and has been called as an "alliance army." During the Cold War, massive numbers of troops from various NATO countries were stationed in the FRG, and the Bundeswehr had a numerous military exercises with them in order to counter the Warsaw Pact troops. After the end of the Cold War, the Bundeswehr participated in the NATO's air campaign against Serbia in 1999.

It is true that the German government can place "national caveats" on overseas Bundeswehr activities, when it decides to dispatch the Bundeswehr abroad. In 2002, for example, Berlin sent Bundeswehr troops to Afghanistan: 100 members of the Special Force (KSK) for Operation Enduring Freedom (OEF) in southern Afghanistan and 3,000 troops to the International Security Assistance Force (ISAF) in northern Afghanistan. However, it placed restrictions on what the Bundeswehr could do there. The KSK, for instance, was about to capture a Taliban commander in cooperation with the Afghan secret service organization (NDS) and the Afghan army in March 2008; however, the Taliban commander escaped. Although the KSK could have shot him, the German government did not authorize them to do so. The German government gave an instruction to the KSK soldiers: "The use of lethal force is prohibited unless an attack is taking place or is imminent." Thus, unlike the Americans or the British Special Forces, the KSK was unable to carry out capture-or-kill missions.[18] In addition, the German government has steadfastly refused the demand made by the United States and Canada that the FRG send more combat troops to southern Afghanistan to fight against the Taliban insurgencies, because FRG leaders have disagreed with American tactics for fighting against the Taliban.[19] Nevertheless, it is becoming increasingly difficult for Germany to dodge the alliance burden by using its national caveats, because the allies are becoming impatient with Germany as the number of casualties in the south has increased.[20] Moreover, since Germany sent Bundeswehr troops to Afghanistan, it has become difficult to withdraw as security conditions have worsened because such an action would negatively affect alliance credibility. To make matters worse, as I explained in chapter 3, Germany has increasingly losing its influence over NATO's operations as the United States has dominated them since the late 1990s. The likelihood of Germany's entrapment into US-led wars, therefore, is much higher than that of Japan.

In this context, it was extremely difficult for German political leaders to support the proposed US attack on Iraq in 2002–2003. The Iraq War was exactly the type of war Germany feared—one led by the United States with a loose coalition of willing, in which Germany would have no input. Germany would not have had any voice over how to carry out either an invasion or postwar reconstruction of Iraq. The Bundeswehr would likely have been used as a "tool" by the United States. If German leaders expressed their support for the US attack on Iraq, it would be difficult to maintain such mere lip service. Eventually Germany would have no choice but to dispatch the Bundeswehr to Iraq. Although the German government might be able to place national caveats on Bundeswehr activities in Iraq, as it did in Afghanistan, it would be difficult to keep the Bundeswehr away from dangerous peacekeeping operations (PKOs) with a high likelihood of casualties in the de facto combat zone. With such a profound alliance security dilemma, then, it was very difficult for German political leaders to express support for a US attack on Iraq in 2002–2003.

III. The Purposes of the Alliances

1. The FRG

During the Cold War, the sole purpose of NATO was to defend member states from a Soviet attack. The FRG was thus only responsible for defending the territories of other member states under Article 5 of the NATO Charter. The Bundeswehr was supposed to operate only within the territory of the member states, and the majority of FRG politicians regarded out-of-area deployment unconstitutional. As a result of the collapse of the communist bloc in 1990, however, the purpose of NATO was altered to include out-of-area PKOs. NATO agreed, on a case-by-case basis, to carry out PKOs based on decisions made by the UN, since there was no UN army to enforce the UN decisions.[21] To support this development, in July 1994, the German Federal constitutional court overturned a previous constitutional interpretation and stated that it was constitutional for the government to deploy the Bundeswehr outside the area of the NATO member states, though the government would have to obtain a Bundestag mandate to do so. During the Cold War, therefore, the security that NATO was producing under Article 5 of the collective self-defense obligation was a private good that only the member states were able to consume. Since the end of the Cold War, however, the type of security produced by NATO became a public good benefitting both member and nonmember states. Consequently, not only has the likelihood of Germany's entrapment into overseas PKOs grown, but, as Joseph Lepgold suggests, the free-riding incentives among member states have also increased, resulting in "nasty burden-sharing squabbles" among them.[22]

The transformation of NATO's purpose began with adoption of the 1991 NATO Strategic Concept.[23] The 1991 Strategic Concept identified several potential outside threats with which NATO should deal. The first threat discussed was from former communist countries in Central and Eastern Europe. "The serious economic, social and political difficulties, including ethnic rivalries and territorial disputes" in those countries were likely to cause instability. Although instability in those countries might not pose a direct military threat to NATO member states, it might involve outside powers and eventually spill over into the member countries. The second threat involved the Soviet Union. The Soviet Union still had substantial military capability, including its nuclear dimension, and whether the Soviet Union would develop into a peaceful democratic country was still uncertain at that time. The third concern was the potential threat stemming from instability in the Middle East and Mediterranean regions. Finally, the document discussed the global risks posing threats to the security of NATO member states—threats such as proliferation of weapons of mass destruction (WMD), disruption of the flow of vital resources, and actions of terrorism and sabotage. The areas covered by the 1991 Strategic Concept, therefore, stretched the entire globe. This expansive tendency was further accelerated in the 1999 Strategic Concept, which emphasized conflict prevention and crisis management as alliance objectives.[24]

In the 2002 Prague Summit Meeting, moreover, member states' commitment to expand the scope of NATO's mission globally was strengthened. The member states formally agreed to "strengthen our ability to meet the challenges to the security of our forces, populations and territory, from *wherever* they may come" [emphasis added].[25] Because they did not specify any particular region or country, NATO's reach could be extended to Pakistan, Indonesia, and the Philippines.[26] One might even imagine a "global NATO," which would continue to admit new members into NATO from all over the world, ranging from Afghanistan to Zimbabwe. And, if the number of members finally reached nearly 200, NATO would merge with the UN General Assembly.[27] The 2003 Defense Policy Guidelines of the Federal Ministry of Defense written by Defense Minister Peter Struck (SPD) reflected this trend. Struck wrote:

> Defense as it is understood today means more, however, than traditional defensive operations at the national border against a conventional attack. It includes the prevention of conflicts and crises, the common management of crises, and post-crisis rehabilitation.

Accordingly, *defense can no longer be narrowed down to geographical boundaries, but contributes to safeguarding our security wherever it is in jeopardy*[28] [emphasis added].

Thus, it became possible for the German government to dispatch the Bundeshwehr anywhere in the world.

Nevertheless, German politicians have raised concerns about the FRG's unlimited commitment to overseas PKOs under NATO, arguing that this would increase the likelihood of Germany's entrapment into a US-led war overseas. Rolf Mützenich (a SPD member of the Bundestag Foreign Relations Committee), for example, wrote that after 9/11, NATO has been searching for an identity. It is uncertain whether NATO is a defense union of democratic states or a global alliance focused on intervention. In his opinion, the purpose of NATO should be to protect its member states, not to act as a world policeman. He is skeptical about the idea of NATO's global alliance with other countries in the Asia Pacific such as Japan, New Zealand, and Australia. Such a global alliance, according to Mützenich, would be just another US-led "coalition of willing."[29]

The CDU member of the Bundestag (a former parliamentary secretary in the Ministry of Defense) whom I interviewed was also skeptical about the expansion of NATO's mission to the Asia Pacific. He stated that at the NATO summit meeting in Riga in November 2006, the United States tried to expand the scope of NATO's mission to the Asia Pacific in order to make it a worldwide organization. However, he maintained, the Germans would not support such a development. When he recently traveled to Japan, a Japanese vice minister of defense—who seemed to believe the US notion of a global NATO—told him that the Bundeswehr would likely act under NATO in the event of an emergency in Korea. This belief, however, is totally absurd from the German point of view.[30]

The prospects for a global NATO seem to be dim, because even NATO in its limited form has already experienced serious difficulties in its out-of-area PKOs. As Joseph Lepgold predicted, when the security produced by NATO changed from a private to a public good, the free-riding incentives among member states increased. As a result, NATO has suffered from incessant disputes among member states over burden sharing. During the Cold War, the member states were willing to sacrifice their autonomy to NATO and make strong commitments to defending their allies under Article 5 of the collective self-defense obligation in exchange for NATO's commitment (or, more specifically, the United States' commitment) to defend their territory. The security produced by NATO, therefore, was a private good consumed by only the member states. On the other hand, the member states do not have as serious a stake in post–Cold War out-of-area PKOs as they did in the defense of their own territory against outside threats during the Cold War, and the benefits produced by the post–Cold War out-of-area PKOs under NATO are no longer limited to the member states themselves. As NATO has begun to work as a quasi-UN army since the early 1990s, the security produced by NATO's PKOs benefits both member and nonmember states alike. The member states, therefore, tend to be reluctant to get involved in out-of-area PKOs in which their armies could suffer a number of casualties. Instead, they try to easy- or free-ride on other member states.

In the present peacekeeping operation in Afghanistan, for example, the disputes over national caveats among the NATO members have been nasty and sometimes even emotional. The United States, Canada, and Great Britain have accused Germany of keeping the Bundeswehr in the relatively stable northern part of Afghanistan and refusing to send combat troops to the south to fight against the Taliban insurgency. However, from the German point of view, sending 3,000 troops to northern Afghanistan is all they can do. Although Defense Minister Peter Struck made a well-known statement in 2002—"Our security must also be defended on the Hindukush (the Afghan mountain range)"[31]—it is still difficult to convince the public of the importance of the Bundeswehr's contributions to the peacekeeping operation in Afghanistan. Thus, no political leaders have dared to send soldiers to combat operations in the south, since that would surely result in a number of casualties. Although the number of German casualties is smaller than those of the other major contributing countries, the significance of war casualties for Germans seems to be greater than for others because of Germany's particular historical past. Each time Bundeswehr soldiers die in Afghanistan, the German government holds funerals for them, which the defense minister, Bundeswehr chief of staff, and other high-ranking party and government officials always attend.

In addition, regarding the national caveats, the high-ranking Bundeswehr officers with whom I conducted interviews argued that *all* NATO member states, including the United States, should remove their national caveats, not just Germany. If the United States wants Germany to remove its caveats, the United States should do the same. The United States has never placed its troops under foreign command, for example, while the FRG has done so many times.[32]

The change in NATO's purpose from the defense of member states to out-of-area PKOs, which began in the early 1990s, therefore, not only increased the likelihood of Germany's overseas entrapment but also brought about constant disputes among the member states over burden sharing and thereby undermined alliance cohesion. German political leaders are especially concerned that NATO will be dragged into the US global strategy with which they do not necessarily agree. Although they think that out-of-area instabilities represent threats to their security at home, stakes in out-of-area PKOs are not as high as were those concerning their own territorial defense during the Cold War. Moreover, most German leaders think that out-of-area problems should be solved using nonmilitary means. For these reasons, German political leaders did not support the US-led attack on Iraq in 2002 and refused to make any commitment to send their troops to Iraq.

2. Japan

In contrast to NATO, the purpose of the US-Japan Security Treaty has not changed significantly since the end of the Cold War. Although the United States has used the Security Treaty to maintain its military bases in Japan, from which it has projected its forces, from East Asia to the Middle East since the Cold War period, Japan has regarded the sole purpose of the Security Treaty as the defense of its territorial integrity regardless of how the United States has used its military bases in Japan. Because the Security Treaty does not oblige Japan to send its troops to overseas PKOs, Japan—unlike Germany—has never experienced "nasty burden-sharing squabbles" with the United States in overseas PKOs in the post–Cold War period. Although Japan has begun to send its troops to overseas PKOs under the UN authority since the Peacekeeping Operation bill was passed in the Diet in 1992, Japan can decide by itself to which UN PKOs it would send the SDF and what kind of support it would provide. Japan can effectively choose to send the SDF to any UN PKO in the world—and so usually opts to involve the SDF only in operations in which it is unlikely to suffer casualties—without affecting the credibility of its alliance with the United States. Therefore, the likelihood of Japan's entrapment into US-led military affairs abroad remains relatively low. Japanese political leaders did not have to worry much about the potentially negative consequences of the US attack on Iraq for their alliance security dilemma with the United States, and they certainly had much less to worry about in this regard than did their German counterparts in 2002–2003.

To be sure, Japan experienced some changes in its alliance relationship with the United States after the end of the Cold War. For example, the "US-Japan Joint Declaration on Security: Alliance for the Twenty-First Century" formally announced by the top leaders of Japan and the United States on April 17, 1996, marked a new development because it stressed the importance of the alliance not just for the security of Japan, but also for the entire Asia-Pacific region for the first time. However, this attempt to expand the purpose of the US-Japan alliance from the sole defense of Japan to regional stability was fairly limited and did not entail significantly new obligations for Japan.

The 1999 Defense Guidelines bill (*shūhen jitaihō*), along with the revisions to the SDF Law, introduced by the Japanese government as a result of the 1996 Joint Declaration, provided a legal framework to mobilize the SDF and provide support for the United States in case of regional contingencies that impact the security of Japan. The Guidelines deliberately defined the term *shūhen*—the area surrounding Japan that would presumably impact Japanese security—in vague terms in order to expand the scope of the alliance's functions to encompass the entire Asia-Pacific region. The Japanese government argued that the definition of *shūhen* was "situational" rather than "geographical," because Japan's security interests could not be marked in a definitive geographical line, although it envisaged that the scope of the alliance's operation was likely to remain close to Japan and would not stretch as far as the Indian Ocean in the Middle East.

Although it seems that the Guidelines succeeded in expanding the alliance's potential range of action, it did not fundamentally change the preexisting nature of the US-Japan alliance system. The security treaty was still an unequal treaty, one in which Japan had no obligation to exercise a right of collective self-defense on behalf of the United States. Japanese action was still limited by Article 9. In the event of an emergency, Japan's role remained confined to rear-area functions. Moreover, because the concept of situational need was vaguely defined, it was still possible for Japan to choose not to support the United States if Japan judged that the matter would not impact its own security.[33]

Evidence of Japan's attempt to protect itself from becoming entangled in US-led overseas military affairs can also be found in its failure to utilize the 1998 Defense Guidelines (shūhen jitaihō) in the wake of 9/11 to provide support for the United States. Japanese political leaders were concerned that if they employed the Guidelines to support OEF in and around Afghanistan, they would ultimately have to break the restrictions placed within the Guidelines, which limited the Self-Defense Forces' support for the United States to sea and airspace operations. (They were considering dispatching the GSDF to Afghanistan or Pakistan at that time.) They also worried that using the Guidelines in this case would undermine the country's advantage in keeping the definition of shūhen vague. Once they created a precedent by sending the SDF to Afghanistan or to the Indian Ocean under the Guidelines, they would lose the ability to employ the opt-out clause to avoid committing Japan to supporting the United States in some future war in which Japan had no interest.[34]

In the end, instead of using the Guidelines, the Japanese government passed the ATSML and dispatched the MSDF to the Indian Ocean. The ATSML was indeed "special" in the sense that it was effective only for two years (though it was renewable). Japan's role under the ATSML was only to provide noncombat and rear-area logistical support. Moreover, the ATSML was not invoked by the US-Japan Security Treaty but as a result of the UN resolutions identifying 9/11 as a threat to international peace and calling on all UN members to counter terrorism. The support that Japan provided under the ATSML, so the logic went, was not just for the United States, but for the international community as a whole to fight terrorism. Thus, the SDF's support for the United States under the ATSML was carried out outside the framework of the Security Treaty.

In fact, the SDF-Iraq bill, which was passed in the Diet in July 2003 and dispatched the SDF to Iraq, was designed using the same logic as the ATSML. The May 2003 UN Resolution 1483, which called upon members to assist in the reconstruction of Iraq, was used as the legal basis for the SDF-Iraq bill, and the bill's "official" purpose was to provide humanitarian and reconstruction assistance in postwar Iraq, not necessarily to help the US forces there. As such, the main purpose of the US-Japan Security Treaty has remained the defense of Japan (at least from the Japanese point of view), and Japan's overseas peacekeeping activities have been carried out outside the framework of the security treaty.

* * *

In sum, while NATO's purpose changed from territorial defense of its member states to out-of-area PKOs after the end of the Cold War, the purpose of the US-Japan Security Treaty remained unchanged. This difference had a substantial impact on the two countries' respective strategic dilemmas with the United States and, in turn, their responses to the Iraq War. As a result of the change in NATO's purpose, the type of benefit that it produced went from a private to public good. Accordingly, as free-riding incentives increased, disputes among the member states over burden sharing in overseas PKOs intensified. Still, while member states have tried to free or easy ride on other members in PKOs, they cannot completely walk away from PKOs, as NATO's success in PKOs affects the credibility of the alliance itself. In addition, the United States has tended to exploit this logic as it has tried to use NATO for its own global strategy. German political leaders thus have expressed concern that NATO would be dragged into US-led overseas wars. Because of this fear of entrapment into US global strategy for the sake of NATO's alliance credibility, the SPD-Green government opposed a US-led attack on Iraq in 2002.

On the other hand, the purpose of the US-Japan Security Treaty has remained constant since the end of the Cold War. Its purpose (from Japan's point of view) continues to be the defense of Japan. Unlike the case of Germany in NATO, Japan had no obligation to send the SDF to overseas PKOs under the Security Treaty. While Japan did (facing pressure from the United States) begin making contributions to overseas PKOs under UN authority after the end of the Cold War, its contributions to these operations were made outside the framework of the Security Treaty. Thus, its commitment to overseas PKOs does not directly affect the credibility of its alliance with the United States. In addition, the geographical scope of the Security Treaty was much narrower than that of NATO. While NATO's mission was extended to reach the entire globe, the Security Treaty's mission covers only the Asia Pacific. Moreover, with Article 9 still in effect, Japanese military action continues to be limited to rear-area support. In contrast to Germany, therefore, the likelihood that Japan would be dragged into US-led overseas military affairs through the Security Treaty framework was relatively low. For this reason, Japanese political leaders were more tolerant of the US attack on Iraq in 2003 than were their German counterparts.

IV. Conclusion

Along with the regional security environments and US security commitment to the regions, the characteristics of alliance institutions have a great impact on the difference in the likelihood of two countries' entrapment in US-led overseas wars, thereby their responses to 9/11 and the Iraq War. The regional security environments, US security commitment to the regions, and the characteristics of alliance institutions have in fact interacted one another. The origins of the different alliance obligations, for example, stemmed from the regional security environments surrounding the two countries during the Cold War. In facing the massive troops of the Warsaw Pact countries, Germany had no choice but to defend its territory with the NATO allies, especially with the United States. In exchange for its strong alliance commitment to exercise the right of collective self-defense under Article 5 of the NATO Charter, Germany was able to secure the US commitment to defend its territory from a Soviet invasion. The Bundeswehr was placed under NATO command, and conducted many military exercises with a massive number of foreign troops from NATO member states stationed in the FRG in order to prepare for a "combat" as a result of the Soviet invasion.

Postwar Japan, on the other hand, was surrounded by a much more favorable regional security environment. The Soviet threat to Japan was not particularly imminent, making it possible for Japan to remain secure simply by permitting US military forces to stay on its soil. Japan did not have to commit to collective self-defense with the United States under the US-Japan Security Treaty. Japanese political leaders used Article 9 of the constitution in order to dodge US demand of rearmament and refuse to involve Japan in any kind of regional collective security organization out of their fear that such an organization would force Japan play a military role in US efforts to fight the Cold War in the region. Because Article 9 prohibited Japan from exercising the right of collective self-defense, it was unconstitutional for the SDF to fight alongside US forces against a third country. Consequently, the SDF's military exercises with US forces were fairly limited, and it was certainly out of the question for the SDF to conduct exercises with US forces for the purpose of "combat" operations. The different characteristics of the two alliance institutions, originated from the respective regional environments during the Cold War, have also shaped the characteristics of the two countries' military institutions (see chapter 5 for detail). And these factors together have influenced the likelihood of the two countries' entrapment into US-led overseas wars.

5

Military Institutions: Bundeswehr versus Self-Defense Forces (SDF)

I. Introduction

The military institutions of the two countries—the Bundeswehr in Germany and the Self-Defense Forces (SDF) in Japan—did not have the power to make a specific decision regarding whether or not their countries would support or oppose the US attack on Iraq. Both Germany and Japan are democratic countries, and such decisions were made by the top civilian leaders. In addition, in both countries, the overseas deployment of troops must be approved by the legislative branch of the government. Yet, the characteristics of the two countries' military institutions had a great influence on what kind of contributions their countries actually made to the US-led war on terrorism in and around Afghanistan, as well as to the reconstruction of postwar Iraq. Thus, they could be the important sources of overseas entrapment, and therefore, along with the regional security environment, US commitment to the regions, and alliance institutions, they represent one of the significant factors influencing the levels of the two countries' alliance security dilemmas with the United States.

The differences in the characteristics of the German Army and Japan's Ground Self-Defense Force (GSDF) have particularly important implications for the two countries' alliance security dilemma with the United States, because a country's ground force is more likely to engage in local combat operations than either its navy or air force.[1] The most significant difference between the German Army and the GSDF is that the German Army is active in expanding the scope of its overseas activities and do not hesitate to take risks of casualties, whereas the GSDF has been very conservative about overseas dispatch, and has taken all measures to avoid sending their troops to places where the likelihood of casualties was high. For example, following 9/11, the German Army did not hesitate to send its troops to Afghanistan. The German Army even sent 100 soldiers from the Special Operations Forces (Kommando Spezialfräfte: KSK) to Afghanistan, along with 3,000 regular troops. On the other hand, in fall 2001, Japan's GSDF aggressively lobbied Diet members to stop the government's plans to dispatch GSDF troops to Afghanistan and Pakistan. In 2003, none of the high-ranking GSDF officers tried to stop the government's plan to dispatch their troops to Iraq; however, what the GSDF had actually done was to send the minimum number of troops to Iraq (600 troops) in January 2004. In addition, the GSDF's mission was solely limited to humanitarian activities in a relatively safe town in southern Iraq far away from Baghdad, and its personnel never engaged in combat operations or suffered any casualty. Because of the GSDF's conservatism on overseas dispatch, the possibility of Japan's becoming entrapped into Iraq (as well as overseas peacekeeping operations [PKOs] more generally) has remained fairly low.

The attitude and policy preferences of the two countries' military institutions toward US-led overseas wars as well as overseas PKOs in general depend on the extent to which they have been integrated into the strategic structure of the alliance forces since the Cold War period. The more closely they have been integrated into the alliance forces, the more likely they have contacts with the alliance troops. Consequently, they tend to develop camaraderie with the alliance troops at the grassroots level, thereby willing to help the alliance forces (including the US forces) and work with other foreign troops in overseas PKOs. The extent of their integration was mostly a result of the respective regional security environments since the Cold War period. The Cold War regional security environments had a great impact not only on the decision of US forces on whether to integrate the two countries' military institutions into their strategic structure, but also on the decision of the two countries' governments on whether to allow their military forces to be integrated into the structure of alliance forces. The decision of US forces to integrate the two countries' military institutions also depended on the capability and usefulness of the two countries' military institutions.

The observations in this chapter draw heavily upon the data from my confidential interviews with a small number of military officers. There are, of course, concerns about drawing broad conclusions from a small, anecdotal sample such as this. However, because most military officers in both countries tend not to open up to the public, it would be exceedingly difficult to conduct a large-scale survey of these officers. Nor are many secondary materials, such as lengthy press interviews, available for examination. Thus, while the data employed in this chapter are somewhat limited, they offer a new and valuable perspective on this important issue.

II. The Bundeswehr (Germany)

The Bundeswehr is called the "alliance army" because it has been placed under NATO command since it was established in 1955. (For this reason, the Federal Republic of Germany [FRG] does not have its own national military command.) Defense Minister Peter Struck (Social Democratic Party [SPD]: in office 2002–2005) wrote in the 2003 Defense Policy Guidelines:

> Multinational preventive security measures are one of the basic factors determining German defense policy. With the exception of evacuation and rescue missions, *the Bundeswehr will conduct armed operations only together with allies and partners in a UN, NATO and EU context.*[2]

The degree of the Bundeswehr's integration into NATO has been very high, and Bundeswehr officers have a great deal of experience working with other allies' officers through NATO. The degree of interaction between Bundeswehr officers and their allies' counterparts is far greater than the level of interaction between officers in the SDF and the US forces. Bundeswehr officers have numerous contacts with both US forces and other European allies. (Indeed, some of the Bundeswehr officers with whom I conducted interviews spoke British English, not American English.) Moreover, their relationships with other allies' officers extend over decades, dating back to the Cold War period.

Regarding the air force, for example, one former general told me that he received two years of jet pilot training in Texas and Arizona in late 1960s. He was one of the 90 German recruits who were sent to the United States at that time, and half of the students in the training were American. (He added that some of his American classmates were going to be visiting him in Germany a week after I conducted the interview. So his friendship with the American classmates lasted for decades.[3]) He also received general staff officer training in Canada. In addition, another active air force colonel specializing in air surveillance spoke fluent English—despite never having lived in a foreign country until the late 1990s when he was assigned to work in NATO headquarters in Brussels—because he worked with NATO servicemen in the air defense controller in Germany from the late 1970s to the mid-1980s.[4]

In the navy, one active vice admiral told me that he worked at NATO's Supreme Allied Commander Atlantic in Norfolk, Virginia (SACLANT) for six years. (The first assignment, which lasted for three of the six years, was during the Cold War.) When he was serving at SACLANT in the 1980s, his boss was a British captain—part of the broad multinational team operating SACLANT.[5] In addition, a former vice admiral, who worked in the NATO branch office in Britain for one-and-a-half years in the mid-1990s, told me that although he held positive feelings toward many countries' navies, he felt that the British, the Dutch, and the Danish navies were particularly close to the German Navy. Geographical proximity has led to frequent interactions between German naval ships and those of the United Kingdom, the Netherlands, and Denmark, and these interactions, the vice admiral suggested, had generated an ethos of cooperation and camaraderie. I asked the vice admiral about the tension that existed between the German and the British navies immediately following World War II.[6] He informed me that the relationship between the two navies was already quite positive and supportive by the time he entered the navy in the early 1960s. (Indeed, many German Navy ships and servicemen have been sent to Flag Officer Sea Training [FOST] hosted by the British Royal Navy in Portland and Plymouth since 1958. In all, 185 German warships and 38,000 German sailors have been trained by the Royal Navy.)[7]

The vice admiral also told me that when German naval officers meet with their American counterparts in a harbor, the Americans board the German ships, and not vice versa, because alcohol is prohibited on US ships. The German and American officers then drink and party together for hours. And it seems that US Navy officers were not the only ones with whom the vice admiral drank. During the interview, he offered an enigmatic observation about Russians and Germans sharing a similar mentality. When asked for clarification he explained that when Russians become emotional while intoxicated, they cry—as do Germans. On the other hand, he suggested, navy officers from countries such as Britain and the United States never cry while drunk. (He had, of course, met the Russian naval officers after the end of the Cold War.)[8] While these stories are certainly amusing anecdotes, they also show just how extensive the relationships are between German Navy officers and their foreign counterparts.

It is often said that during the Cold War the army was fixed on German soil and, as a result, army officers' views tended to be narrow and parochial, though they became more internationally oriented once they began to participate in overseas PKOs after the end of the Cold War. However, even during the Cold War, German Army officers had significant experiences working with their allies' because many troops from other NATO member states were stationed in the FRG and often held exercises with the German Army there. I met one active army colonel who spoke fluent British English. I asked him whether he had ever lived and worked in England. Though he had not, when he was chief of staff of a brigade in the FRG for two years in the mid-1980s, he worked extensively with British and Belgian troops. In addition, he had lived and worked at NATO headquarters in Brussels for eight years in the late 1990s and early 2000s.[9] While serving in these positions, he learned British English.[10]

I met another active army colonel whose curriculum vitae indicated that he worked with US forces for the transportation and protection of "special weapons" in the FRG in the mid-1980s. When questioned about the "special weapons," he clarified that they were actually nuclear weapons. It was the Bundeswehr's duty to provide infrastructure and personnel to maintain US nuclear weapons on German soil, though it was the United States that would ultimately decide on the use of the nuclear weapons should they ever be needed. He also told me that he had studied in a French military school and often worked with the French Army because he was born in a town near the French-German border and was fluent in French. Moreover, he worked for the UN for two years in the mid-1990s as a planning officer specializing in Africa, the Middle East, and the Balkans and attended an officer-training course in the United States in 2001. He also had experiences serving in overseas PKOs in places such as Somalia, Bosnia, Albania, Macedonia, and Kosovo throughout the 1990s.[11]

A former army general provides another good example of how extensive the army officers' relations with other NATO officers were. In my interview, he explained that even in his earliest experiences he worked with the US troops in Germany at the platoon and company levels, but his contacts with the United States and other allied troops became more frequent after he passed the general staff course in the late 1970s and became a chief of a panzer brigade. He participated in an exercise every autumn with the allied forces called "autumn Reforger" in which 60,000 German soldiers and allied forces exercised together in the FRG based on the General Defense Plan. The German Army also had an exercise with the allied forces in winter every 2–3 years on German soil called the "Wintex." This exercise included simulations of nuclear war.[12]

The general also told me that he studied at the army staff college in Great Britain in the early 1980s. During that time, he established important friendships with future colleagues. For example, General Sir Michael David Jackson—a commander of the NATO-led implementation force (IFOR) in Bosnia-Herzegovina, as well as the Kosovo Force (KFOR) in the 1990s—was his classmate in the army staff college. So, when the German Army general took charge of the Stabilization Force (SFOR) in Bosnia-Herzegovina in the late 1990s, he had a very good working relationship with General Jackson during the operation. Moreover, when he was working for SFOR, the future US Army chief of staff (1999–2003) General Eric K. Shinseki was also serving as a commander of SFOR, and the two established a friendship.[13] As we can see then, all three forces of the Bundeswehr have been thoroughly integrated into NATO, and their officers have had very extensive relations with the NATO allied forces since the Cold War period.

How did these Bundeswehr officers view the SPD-Green government's opposition to the possible US attack on Iraq in summer 2002 and the Iraq War in 2003? How deep was their feeling of camaraderie toward their US counterparts? One SPD member of the Bundestag Defense Committee told me that Bundeswehr officers tended to be pro-American, because many of them were trained in the United States and exercised many times with US forces through NATO.[14] However, my interviews with the Bundeswehr officers revealed that there were some differences in their attitudes toward the Iraq War and US foreign policy in general. It seems that the army officers were the most pro-American and very sympathetic toward the US Army. The navy officers were not as enthusiastic as were the army officers, but they were still supportive of the United States. The air force officers, on the other hand, were quite critical about the US decision to attack Iraq and were skeptical about the efficacy of the use of force.

When I raised questions about the Iraq War, all three army officers answered that they thought that the FRG government should have supported it, at least during summer 2002, at the time of the Bundestag election campaign. One army colonel told me that because Chancellor Schröder said "no" to the Iraq War in summer 2002, deterrence against Iraq did not work. If deterrence had worked, he argued, Saddam Hussein might have left his country and the war might have been avoided. In addition, he observed that other NATO members were disappointed with the German and French opposition to the war, and German opposition to the war made it difficult for the German delegates in NATO's Brussels headquarters (including himself) to work during the Iraq crisis of 2002–2003. The Germans were excluded from many informal meetings during that time. He also expressed his strong feelings of attachment toward the United States. He identified himself as an Atlantist, saying that Germany had a special relationship with and owed a lot to the United States. Not only did the United States resolve the mistrust other European countries felt for Germany after the end of World War II, but the United States also supported Germany's unification in 1990. He did mention, however, that he was not convinced by US secretary of state Colin Powell's photo presentation at the UN in February 2003, which argued that Iraq had weapons of mass destructions (WMDs).[15] Nevertheless, he seemed convinced that solidarity among NATO member states was the key to solving the Iraq problem and that it was not a wise decision for the SPD to express its opposition to the possible US attack on Iraq during summer 2002. More importantly, his answers revealed that he and other German delegates in NATO headquarters were under strong pressure from the United States during the Iraq crisis.

Another army colonel explained that during the summer of 2002 he was also convinced that the FRG should send some troops to Iraq. He changed his mind later, however, when it became apparent that the United States was failing to maintain security and stability in Iraq. But he attributed the US failure in Iraq to the civilian political leadership of the Bush administration, not to the military leadership of the US Army. US Army chief of staff General Eric Shinseki gave the right advice to the civilian leaders, the German colonel contended, but they did not listen to Shinseki.[16] (General Shinseki advised that massive troop numbers were necessary to successfully carry out the occupation in Iraq after the invasion; however, Secretary of Defense Donald Rumsfeld and Deputy Secretary of Defense Paul Wolfowitz rejected his advice.) [17]

The other army general made a similar argument. He maintained that the US failure in Iraq was a political failure. The US forces did an excellent job at first. They won a victory in a very short period of time. However, they lacked the "escalation of dominance." Lacking sufficient troop numbers, the US forces were unable to prevent widespread looting in Iraq following the invasion. The army was overstretched and underfinanced. Because of the political failure, the wonderful military victory was lost.[18] These two German Army officers were very sympathetic toward the US Army, particularly toward General Shinseki. From their point of view, there was nothing wrong with the US decision to attack Iraq, but the United States failed in Iraq because of the shortsightedness of the American civilian political leaders. If the operation had been carried out as the US Army generals advised, the occupation of Iraq would have been successful.

A touching story tells us a great deal about the camaraderie felt between the American and the German navies right after 9/11. At that time, a German Navy ship saluted the USS. Winston S. Churchill by flying an American flag at half-mast and hanging a banner saying "We stand by you" as the ships parted ways after exercising together off the coast of Plymouth in Britain.[19] The story says much about the feelings of the German Navy toward the United States at that time. The German Navy was willing to do whatever it could to help the United States. However, when it came to the question of the Iraq War, the answers of the two high-ranking navy officers with whom I spoke were more tempered than those of the German Army officers.

One former vice admiral said that early on he believed that the FRG should provide some degree of support for the United States during the Iraq crisis of 2002–2003. It was a serious mistake for Germany to stand with Russia against the United States (he did not mention France), as, he felt, it left a very bad impression for the Americans. Nevertheless, he later decided that Germany was right not to participate in the Iraq War, because it turned out to be a failure. The United States failed to stabilize Iraq.[20]

Another vice admiral was more cautious about my questions. He refused to directly answer a question about his opinions regarding Chancellor Schröder's opposition to the possible US attack on Iraq in summer 2002. However, he stated that the United States had made a mistake by not ousting Saddam Hussein from Iraq in the Persian Gulf War of 1990–1991. As long as Saddam Hussein was controlling Iraq, he would have to be removed sooner or later, the vice admiral felt. His answer seemed to imply that the US decision to attack Iraq was not necessarily a bad one. Though reluctant to offer his opinions on the Iraq War, the vice admiral kindly answered my questions about his experiences working at NATO's office in Norfolk, Virginia, for three years in the mid-2000s. I asked whether he felt uncomfortable going to the United States in 2003 when relations between the United States and the FRG were strained because of German opposition to the war. He responded that, no, he did not worry about it at all. He had worked in Norfolk before and was quite happy to return in 2003. After all, he explained, Germany's opposition to the Iraq

War was a political decision, and the Bundeswehr had to follow the decision made by the Chancellor. Even though the German government opposed the Iraq War, German naval officers were still members of the NATO naval community, and camaraderie and professionalism remained strong among NATO naval officers throughout this period. During his stay in Norfolk, the vice admiral had a number of informal conversations with American naval officers about the Iraq War and said he did not feel any discomfort in talking to the Americans about the subject.[21]

The reactions of the two German vice admirals may have been more tempered than those of the army officers in part because the US Army, as the main actor in the invasion and occupation of Iraq, has suffered a number of casualties since 2003, and the German Army officers may have felt particular sympathy for their American counterparts. The vice admiral did not have any difficulties working in Norfolk, nor in having conversations with American naval officers about the Iraq issue, because the US Navy did not suffer nearly as many casualties in Operation Iraqi Freedom (OIF) as did the US Army. (As of February 25, 2012, the US Army suffered 18,928 casualties, the US Navy 613, the US Marine Corps 8,451, and the US Air Force 413 in OIF.)[22]

One might expect German Air Force officers to be the most pro-American, since many of them have trained in the United States and have developed extensive contacts with the Americans. (The German Air Force has its own training center at the Holloman Air Force Base in New Mexico). However, the two air force officers with whom I spoke did not hesitate to express critical opinions regarding the US decision to attack Iraq. One former air force general, who spent two years training as a jet pilot in the United States in the late 1960s and who, since then, has frequently visited the United States, told me that he fully supported Chancellor Schröder's decision to oppose a US attack on Iraq in summer 2002, though he added that the chancellor's way of expressing his view and communicating with the United States was not ideal. There was no evidence that Iraq supported al-Qaeda, he contended, and the argument linking Iraq and al-Qaeda was not credible. It was unthinkable, according to the general, that Saddam Hussein would have supported al-Qaeda, since al-Qaeda posed a threat to Hussein's own regime. The general also said that he talked with one high-ranking American military officer about the Iraq War after March 2003. At that time, the German Air Force general told the American officer that the United States should not create a power vacuum in Iraq, because that would generate instability in the Middle East. Iran, for example, might capitalize on the situation to realize its own ambitions for dominance in the region.

The general may have been so critical of the United States' policies precisely because he lived in the United States and understood American society and politics very well. When I asked him how he felt about American society in general while he lived in the United States in the late 1960s, he answered that the Americans were inward looking. They thought only about themselves. They did not care about Europe, Asia, or any other parts of the world. And, regarding the Iraq War, he continued, there were disagreements among the Americans themselves—within the Bush administration, between the bureaucracies, the military, the media, and the public. Moreover, when I asked him to rate the warmth of his feelings toward different NATO member states, he responded with a 50 toward France, 47 toward Italy and the Netherlands, and 30 toward the United States. Thus, even though he spent significant time in the United States and had many contacts with the Americans throughout his long military career, he still feels closer to Europeans than to the Americans.

Finally, when I asked the general about his impressions of the ongoing PKO in Afghanistan (he was in charge of the International Security Assistance Force [ISAF] in Afghanistan as a NATO officer for two years), he responded that the present operation in Afghanistan was very similar to the Vietnam War in the late 1960s. According to him, the problem with the American strategy in Vietnam was that the US forces were unable to capture the Vietcong in South Vietnam once they escaped to North Vietnam. The Vietcong were thus able to return to the south and continue their insurgencies, making the fight with the Vietcong endless. The same problem exists in Afghanistan, he contended. The Taliban are hiding in the border region between Afghanistan and Pakistan. Even though the ISAF and the Operation Enduring Freedom (OEF) forces have fought the Taliban insurgency in Afghanistan, the Taliban fighters can withdraw to Pakistan. Neither the ISAF/OEF nor the Pakistan government is able to capture the Taliban fighters who escaped to the Afghan-Pakistani border. Thus, the Taliban are able to return to Afghanistan to carry out insurgencies.

The general suggested that the problem cannot be solved militarily. Instead, the ISAF/OEF needs a "comprehensive approach," employing both military and political means. Although foreign troops are necessary to maintain security in Afghanistan, he argued, the allied countries need to change the social structure of Afghanistan. They need to establish financial, judicial, and police institutions. At the same time, the general was quite pessimistic about the future of the comprehensive approach. He maintained that it would be difficult for Western countries to force the Afghan people to adopt a (Western) way of life that they did not desire.[23] Interestingly, the former air force general's perspective was shared by a senior Leftist Party member of the Bundestag whom I interviewed. The Leftist Party member also said that the war in Afghanistan was like the Vietnam War, because it is a guerrilla war. We do not know who is on our side.[24] Thus, even though the German Air Force general had trained in the United States and had many contacts with American officers through NATO, he is still very critical of US foreign policy, much like the Leftists.

Another active air force colonel was also critical about the US decision to attack Iraq. Before beginning the interview, he brought me to the center of the Ministry of Defense (MOD) building in Berlin, which was surrounded by a circular staircase. There was a large carpet on the bottom floor, which could be seen from the upper part of the staircase. The carpet looked like an abstract image, colored with orange, red, yellow, and black. But the colonel explained to me that the carpet depicted the air map of Berlin in 1944. Indeed, upon closer inspection, I could recognize the river (*Spree*) that runs around the Bundestag. He explained that in 1944 all but a few buildings were bombed and destroyed in Berlin. The present MOD building was the army headquarters during World War II and was one of the few buildings that survived the allied bombings. He showed me the carpet to convey the devastating effects of World War II on Germany and to explain why Germans are typically very skeptical about the efficacy of the use of force. During the war, Berlin and many other major cities, such as Dresden and Hamburg, were bombed and totally annihilated. The colonel suggested that US political elites do not consider the historical legacy of Germany. Of course, the Germans first started the war, he stipulated. However, because of this historical experience, the Germans—unlike the Americans—are extremely pessimistic about the use of force and war in general. Regarding the Iraq question, the colonel was very stern. He maintained that Iraq had nothing to do with 9/11 and that the US decision to attack Iraq was totally "out of the blue."[25]

From these interviews we can see, then, that although the Bundeswehr has been closely integrated into NATO, there are still some differences among the three forces. The most likely source of Germany's entrapment into US-led overseas military operations would seem to come from the army because German Army officers not only have rich experiences working with the US Army, but they also have very strong feelings of camaraderie for their American counterparts.

There are some concrete indications that the likelihood that the FRG would become entrapped into the US-led invasion and occupation of Iraq was high. First of all, the German Army did have the ability and willingness to take part in the invasion and occupation of Iraq in 2002. Some have argued that even if the German government had supported the US invasion in Iraq, the Bundeswehr would not have enough troops to send to Iraq, since its forces were already stretched too thin on various missions around the world. However, one former army general told me that it would have been possible to send troops to Iraq if they had received a six-month training period. He knew that the United States and Britain had already begun training their soldiers in summer 2002, so the invasion would take place sometime in spring 2003. If the German Army had started training their soldiers in summer or early fall 2002, it would have been possible for them to participate in the invasion of Iraq in March 2003.[26] The German Army could have taken part in the invasion of Iraq in March 2003 if the government had ordered the army to start training, even if a Bundestag mandate did not come until later. And, as discussed above, the high-ranking German Army officers with whom I spoke supported the possible US invasion of Iraq in 2002 and were willing to help US forces.

Second, German Army officers (at least those in the upper echelon) seek to expand the scope of the army's activities overseas and are willing to take risks to realize this ambition. I asked the former army general whether the US request was the main reason that the German Army sent approximately 100 soldiers from the KSK to Afghanistan in December 2001. He responded, no, that even if the United States had not asked Germany for KSK support, the German Army would have sent the KSK to Afghanistan, because it was a good opportunity for KSK soldiers to experience real combat operations. KSK officers had undergone substantial training since the force's creation in 1996; however, they had never experienced real combat. I also asked the general about the statement made by General Reinhard Günzel, the head of a KSK brigade, regarding NATO's plan to send member states' special forces to Afghanistan to hunt down Osama bin Laden in September 2001. General Günzel remarked that it would be almost impossible to complete the mission successfully without severe losses to his special troops and those of other allied nations.[27] The former general responded that Günzel had not been thinking strategically at that time. He and other generals convinced Günzel, as well as other KSK soldiers, that the operation in Afghanistan would be beneficial.

The upper echelon of army officers also thinks that the army has no choice but risk casualties in overseas operations. The former army general told me that the possibility of casualties would not preclude the army from sending its troops to overseas operations. Because it is dangerous, the government would send soldiers there. If it is safe, other civilian organizations should go. The Bundeswehr has the highest standard of medical service, he explained. It has planes with hospitals. So it is well prepared for treating injured soldiers. The Bundeswehr even has refrigerators to store dead bodies.[28] Similarly, one army colonel said that once one becomes a Bundeswehr soldier, there is always the risk that he or she might die in an operation.[29] Another army colonel also said that Germany has a responsibility to help maintain global security. Germans have to share the burden, he argued.[30] The high-ranking army officers thus do not hesitate to send army soldiers to overseas military operations, despite the prospect of casualties.

The German Army officers' willingness to participate in overseas operations even with risks of casualties seems to reflect the transformation of the Bundeswehr from a traditional territorial defense army to an out-of-area expeditionary force.[31] Until 2000, the Bundeswehr reform remained stymied between "old" and "new" security thinking. German policymakers understood that the Bundeswehr should be transformed from a manpower-heavy territorial defense force to a more flexible, deployable, and interoperable force as a result of changes in the regional security environment in the 1990s. However, they were unable to shed the old idea that national defense within the alliance context was the fundamental task of the Bundeswehr defined in the Basic Law (German constitution). In 1999, for example, a commission headed by Richard von Weizsäcker (former Federal president) demanded a "fundamental renewal of the Bundeswehr"; whereas those headed by Rudolf Scharping (defense minister) and Hans-Peter von Kirchbach (chief of staff Bundeswehr) still defined the primary task of the Bundeswehr as territorial defense within the alliance context.[32]

9/11 and the subsequent US-led war on terrorism, however, eliminated the residues of old security thinking and accelerated a more radical reform of the Bundeswehr. The 2003 Defense Policy Guidelines (DPG) written by Defense Minister Peter Struck would be the best articulation of this trend of the Bundeswehr transformation from a territorial defense force to an expeditionary force. In the DPG, Struck stated, "At present, and the foreseeable future, there is no conventional threat to the German territory. The Bundeswehr's spectrum of operation has changed fundamentally,"[33] and "defense can no longer be narrowed down to geographical boundaries, but contributes to safeguarding our security wherever it is in jeopardy."[34] Further, he stated, "The necessity for the Bundeswehr to participate in multinational operations may arise anywhere in the world and at short notice and may extend across the entire spectrum down to high-intensity operations."[35] According to the DPG, therefore, the Bundeswehr can be deployed anywhere in the world, and its tasks include high-intense combat operations.

In addition, the German government's attempts to cut military spending since the end of the Cold War have further encouraged German Army officers to expand their overseas mission (figures 5.1 and 5.2). Although Defense Minister Peter Struck advocated the necessity to restructure the Bundeshwer, the Bundeswehr in fact has been suffering from the lack of funding to restructure itself.[36] No longer facing a threat from the Soviets, the German Army had to actively go abroad in order to justify its budget. Chief of Staff Gert Gudera (in office 2001–2004), for example, resigned in January 2004 because he disagreed with the decision made by Defense

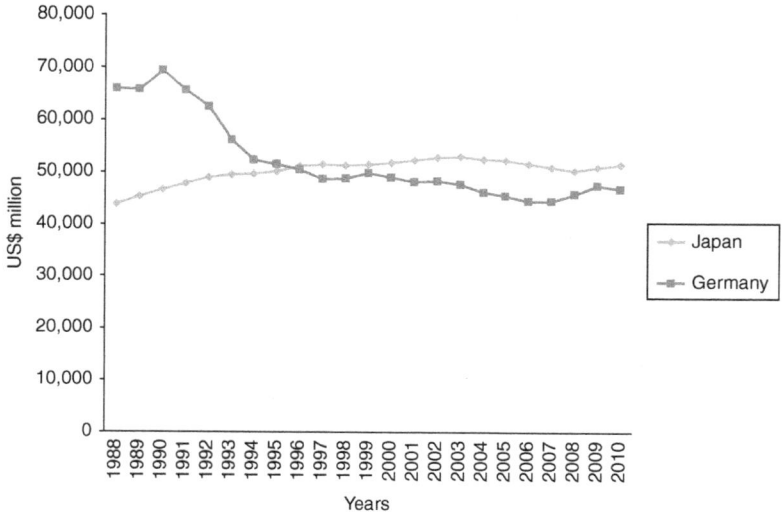

Figure 5.1 Military Expenditures of Germany and Japan in Constant (2009) US$ m., 1988–2010.

Source: SIPRI, http://www.sipri.org/, accessed September 5, 2011.

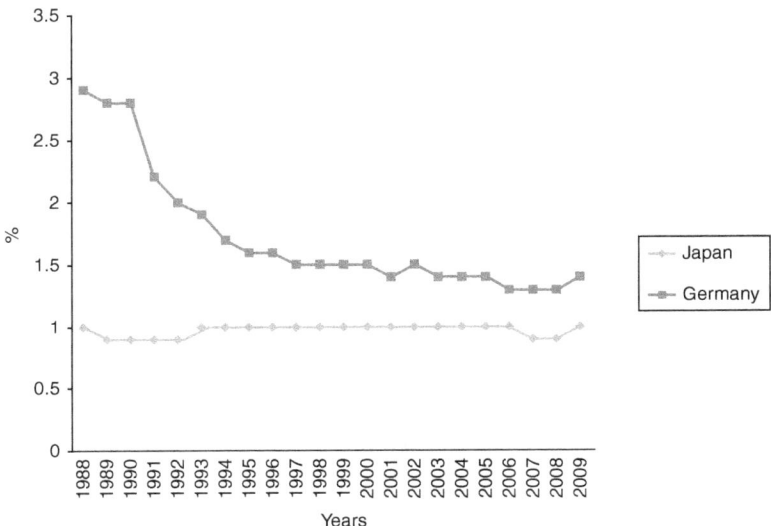

Figure 5.2 Military Expenditures of Germany and Japan as Percentage of Gross Domestic Product, 1988–2009.

Source: SIPRI, http://www.sipri.org/, accessed September 5, 2011.

Minister Peter Struck to reduce the army budget and personnel. Struck decided to trim 26 billion Euros from the defense budget—with 15 billion of that coming from the army budget—and to cut 35,000 personnel.[37] Gudera had already complained in October 2003 that reduced payments to the regular soldiers—in the form of cuts to holiday and Christmas bonuses and increases in the price of lunch—would decrease the soldiers' morale.[38] Moreover, Gudera wrote a 42-page confidential paper entitled "The German Army 2020" and distributed it to the high-ranking officers. In the paper, he advocated the expansion of the Bundeswehr mission overseas. He wrote that in the future, the army "must be able to react flexibly in time and, on principle, all over the world to a range of risks that has become wider and more complicated." He also stated that, in order to "keep pace with the most important alliance partners," the army needed to improve its weapons systems and information technologies, and demanded purchasing a series of modern weapons such as missiles for piercing bankers, combat robots for reconnaissance and mine cleaning, and so on.[39] Thus, budgetary constraints provided a strong incentive for the German Army to expand its out-of-area operations.

The last reason for the likely entrapment of the FRG was the general difficulty the Bundestag faces in effectively overseeing the Bundeswehr's activities abroad. The case of the KSK activities in OEF in Afghanistan provides a good example. Although a 1994 Federal constitutional court decision stipulated that the government has to obtain majority approval from the Bundestag to dispatch the Bundeswehr abroad, the Bundestag mandate that authorized the government to send the KSK to OEF in Afghanistan was rather vague.[40] Indeed, one Free Democratic Party (FDP) member of the Bundestag complained to me that the contents of the document that members of the Bundestag received from the government about the potential Bundeswehr dispatch in fall 2001 was very vague and did not contain a detailed explanation about the kind of operations the KSK would carry out in Afghanistan because these operations were to be covert.[41]

Because the KSK's job is to carry out covert operations, the Bundeswehr will not make the contents of KSK operations public in order to ensure the safety of soldiers as well as the success of their missions. Although the Bundestag has the power to authorize overseas Bundeswehr dispatches, there are no formal procedures for the Bundeswehr to report to the Bundestag regarding KSK activities. The decision on whether or not the KSK would ultimately be deployed overseas was solely up to the discretion of the Bundeswehr leadership, and only members of a special Bundestag committee were informed of the decision.[42] This committee comprises approximately ten people, including the speakers of the Foreign Relations and the Defense committees, as well as the speakers of each party (including the Leftist Party).[43] Only the members of this committee receive (supposedly) full information about KSK operations before they take place, and all other members of the Bundestag (including the members of the Defense and the Foreign Relations committees) are informed after the missions are completed.[44]

Ultimately, this allows the Bundestag very little oversight over the KSK. Although the members of the Bundestag Defense Committee, for example, were informed in January 2002 that about 100 KSK soldiers were ready for deployment,[45] most KSK soldiers in fact had already been sent to a camp next to the US military base on Masira (a small island off the coast of Oman) in December 2001 and were transported to Afghanistan by US planes from mid-December to early January 2002 in order to participate in a number of offensive operations against the Taliban and al-Qaeda alongside US forces.[46]

Moreover, there are some allegations of KSK misconduct in Afghanistan. The most remarkable case is that of Murat Kurnaz, a

German-born Turkish citizen who spent four years in the Guantanamo Bay prison. Kurnaz, who was born and raised in Bremen, Germany, was arrested in Pakistan in October 2001 as a suspected member of al-Qaeda and was held in an American prison in Afghanistan until 2002. He was then transferred to Guantanamo before being released in August 2006. After being freed from Guantanamo, Kuranz publicly accused two KSK soldiers of abusing him while he was being held in a US prison camp in Kandahar in 2002.[47] The Bundestag commission tried to investigate this case; however, the MOD informed the commission that they "accidentally" destroyed a large number of files on the KSK mission during the period in question. Consequently, the commission was unable to thoroughly carry out its investigation.

In sum, the Bundeswehr is likely to be entrapped into overseas military operations under NATO because it is highly integrated into the organization. Bundeswehr officers have had long-term relations with the officers of other NATO member states since the Cold War period as a result of working together in NATO offices, holding joint military exercises, receiving overseas training, and conducting actual peacekeeping (including combat) operations abroad. Although the officers of the three forces in the Bundeswehr expressed differences in their views regarding the US attack on Iraq, the army and the navy officers were generally supportive, and the German Army officers were particularly sympathetic toward the US Army. In addition, the possibility of German entrapment into the Iraq War was high not only because the army had the capability to participate in the invasion and occupation of Iraq but also because its officers carried a strong desire to expand the army's overseas activities. Finally, it is difficult for the Bundestag to control the activities of Bundeswehr soldiers once they are dispatched abroad. Although the United States did not have a clear mandate from the UN when it launched its attack on Iraq in March 2003, it was possible that the United States could start the war under NATO if Germany or France acquiesced, as with the case of the Kosovo War.[48] Alternatively, even if the United States started the war without NATO, it was possible that the occupation of Iraq would be carried out by NATO later, as had happened with the ISAF in Afghanistan since the UN endorsed the postwar reconstruction of Iraq. As a result of each of these factors, the FRG political leaders could not support a US attack on Iraq in 2002. Such support would have inevitably resulted in the dispatch of the German Army to Iraq, which, in turn, most likely would have led to Germany's entrapment into the war.

III. The Self-Defense Forces (SDF)

One of the reasons for Japan's low likelihood of entrapment into US-led overseas military affairs—and therefore its support for the US decision to attack Iraq in March 2003—relates to the conservatism of the GSDF concerning overseas PKOs. The GSDF's conservatism stems from the fact that the forces have not been integrated into the strategic structure of the US Army Japan (USARJ), as well as the fact that there is no court-martial in Japan. In the pages that follow, I will begin by discussing the roots of the GSDF's conservatism regarding overseas PKOs by comparing it with the Maritime SDF (MSDF) and the German Army, and present a detailed description of the GSDF's response to 9/11 and the Iraq War.[49]

In contrast to the Bundeswehr, which is firmly integrated into the multinational collective alliance system of NATO, the SDF has been fairly isolated from contacts with foreign troops. Japan has only one ally—the United States under the US-Japan Security Treaty. But even the SDF's relations with US forces are not as close as those of the Bundeswehr, because Article 9 of the Japanese constitution prohibits Japan from exercising the right of collective self-defense. Article 9 does not allow the SDF to fight side-by-side with US forces in order to carry out offensive operations against any third country. The scope of joint operations and exercises between the two forces is therefore quite limited.

The limits placed on relations between the SDF and US forces are exemplified by the "Coordinated Joint Outline Emergency Plan" (CJOEP)—a confidential emergency plan cowritten by the Joint Staff Council (JSC) of the SDF and the head of the United States Forces in Japan (USFJ) every year between 1952 and the mid-1970s. The CJOEP laid out plans for the joint defense of the northern island of Hokkaido in the event of a Soviet invasion. In that plan, the GSDF was charged with holding the Soviet forces in Hokkaido by itself for a time until the US forces, along with the MSDF and the Air SDF (ASDF), could come to assist. However, the CJOEP was never authorized by any of Japan's prime ministers over the years. Even though the JSC submitted the plan to the directors of the Defense Agency, the directors never shared it with the prime ministers, knowing that any prime minister to sign off on such a plan risked the public's wrath at a time when even discussing the possibility of war was taboo. At the same time, the USFJ thought that it was unlikely that the Soviet Union would actually invade Japan. Instead, the USFJ was more interested in how the SDF would help US forces in the event of an emergency in the Korean Peninsula, and thus demanded the JSC consider that case. But the JSC refused to even consider such a plan, fearing that it would violate the Article 9 prohibition on collective self-defense.

The JSC and the USFJ stopped writing the confidential military plan in 1978 when both the US and the Japanese governments formally agreed upon the Guidelines for Japan-US Defense Cooperation as a result of the increased presence of Soviet forces in the Far East and of the US decision to decrease the number of its troops abroad as a part of the Nixon Doctrine. The number of joint exercises between the SDF and US forces has increased since then.[50] However, Article 9 still continues to limit the extent of joint exercises, as well as the overall activities of the SDF.

Although all the three different forces of the SDF have been equally under the same constraint of Article 9, there are noticeable differences among the extent to which they have been integrated into their US counterpart. The relationship between the MSDF and the US Navy is very close, whereas that between the GSDF and the US Army is distant, and the relationship between the ASDF and the US Air Force is in between. These differences are reflected in the degree of each force's willingness to make contributions to the US-led war on terrorism following 9/11. When the Cabinet Secretariat started drafting the Anti-Terrorism Special Measures Law (ATSML) right after 9/11, one of the Ministry of Foreign Affairs (MOFA) officials drafting the bill called the defense sections of the three forces in order to ask what kind of support they could provide. At that time, the MSDF was very enthusiastic about providing support for the US Navy. The ASDF was less enthusiastic, but still willing to provide support, while the GSDF was extremely cautious on the matter.[51]

The MSDF has historically close relations with the US Navy, because it owes its birth to the US Navy. During the postwar occupation, a group of former Japanese naval officers set out to recreate a navy similar to the prewar Imperial Navy. However, the Japanese government, led by Prime Minister Yoshida Shigeru, was not interested in large-scale rearmament at the time. As such, two of the former Japanese Imperial Navy officers—Admiral Nomura Kichizabro and Colonel Yoshida Eizo—approached the US Navy. With the recent outbreak of the Korean War in mind, the US Navy embraced the Japanese officers' idea. In 1952, the Americans helped them establish a semi-independent naval organization called the Costal Safety Force (CSF) within the Japan Coast Guard (JCG). Two years later, the CSF became completely independent from the JCG and was renamed the

MSDF.[52] The US Navy also provided the MSDF with ships and training. One of the MSDF officers who served during the 1950s and 1960s described the MSDF's relationship with the US Navy as *"onbu ni da'kko,"* which means that the MSDF was totally dependent on the US Navy for everything.[53]

It is important to note, however, that the relations between the US Navy and the MSDF were not a teacher-student relationship because the prewar Japanese Imperial Navy had a high level of skills to maneuver battleships, and therefore, US Navy officers showed their respect to the Japanese Imperial Navy and its officers such as Togo Heihachiro and Yamamoto Isoroku.[54] They have appreciated a high level of skills that the MSDF possessed, such as minesweeping and submarine detection, which no other Asian navies were comparable with. One retired high-ranking MSDF officer told me that maneuvering ships required a high level of skills. Even if a certain Asian country's navy had been rented ships from US Navy in the 1950s, they would not have been able to use them because they did not have enough skills. MSDF officers were able to use the ships rented from the US Navy because they acquired the skills from former imperial navy officers.[55] Indeed, the US Navy decided to help the former Japanese Imperial Navy officers establish the MSDF in the 1950s because it appreciated that MSDF ships went to the Korean coast for minesweeping during the Korean War so that US Navy ships could sail safely around that area.[56] Camaraderie between the MSDF and the US Navy, therefore, has developed from the mutual respect between them.

Moreover, since it was established, the MSDF was designed to function as a part of the overall operational structure of the US Navy's Seventh Fleet in Yokosuka. The MSDF complements the operations carried out by the US Seventh Fleet and is, therefore, not a fully independent military entity. The MSDF certainly has advanced defensive capabilities. It is adept at minesweeping and detecting foreign submarines intruding into Japanese waters, and has recently acquired fleets with the Aegis air defense system. Such MSDF's capabilities, however, are in fact designed to clear Japanese waters so that US Navy ships can sail and carry out its operations safely around Japan. Additionally, the MSDF does not have ships traditionally used for offensive operations such as aircraft carriers or nuclear-powered ships, since these would violate Article 9. Ultimately, then, the MSDF is not a self-reliant, independent force, but a complement to the Seventh Fleet.[57]

MSDF officers have developed a strong sense of camaraderie with US Navy officers in the Seventh Fleet through a series of joint exercises and daily contacts. One high-ranking MSDF officer said in my interview that he had numerous small exercises with US Navy when he belonged to one of MSDF escort flotillas. He also told me that he met US Navy officers many times not only in exercises but also in parties, and it was a part of his job (*shigoto no uchi*) to associate with them.[58] One MSDF rear admiral in the MSDF defense section in Ichigaya, Tokyo, also told me during an interview that he communicates with the Seventh Fleet in Yokosuka on a daily basis. But what struck me at that time was that he looked so happy when he talked about the Americans.[59] Similarly, when I conducted an interview with a vice admiral in MSDF headquarters in Yokosuka, he claimed that Japan has had a special relationship with the United States since American whalers came to Japan and asked for water in the nineteenth century.[60] And it is important to note that the MSDF headquarters is located right across from the US Navy base in Yokosuka. Similarly, the MSDF is located very close to the US Navy base in Sasebo. Indeed, they are sharing the same harbor in Sasebo. Thus, it is not difficult to imagine that MSDF and US Navy officers and servicemen have numerous contacts, and understand what each other is doing by seeing off and receiving each other's ships in the same harbor on daily basis.

Among the three forces of the SDF, therefore, the MSDF was the most enthusiastic about making contributions to the United States right after 9/11. The MSDF was willing to send its ships to escort the USS *Kitty Hawk*, as well as to support US naval operations in the Indian Ocean. In the wake of 9/11, MSDF officers in the defense section quickly drafted a support plan in which the MSDF would send its ships to the Indian Ocean to provide the US Navy and other foreign ships participating in OEF with fuel for free. The support plan that Prime Minister Koizumi formally announced on September 19, 2001, was in fact based on that draft.[61] High-ranking MSDF officers also visited with Liberal Democratic Party (LDP) members of the upper and lower houses of parliament in order to convince them that Japan should make contributions to the United States as quickly as possible. This extraordinary action broke normal policymaking procedures. As a rule, contact with Diet members was made exclusively by civilian officials in the Defense Agency, not uniformed officers.[62]

MSDF ships escorted the US aircraft carrier *Kitty Hawk* for the first time ever when it sailed from Tokyo Bay on September 21, 2001.[63] In addition, high-ranking MSDF officers pressed the government to allow them to send Japanese fleets with the Aegis air defense system to the Indian Ocean. The MSDF wanted to send the Aegis to the Indian Ocean because the US Seventh Fleet requested the MSDF to assume the air defense of the Diego Garcia islands in the Indian

Ocean, which the US forces were using as an air base to attack the Taliban in Afghanistan.[64] The Japanese government resisted at first, as some senior LDP and Komeito politicians expressed concern that the US forces might use the information collected by the Aegis system for offensive purposes—a clear violation of Article 9.[65] Yet the MSDF persisted. They continued to approach politicians to stress the urgency of this matter.[66] The MSDF felt such urgency because they feared that if action did not come by the time the US launched an attack on Iraq, Japanese politicians would never authorize deployment of the Aegis system to the Indian Ocean for fear of entrapment into the Iraq War.[67] As a result of the yearlong, continuous lobbying efforts of MSDF officers and Japan Defense Agency (JDA) civilian officials, the MSDF finally succeeded in sending the Aegis fleet to the Indian Ocean in December 2002.

The MSDF's active, and sometimes even aggressive, lobbying activities were extraordinary, even when compared to the German Navy's reactions to 9/11. The German Navy sent two frigates and four support ships with 750 servicemen to OEF in January 2002 to patrol the seas off the Horn of Africa, which was the biggest German naval deployment since World War II. The top officers in the German Navy, however, were not as anxious to provide support for the US Navy as were those of the MSDF. In fact, the German Navy did not take any initiatives to support the United States efforts in Afghanistan right after 9/11. None of its officers approached members of the Bundestag. (To do so would have breached normal protocol, but as we have just seen, Japanese MSDF officer were willing to breach the same protocol in this case.) The German Navy chief of staff did not take action, and Bundeswehr chief of staff General Harald Kujat did not ask him to do so. Immediately after the 9/11 attacks, German defense minister Rudolf Scharping, parliamentary and state secretaries, chiefs of law and social departments, Bundeswehr chief of staff General Kujat, and the chiefs of staff of the three forces attended an emergency meeting in Berlin. Even in that meeting, however, the navy chief of staff did not propose any action on the part of the German Navy.[68]

Though the navy did eventually provide support for the American-led efforts in Afghanistan by sending ships to the Horn of Africa, the German Navy itself was not behind the push for this action. Instead, after planning the operation in Afghanistan, the United States informally approached one high-ranking German Navy officer who was working in a NATO branch office and asked him what kind of support the German Navy was capable of offering. The German Navy officer then passed along the American inquiry to the navy's chief of staff, who replied that the navy could likely supply frigates, fast patrol boats, and other support. Later, the US government sent a formal request to the German government for this support. At the same time, the German Navy also informed Bundeswehr chief of staff General Kujat about the possible form of their support. General Kujat then contacted State Secretary Walter Stützle, and Stützle contacted the spokespeople of the Bundestag Defense and Foreign Affairs committees, (since the Bundestag would have to approve any support provided to the Americans in Afghanistan). At that time, the Bundestag prohibited the navy from sending fighter bombers, as they opposed the use of German forces for aerial bombings in Afghanistan.[69] As we can see then, the Japanese MSDF went much further in pushing the government to provide the United States with support after 9/11 than did the German Navy.

The MSDF's active support for the US Seventh Fleet following 9/11 seems to show that the MSDF was the most likely source of Japan's entrapment into US-led overseas military operations. Indeed, the MSDF faced one allegation that one of its fuel supply ships operating in the Indian Ocean was indirectly involved in US offensive operations in Iraq. In September 2007, a Japanese peace group called Peace Depot, which obtained internal US Navy documents, accused the MSDF of violating both the ATSML and Article 9 of the constitution. The ATSML was designed to allow Japan to provide support for antiterrorism operations in and around Afghanistan only, not in Iraq. Peace Depot revealed that the same amount of fuel (18,704 barrels) that the US Navy oiler Pecos received from an MSDF fuel supply ship called Tokiwa on February 25, 2003, was transferred to the USS *Kitty Hawk* on the same day and that the *Kitty Hawk* later moved into the Persian Gulf and took part in the offensive operations against Iraq.[70] As a result of this scandal, along with the opposition parties' success in controlling the upper house after the July 2007 election, the government failed to renew the ATSML in November 2007, and subsequently, all MSDF ships operating in the Indian Ocean were ordered to return to Japan.[71] (The government later succeeded in passing a new antiterrorism law in January 2008, and the MSDF resumed the fueling mission in the Indian Ocean.)

This allegation shows how difficult it was for the government to control the activities of the MSDF ships once they sailed out to the Indian Ocean. It was difficult for the Japanese government to check how the oil that the MSDF ships gave to the United States and other foreign navy ships supposedly participating in OEF was actually used later. Any foreign ships could request fuel from the MSDF for use in OEF but then transfer the fuel to other ships taking part in non-OEF activities. The Tokiwa incident, however, was ultimately only one incident, and the overall likelihood of Japanese entrapment in Iraq seems to remain quite limited. Although the MSDF did get involved indirectly in the US offensive operations against Iraq as Peace Depot claimed, the fuel supply took place in February 2003—before the United States launched the offensive attack on Iraq in March. One might argue that the fueling contributions, along with the Aegis dispatch to the Indian Ocean, could set a precedent for the MSDF to expand its activities in the future and thereby increase the chances of Japan's overseas entrapment. However, any such increase seems to be small. After all, it is armies, not navies, that suffer serious casualties in overseas PKOs. As of June 20, 2009, for example, the number of casualties suffered by the US Army in OEF stood at 2,458, whereas the US Navy suffered only 96 casualties.[72] Similarly, of the 33 casualties suffered in Afghanistan among the Bundeswehr, 29 come from the army.[73] Thus, the most likely source of overseas entrapment comes from an army, not from a navy.

Yet the Japanese GSDF has—unlike either the German Army or the Japanese MSDF— essentially operated as an isolated, independent, self-reliant military force and has established very few contacts with foreign troops since the Cold War period. GSDF personnel have developed a strong sense of camaraderie only among themselves, not with any other foreign troops. And the main task of the GSDF has remained the defense of Japan. The GSDF thus tends to be reluctant to work with foreign troops in overseas PKOs and conservative about dispatching its servicemen to overseas missions that are likely to result in casualties. The possibility of the GSDF's entrapment into any US-led overseas war is therefore much lower than that of its German counterpart.

There are several factors that have contributed to the conservative character of the GSDF. First of all, the US Army has not been interested in the defense of Japan since the Cold War period, because, as the case of the CJOEP shows, the US Army presumed that Soviet forces were unlikely to invade Japan. If we compare the number of US Army personnel in the FRG to that in Japan during both the Cold War and post–Cold War periods, we can get a sense of the Americans' relative disinterest in Japan. In 1976, for example, the US Army had 189,437 personnel in the FRG; in 2001, this number was 55,149. In Japan, by contrast, there were 3,908 US Army personnel in 1976 and 1,827 in 2001 (tables 5.1 and 5.2, figures 5.3 and 5.4). The rank of

Table 5.1 Number of US Military Personnel in the FRG

	Army	Air Force	Navy	Marine Corps
1976	189,437	29,974	285	81
1986	186,548	50,560	352	92
1993	87,030	17,767	313	144
1997	44,394	15,171	322	166
2001	55,149	15,248	322	279

Source: Department of Defense, *Selected Manpower Statistics* (Washington, DC: Washington Headquarters Services, 1977, 1986, 1993); Department of Defense, *Worldwide Manpower Distribution by Geographical Area* (Washington, DC: Washington Headquarters Services, September 30, 1997; September 30, 2001).

Table 5.2 Number of US Military Personnel in Japan

	Army	Air Force	Navy	Marine Corps
1976	3,908	14,061	7,926	19,953
1986	3,767	23,095	11,146	6,268
1993	1,961	15,403	7,247	21,520
1997	1,817	14,027	6,649	16,764
2001	1,827	13,128	6,189	19,073

Source: Department of Defense, *Selected Manpower Statistics* (Washington, DC: Washington Headquarters Services, 1977, 1986, 1993); Department of Defense, *Worldwide Manpower Distribution by Geographical Area* (Washington, DC: Washington Headquarters Services, September 30, 1997; September 30, 2001).

US Army officers assigned to Japan is also telling. The commander of the USARJ is a two-star major-general, while the commanders of the other two forces are a three-star lieutenant-general (US Air Force) and a vice admiral (US Navy). Compare this to the US Army Europe, where the commander is a four-star general.

Consequently, the GSDF is not integrated into the operational structure of the USARJ, thereby independent from the US Army. According to one high-ranking GSDF officer, the GSDF is like a "small but warm family." While the MSDF is one of the family members of the US Seventh Fleet, the GSDF itself is one complete, independent family.[74] The relationship between the GSDF and the US Army is thus much more distant than that between the MSDF and the US Navy, and is also much more distant than the relationship between the German Army and the armies of other NATO member states.

Moreover, unlike the US Army Europe—whose operational scope extends beyond Europe to the Middle East—and unlike the US

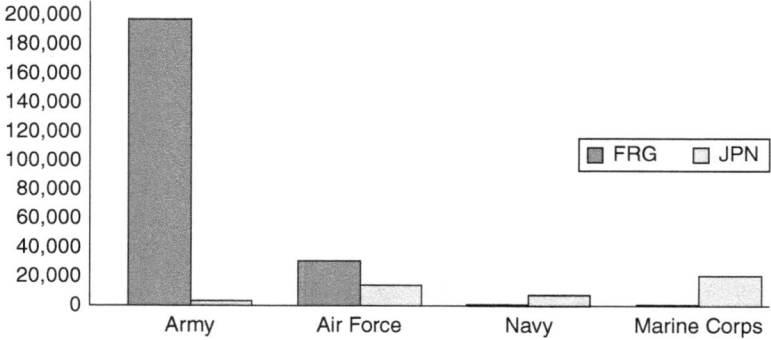

Figure 5.3 Number of US Military Personnel in the FRG and Japan (1976).
Source: Department of Defense, *Selected Manpower Statistics* (Washington, DC: Washington Headquarters Services, 1977).

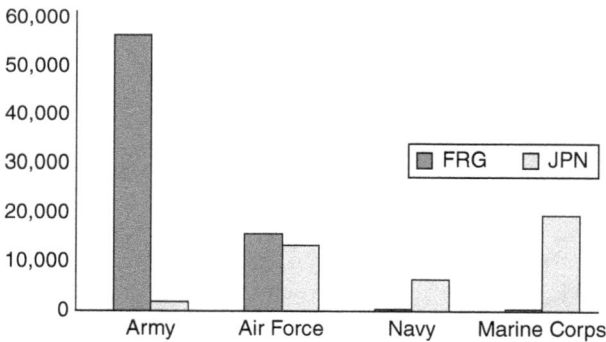

Figure 5.4 Number of US Military Personnel in the FRG and Japan (2001).

Source: Department of Defense, *Worldwide Manpower Distribution by Geographical Area* (Washington, DC: Washington Headquarters Services, September 30, 2001).

Seventh Fleet—whose operational scope extends beyond Japan to the Persian Gulf—the scope of USARJ's activities is limited to Japan. In fact, those in the USARJ in Camp Zama are not combat troops, but administrative staffs. Although the GSDF has conducted a number of exercises with the US Army since 1981, US Army soldiers with whom the GSDF actually conducted exercises in Japan came from Hawaii and Fort Lewis, Washington, not from the USARJ in Camp Zama. There is also the US Marine Corps (USMC) in Okinawa. The USMC is an expeditionary force that projects its troops to overseas, and the GSDF has also exercised with the USMC in Japan. One retired high-ranking GSDF officer in fact told me that it was very useful for the GSDF to exercise with the USMC because the USMC's combat skills was very high, and therefore, the GSDF could learn a lot from the USMC. Yet, the USMC is basically an independent force that does not work with the GSDF in an actual military operation.[75] Thus, in contrast to the case of the US Seventh Fleet, which left Yokosuka for the Indian Ocean, the soldiers of the USARJ did not leave Japan to participate in the Middle East operations following 9/11; nor did the GSDF have to accompany the USARJ or the USMC to assist them in overseas military operations.[76]

The same retired high-ranking GSDF officer also pointed out that the GSDF's exercises with the US Army are not "joint" but "bilateral" exercises. Because of the restriction posed by Article 9 of the Japanese Constitution, the US Army and the GSDF work under their respective command, not under the same unified command. In a "bilateral" exercise, according to him, both the GSDF and the US Army try to attain the same goal, but each of them set up a different strategy. For example, in an exercise during the Cold War, the US Army and the GSDF worked for the same goal that was to stop the Soviet invasion from Wakkanai, Hokkaido; however, each of them set and carried out their own different strategy. Although the US Army and the GSDF adjusted their strategy each other, they did not work together under the same unified command.[77] This nature of exercise has also contributed to the distant relationship between the US Army and the GSDF.

In short, the GSDF has become a fairly isolated military force, independent from the US Army. Although its overseas peacekeeping activities have been gradually expanded since the early 1990s, the main purpose of the GSDF still remains national defense. Moreover, GSDF personnel have developed a sense of camaraderie only among themselves. Due to the USARJ's relatively small size, the GSDF had to become self-reliant. Under the scenario of the CJOEP, the GSDF was to fight against the Soviet forces in Hokkaido by itself until other Japanese and American forces could come to aid. GSDF personnel thus came to believe that, should the country face a military emergency, the only people whom they could trust and rely on were themselves.[78] As a result, GSDF personnel developed a sense of camaraderie only among themselves, not with the US Army or any other foreign armies. Although the number of the GSDF's contacts with foreign troops has increased since it started to participate in overseas

PKOs in the early 1990s, the basic characteristics of the GSDF remain unchanged. During an interview with one GSDF officer in the MOD in Ichigaya, Tokyo, he bluntly told me that the GSDF disliked foreigners (*gaijin kirai*).[79]

Because the nearly exclusive purpose of the GSDF is to defend Japan, and because the force has developed a strong sense of camaraderie only among its own personnel, the GSDF is very conservative about dispatching its personnel to overseas PKOs that might endanger lives. The GSDF's conservatism regarding casualties in overseas PKOs can also be explained by the GSDF's lack of alliance obligations. One of the reasons why high-ranking German Army officers think that it is necessary to send their soldiers to overseas missions, even where the likelihood of casualties is high, is their strong sense of identity and obligation as part of the NATO alliance. It is hard for the German Army to keep their soldiers behind while the soldiers of other NATO allies are killed or wounded in overseas operations, not just because they want to keep the alliance solidarity but also because they have a strong sense of history. Remembering that the United States and other NATO member states sent a number of ground troops to the FRG to defend it against Soviet invasion during the Cold War, it is difficult for German Army officers to ignore the suffering of their foreign comrades in overseas PKOs. On the other hand, because of the distant relationship between the GSDF and the US Army and without a sense of camaraderie toward the US Army, the GSDF does not particularly feel obliged to jeopardize the lives of its servicemen in order to help the US Army in overseas operations.

The absence of a court-martial in Japan has further caused the GSDF to hesitate to send its servicemen to overseas PKOs. Because of Article 9 of the Japanese Constitution, the legal status of the SDF as well as legal treatment on use of force by SDF servicemen are ambivalent. Most SDF officers (regardless of Air, Ground, or Marine) with whom I conducted interviews stressed that the SDF is not regular *guntai* (armed forces) like the US forces or the German Bundeswehr since there is no court-martial in Japan. Because there is no court-martial, SDF servicemen who killed somebody in an operation inside or outside Japan will be tried for murder for self-defense in a regular court as ordinary citizens. Although the majority of the Japanese public has seen the SDF as constitutional,[80] there is no widespread support among the public for constitutional revision to explicitly make the SDF constitutional or establish a court-martial for the SDF. All the three forces of the SDF have been equal under this legal ambivalence; however, the GSDF might be particularly concerned about the legal ambivalence since a ground force is the most likely to face a situation in which its servicemen have to use force among the three forces.

The characteristics of the GSDF had a significant impact on the extent and form of Japan's contributions to the US-led war on terrorism in Afghanistan and to the postwar reconstruction of Iraq. In contrast to the MSDF, the GSDF aggressively lobbied the LDP Diet members to *stop* the government's plans to dispatch GSDF troops to participate in OEF in fall 2001. In early October 2001, the government was considering a plan to dispatch the GSDF to the Afghan-Pakistani border to provide medical services for war refugees from Afghanistan. The high-ranking GSDF officers, however, told the government that they could not dispatch their servicemen to the refugee camp, because it would be too difficult to ensure the safety of their personnel. They argued that the region was very unstable and that GSDF servicemen could not protect themselves due to the restriction on the use of force placed on them by Article 9. The officers also added that it was difficult to transport food and other necessities from the sea ports to the border region. Later, the government considered a plan to dispatch the GSDF to Afghanistan to remove mines as a part of Japan's contribution to the postwar reconstruction of that country. Again, the GSDF lobbied against the plan. GSDF representatives argued that the force could remove mines on the roads to secure them for tanks; however, it could not remove all the mines around residential areas. That kind of job should be taken care of by NGOs or the local population, they contended. GSDF officers also argued once again that they could not secure the logistical supply routes in Afghanistan. They tried to make their case by appealing to Diet members during visits to their offices, as well as to their private residences.[81] Thus, while the MSDF aggressively lobbied the government in order to make contributions to OEF in fall 2001, the GSDF aggressively lobbied *against* all the government's attempts to dispatch the GSDF to OEF (and won).

The GSDF's negative response to the war on terrorism following 9/11 was also strikingly different from that of the German Army. The first priority for GSDF chief of staff Nakatani Masahiro was the safety of his troops. He even remarked later that he was considering resigning from his post if the government forced the GSDF to deploy to Afghanistan or Pakistan.[82] The United States' need for support in Afghanistan was not one of the chief of staff's primary concerns. In sharp contrast, the German Army chief of staff Gert Gudera asked his men to write letters to their American counterparts to express their condolences following 9/11 and had already begun informal discussions with the German defense minister and other NATO allies about what kind of support the German Army could offer to the United States in September. Unlike GSDF chief of staff Nakatani, who tried to avoid sending his soldiers to Afghanistan at all costs, the German Army chief of staff began considering whether his soldiers were *combat-ready*. And, as I discussed earlier, the high-ranking German Army officers even pushed the reluctant officers of the KSK to go to Afghanistan. In November 2001 (a month before UN Resolution 1386 calling for the ISAF mandate was passed), the German Army chief of staff had already begun making plans by sending fact-finding teams to Afghanistan in order to find a place to stay in Kabul, providing special training for soldiers, and so on. In addition, he requested the following from Defense Minister Rudolf Scharping: (1) that the Bundeswehr's freedom of movement in Afghanistan be guaranteed; (2) that German law be applied to German soldiers in Afghanistan; (3) that logistics (medical support, communication support, etc.) be secured; (4) that an exit plan (how to withdraw from Kabul if that the operation failed) be drawn up; and (5) that the German troops be equipped with heavy tanks and artillery. Scharping accepted all of these terms except the last.[83] As we can see then, there was a significant difference between the top officer of the GSDF and his German counterpart in terms of their response to the war on terrorism in Afghanistan, and this difference resulted in the disparity in their countries' contributions to OEF.

In sum, the differences between the GSDF and the MSDF, as well as those between the GSDF and the German Army, in terms of their responses to OEF reveal the important explanatory variables for the GSDF's cautious attitude toward OEF, as well as its conservatism on overseas PKOs in general. The comparison between the GSDF and the MSDF in their responses to 9/11 shows that the factors particular to Japan (Article 9 of the constitution and the regional security environment of East Asia) are not adequate to explain the behavior of the GSDF. Both the MSDF and the GSDF were under the same domestic and international constraints; however, the MSDF was extremely enthusiastic about participating in OEF, whereas the GSDF refused to take part in that operation. The difference between the two forces in terms of their response to 9/11 can be explained by the degree of their integration with their US counterparts (and thereby the degree of their sense of camaraderie with those forces) and by the likelihood of casualties in overseas operations.

Concerning the GSDF and the German Army, both are ground forces and both face a high likelihood of casualties in overseas PKOs;

however, the German Army is active in expanding its overseas PKOs, while the GSDF is reluctant to deploy. Not only is the GSDF's relationship with the US Army much more distant than is the German Army's relationship with the armies of NATO member states, but it was also concerned about a consequence of its servicemen's use of force since there was no court-martial in Japan. Additionally, the GSDF did not have any alliance obligations that it had to satisfy by engaging in overseas PKOs. Nor did it have a particularly strong incentive to do other than national defense in order to justify its budget to the government.

The GSDF attributed its refusal to deploy to Afghanistan and Pakistan in fall 2001 to restrictions on the use of force placed on it by Article 9 of the constitution and to the difficulties inherent in securing logistical supply routes. However, the German Army faced similar constraints in Afghanistan, yet was able to undertake operations there. Certainly, because of the restrictions imposed by Article 9, the GSDF could not have engaged in counterinsurgency combat operations in southern Afghanistan as did the German KSK. However, the GSDF could have undertaken PKOs similar to those carried out by the German Army under the ISAF in the relatively stable northern part of Afghanistan—especially considering that the German Army under the ISAF is limited to the use of force only for defensive purposes. As for the difficulties securing logistical supply routes, the GSDF might have followed the Bundeswehr in using the Termez airfield close to the Uzbek-Afghan border.[84]

Two years later, the GSDF again showed no enthusiasm for dispatching troops to Iraq to aid in the US effort to stabilize postwar Iraq in 2003. It is true that none of the high-ranking GSDF officers lobbied to kill the government's plan to dispatch GSDF servicemen to Iraq. However, their silent acquiescence to the government's plans reflected the officers' fear that if they refused to go to Iraq (after already refusing to deploy to Afghanistan and Pakistan), the government might deem the GSDF essentially ineffectual and cut its budget.[85] Moreover, GSDF chief of staff Massaki Hajime realized in May 2003 that the Japanese government was facing too much pressure from the United States for it to refuse to send the GSDF to Iraq.[86]

The GSDF's cautious attitude toward the dispatch of its personnel to Iraq can be explained by its distant relationship with the US Army. While the German Army officers expressed their sympathy toward the US Army and Chief of Staff Eric Shinseki, and supported the possible US attack on Iraq at least at the time of year 2002, none of the GSDF officers with whom I spoke expressed the same degree of sympathy for the US Army or its chief of staff as did their German counterparts.

The fact that high-ranking GSDF officers rarely referred to the US-Japan alliance when working to justify the Iraq deployment to their servicemen provides further evidence of the distance and lack of camaraderie between the GSDF and the US Army. GSDF chief of staff Massaki, for example, remarked in an interview with *Asahi Shinbun* that it was difficult for him to explain to his servicemen why they had to go Iraq, though he stressed that it was important for them to provide the Iraqis with water.[87] Similarly, Banshō Koichirō, a GSDF officer who led the GSDF unit in Iraq, explained the justifications for deploying to Iraq as follows: The first reason was to help the Iraqis; the second, to secure oil in the Middle East; the third, to stabilize the world by securing one of the world's most important sources of energy—the Middle East; lastly, to maintain the US-Japan alliance.[88] The GSDF officers and servicemen who went to Iraq must have understood that the primary reason that the Japanese government would dispatch the GSDF to Iraq was not actually to provide humanitarian support for the Iraqis, but to maintain a good relationship with the United States. However, because they lacked a sense of camaraderie with the US Army, the high-ranking GSDF officers could hardly use the maintenance of the US-Japan alliance as a primary reason to motivate their men to risk their lives in Iraq.

Although the GSDF was ultimately dispatched to Iraq as a part of Japan's symbolic show of support for the United States—its contribution to the "Coalition of Willing," the GSDF's primary concern remained securing the safety of its servicemen, not helping the US Army in Iraq. Consequently, they undertook a humanitarian mission in Samawah, a remote town in southern Iraq, where the GSDF was less likely to suffer causalities. Indeed, the GSDF chose Samawah, according to one high-ranking GSDF officer, because the GSDF concluded that it would be wise to keep its distance from the US forces in Baghdad. The US forces were frequently attacked by the Iraqis and other insurgents, and the GSDF did not want its servicemen to be put in harm's way by working alongside US forces.[89]

To sum up, the GSDF's refusal to send its servicemen to Afghanistan and Pakistan in fall 2001, as well as its cautious attitude toward the dispatch of troops to Iraq in 2003 stemmed from its relative isolation and lack of contacts with foreign forces since the Cold War period. The USARJ is quite small, and does not project its forces beyond the country. More importantly, the GSDF has always been independent from the USARJ and has not been integrated into the overall structure of the US Army. As a result of its distant relationship with the US Army, along with the absence of court-martial and of budgetary pressures that might encourage it to expand overseas PKOs, the GSDF's responses to the war on terrorism in the fall of 2001 and to the Iraq War in 2003 were reluctant and cautious.

VI. Conclusion

Although Germany's and Japan's alliance security dilemmas in their relations with the United States have stemmed from the regional security environments surrounding the two countries and the characteristics of the respective alliance institutions to which they belong, it is important to understand how these variables have affected the two countries' military institutions themselves. It is especially important to examine how these variables have affected the capabilities and willingness of the two countries' military institutions to carry out joint operations with their allies abroad, since these institutions actually implement the government's decisions and, thus, have significant influence on the actual contributions that each country makes. For this reason, in addition to the regional security environments and the characteristics of alliance institutions, the military institutions themselves can be a source of overseas entrapment and thereby increase or decrease the level of their countries' alliance security dilemma with the United States.

6

ALTERNATIVE EXPLANATIONS

In this chapter, I will examine the hypotheses discussed in the Introduction, drawn from the major theoretical frameworks of international relations: (1) realism, (2) domestic institutions, (3) liberalism, and (4) constructivism. Although the major theories of international relations suggest a number of variables that may help explain why Germany and Japan pursued different policies regarding the US attack on Iraq, only a few of these survived the process of hypothesis testing, and none of them can explain the outcome alone.

I. EXAMINATION OF HYPOTHESES

1. Realism

(i) External Threats

Japan needed (or would need in the future) US help to cope with external threats more than did Germany.

Beginning with the realist explanation, as we have seen, the mere presence of external threats is not the main reason that Japan supported the US decision to attack Iraq. It is commonly believed that Japan supported the Iraq War because Japan needed the United States to cope with the threat from North Korea, whereas Germany opposed it because Germany did not have any imminent threat. It is true that the North Korean nuclear weapons development and the rise of China and its future uncertainty were serious concerns for Japan. Nevertheless, these external threats did not directly influence Japan's alliance behavior. Rather, they were filtered through the US alliance commitment to Japan. The US alliance commitment to Japan as well as its overall interest in the Asia Pacific did not decline even after the collapse of the Soviet Union, while its interest in European affairs declined. More importantly, despite the presence of tensions in East Asia, these tensions did not develop into actual military conflicts. As a result, the post–Cold War regional security environment in East Asia was much more peaceful than that in Europe, where EU countries had to deal with a series of civil wars in former Yugoslavia. Different from their German counterparts, who experienced difficulties in working with the United States in the 1999 Kosovo War, Japanese politicians and officials were able to acquiesce in the US decision to attack Iraq because the relatively stable regional environment had prevented Japan from having a negative experience of US unilateralism.

(ii) Dependence on the US Market
Japan's economy was more dependent on the US market than was Germany's economy.

Did Japan support the US attack on Iraq while Germany opposed it because the level of Japan's economic dependence on the United States was higher than that of Germany? It is not very clear whether the two countries' different responses to the US attack on Iraq stemmed from the differences in the level of their economic dependence on the United States. Although the level of Japan's dependence on the US market is higher than that of Germany, it seems that the difference between the two countries is not very substantial. The two countries' economies are closely interconnected with that of the United States. Not only have both countries been dependent on the US market, but the United States has also been dependent on both the German and Japanese markets.

In 2005, for example, Germany's merchandise exports to the United States totaled 8.7 million dollars, while its exports to the EU (25 countries) totaled 62 million dollars. In the same year, Germany's merchandise imports from the United States reached 6.3 million dollars, whereas its imports from the EU were 57.7 million dollars. On the other hand, Japan's merchandise exports to the United States totaled 22.9 million dollars and its imports from the United States, 12.7 million dollars.[1] Therefore, at least in the area of merchandise trade, Japan's economic dependence on the United States is higher than that of Germany, and it seems that what one German official at the Federal Ministry of Economics and Technology told me is correct: The EU is creating a kind of "shield" that protects Germany from fluctuations within the world economy.[2] Nevertheless, when the EU is broken down into single countries, the United States (87.0 million Euros) is Germany's second largest export destination next to France (86.1 million Euros), as well as its fourth largest source of imports.[3] Moreover, Germany's trade-to-GDP ratio (2003–2005) is 71.3, whereas Japan's is 25.6. This means that Germany is much more dependent on foreign trade for its economic growth than is Japan.[4] In addition, although the United States is an important trading partner for Japan, it is not Japan's *only* important trading partner. Other partners, such as the EU and China, are also extremely important for Japanese economic growth. While the United States (22.9 million dollars) was the top destination for Japanese exports in 2005, the EU was the second largest recipient of Japanese goods (14.7 million dollars) and China the third (13.5 million dollars). Moreover, China is Japan's top source of imports (21 million dollars), with the United States (12.7 million dollars) second, and the EU (11.4 million dollars) third.[5]

Although some Liberal Democratic Party (LDP) politicians justified their support for the US attack on Iraq by emphasizing the importance of Japan's economic relations with the United States, it is not very clear whether Japan's opposition to the Iraq War would really have had a negative impact on its economic relations with the United States. Kyuma Fumio, the chairman of the LDP's Policy Research Council, stated in February 2003, for example:

> In light of the U.S.-Japan alliance, I can neither oppose nor support a potential U.S. military attack on Iraq. All I can do is to "understand" the U.S. decision... Not only can Japan not solve the problem of North Korea without the United States but also its economy is closely tied to the U.S. economy. Japan cannot do anything without the United States... Japan has no choice but to understand the U.S. decision, because Japan is like one of the American states.[6]

One of the LDP politicians whom I interviewed made similar remarks. He said that the well-being of the Japanese economy was closely related to the US market, because Japan held a large number of US treasury bonds.[7]

Yet, it is not entirely clear why the strong economic ties between Japan and the United States led these senior LDP politicians to support for the US attack on Iraq. One young LDP member of the lower house told me that if Japanese political leaders were really concerned about the future of US economy, they should have advised their US counterparts to refrain from going to war against Iraq.[8] Some DPJ members also stated that Japan's close economic ties to the United States could not explain why Japan had to support the US action, since the Japanese and American economies are fundamentally *interdependent*.[9] Japan is dependent on the US market, but the United States is also dependent on the Japanese market. Thus, Japan's dependence on the US market would not necessarily increase the likelihood of its abandonment.

These views were further elaborated by one high-ranking official of the Ministry of Economy, Trade, and Industry (METI), who was working to support Japanese companies doing business in the United States from 2001 to 2003. While Okuda Hiroshi, a leader of the Japan Business Federation (*Keidanren*) and president of Toyota Motor Company, publicly supported the Iraq War by saying, "Japan had no choice but to follow the United States" on March 9, 2003,[10] the METI official said that he had never heard concerns from leaders of Japanese companies operating in the United States that if Japan opposed the US attack on Iraq, an anti-Japanese movement would occur in the United States. The METI official argued that because a government basically cannot change the flow of money and goods, even if Japan opposed the Iraq War, the US government could not affect the flow of Japanese products to and from the United States. To be sure, Japan has depended on the United States because of the vast export market it represents, but, the official contended, Americans buy Japanese products because they like those products, not because they like Japan. Similarly, Americans buy Japanese stocks, not because they like Japan, but because they want to make money. They would buy Japanese stocks as long as they can make profits, regardless of whether the Japanese government supported the Iraq War or not.[11]

Additionally, one senior LDP member of the lower house, who served as a minister of defense twice before, expressed his concern that if Japan opposed the Iraq War, important technology and information about missile defense would not flow from the United States to Japan.[12] Codevelopment with US companies has certainly become increasingly important for Japan's defense industry. One high-ranking METI official (a former chief of the division of aerospace and defense industry) told me that codevelopment with foreign companies would be the best way for Japanese defense companies to survive, because pure "made-in-Japan" products are very expensive and costly, and there is little to learn from the license production. Moreover, US companies are the best partners for Japanese companies to codevelop new products, because the former have the most advanced technologies. The same METI official, however, adamantly denied the possibility of a causal linkage between the Japanese government's support for the Iraq War and the future of codevelopment between Japanese and American companies.[13]

Another METI official working in the division of aerospace and defense industry suggested that the government's opposition to the

Iraq War could possibly have a negative impact on codevelopment between Japanese and American defense companies, but it was uncertain. On one hand, because the defense industry tends to be influenced by politics, the government's opposition to the Iraq War could negatively affect codevelopment. For example, he stated, the Japanese Air Self-Defense Force (ASDF) wants to purchase F-22 fighter aircraft from the United States; yet, the US Congress will not permit the purchase out of fear that the United States will lose the technology race to Japan. On the other hand, the METI official suggested, even if Japan had not supported the Iraq War, it would likely have little impact on codevelopment of missile defense, which is essentially based on relationships and agreements between private companies. If American companies judged that they could benefit from codevelopment with Japanese companies, they would work with Japanese companies—regardless of the Japanese government's position on the Iraq War. Thus, the concern about Japan's economic relations with the United States cannot decisively explain why Japan supported the Iraq War. The concern among the Japanese about the potential negative impact on economic relations with the United States should their government decide to oppose for the Iraq War was effectively psychological.[14]

How did German business interests react to their government's opposition to the US preventive war on Iraq? Early on, the German business community was clearly concerned about the potential negative consequences for business with the United States. One Volkswagen manager in Wolfsburg stated, "If an anti-German attitude became common in the USA., it would be a severe problem."[15] Still, an executive of a polling company that conducted a survey in the United States in March 2003, noted, "I have not seen any survey where people were adverse to buying a particular make of a vehicle due to a war [Iraq War]. It's so common for Americans to be detached from what's happening in the world."[16] In addition, by emphasizing the jobs they produce locally and for the US economy as whole, German companies tried to promote the concept that boycotting German goods would hurt the US economy more than it would help US foreign policy. Volkswagen, for example, received fewer than 50 letters and emails on the war issue but still responded to each of them by noting that the company has been operating in the US for 50 years and employs 50,000 Americans.[17]

A high-ranking member of the International Department in the Association of German Chambers of Commerce and Industry told me that he expected that the German government's opposition to the US attack on Iraq could have a negative impact on German-US business relations. Yet he also believed that US investments in Germany were made with a long-term perspective in mind, which meant that such investments might not be affected by short-term political turmoil.

As he saw it, there was a wide range of opinions within the German business community at the time. Some people opposed the war on Iraq; others supported it. But there were many people in the business community who preferred to avoid the war primarily because the Germans had paid such a bitter price for the two world wars. He explained that German business lobbies usually stay out of politics. They do not finance specific political parties (though each private company has done so). Private companies do not want the business lobbies to finance political parties.[18] Accordingly, during the Iraq crisis, German business leaders tried to stay out of politics, to continue business as usual.

However, this does not mean that German business leaders did not worry about the consequences of their government's decision to oppose the Iraq War. In order to minimize negative impacts, they held many conferences and meetings with their American counterparts. Yet during these meetings, they never openly discussed the Iraq issue (though they often engaged in informal discussions on the topic during breaks). There was no problem in the relationship between German and American businessmen during this time, because both sides wanted to maintain positive relationships.[19]

Finally, one high-ranking official working in the Division of External Economic Policy toward North America in the Federal Ministry of Economics and Technology remarked that he and his colleagues did not really expect negative consequences for the government's opposition to the US attack on Iraq, because economic relations between Germany and the United States are so densely connected. In fact, he could only cite one example of a negative consequence to German business as a result of the government's opposition to the United States: When repainting its walls in the summer of 2002, the Pentagon refused to use German paint, instead ordering an American product.[20]

In sum, the two countries' economic relations with the United States are not a significant factor in explaining their divergent responses to the US war on Iraq. Although there are some differences between Germany and Japan in terms of their dependence on the US market, both countries' economies have been closely intertwined with the American economy. Moreover, my interview data suggests that even if the Japanese government had opposed the US attack on

Iraq, such a decision was unlikely to have the serious negative effects on Japan's economic relations with the United States that the senior LDP politicians claimed it would. The LDP politicians' claim seems not to be rooted in an objective assessment of reality, but rather a token excuse to convince the public after the likelihood of the US attack of Iraq became inevitable.

(iii) Dependence on the Middle Eastern Oil
Japan was more dependent on Middle Eastern oil than was Germany.

Although Japan is much more dependent on Middle Eastern oil than is Germany, Japan's dependence on Middle Eastern oil cannot explain why Japan supported the US attack on Iraq and Germany did not. In 2006, petroleum accounted for 44.1 percent of Japan's total energy supply, while it accounted for 35.7 percent in Germany.[21] Moreover, in 2001, Japan imported 89 percent of its petroleum from the Middle East, while Germany imported only 11 percent from the Middle East that same year.[22] Saudi Arabia was Japan's largest source of petroleum in 2005 (accounting for 30 percent of total imports), followed by the United Arab Emirates (24 percent), and Iran (14 percent).[23] Germany's largest source of oil was Russia (30 percent), followed by Africa (including the Middle East) (19 percent), Norway (15 percent), and the United Kingdom (13 percent).[24]

Japan's heavy dependence on Middle Eastern oil, however, created competing and contradictory impulses with respect to the Iraq War. Because the US Navy contributes to security in the Persian Gulf and thereby secures Japan's energy supply line, Japan certainly had incentive to support the United States' efforts in Iraq. In fact, this was the argument employed by American political leaders to force Japan to make huge financial contributions to the US-led allied forces during the Persian Gulf War of 1990–1991.[25] On the other hand, Japan dependence on Middle Eastern oil might lead it to keep its distance from the United States in order to maintain good relations with Organization of Petroleum Exporting Countries (OPEC).

In any case, it seems that Japan's dependence on Middle Eastern oil had little to do with its support for the Iraq War. As one high-ranking METI official (who worked in the Agency for Natural Resources and Energy [ANRE] in 2003) noted, as long as the oil supply from both Saudi Arabia and the Strait of Hormuz was secured, the Iraq War would have likely had little effect on the flow of oil to Japan. Iraq did not possess the military capability to close the Strait of Hormuz, and it was unlikely that the war in Iraq would spill over into neighboring countries. This same official suggested that there were only two (highly unlikely) circumstances—one political, the other physical—under which the supply of oil from the Middle East to Japan might be interrupted. For political reasons, the OPEC countries might stop selling their oil to foreign countries. However, because the economies of the oil-producing countries cannot survive without oil exports, it was virtually unthinkable that OPEC would refuse to export to Japan. The other possibility was that oil fields might be destroyed in the war. In that case, the oil supply might be interrupted temporarily. However, the official argued, the oil fields would quickly be restored and, as a result, Japan's oil supply would not be interrupted for long.[26] This view was endorsed by another high-ranking METI official (who also worked in the ANRE during the Iraq crisis of 2002–2003). He remarked that even if the Japanese government had not supported the Iraq War, there would likely not have been dramatic consequences for Japan's Middle Eastern oil supply.[27] A senior researcher at the Institute of Energy Economics Japan also concurred with this view (although he added that the maintenance of the US-Japan Security Treaty was much more important than securing the oil supply to Japan from the Middle East).[28] Therefore, the fact that Japan is substantially more dependent on Middle Eastern oil than is Germany cannot ultimately explain the difference in the two countries' responses to the US attack on Iraq.

2. Domestic Institutions

(i) Formal Institutions (Article 9)

Article 9 of the Japanese Constitution prohibits Japan from exercising the right of collective self-defense; whereas the Federal Republic of Germany (FRG) does not have such a law.

Article 9 of the Japanese constitution has played an important role in protecting Japan from becoming entrapped in US-led overseas wars ever since the US occupation authority introduced the constitution to Japan in 1946. As I discussed in chapters 4 and 5, Article 9 substantially contributed to the unequal alliance obligation between Japan and the United States under the US-Japan Security Treaty as well as to the distant relationship between the Ground Self-Defense Forces (GSDF) and the US Army, leading to the GSDF's conservatism on overseas dispatch. Not only does Article 9 prohibit Japan from exercising the right of collective self-defense, but it has also contributed to the legally ambivalent status of the Self-Defense Forces (SDF) and to absence of a court-martial in Japan. These are the most important differences between the FRG and Japan.

Article 9 was able to so effectively keep Japan's alliance security dilemma with the United States low only because other factors provided favorable conditions. To begin, Article 9's renunciation of war has been widely accepted and supported by a large segment of the Japanese public, which holds a strong antimilitarist sentiment as a result of the devastating experience of the Pacific War. Even with generational change, the majority of the Japanese public still opposes revising Article 9 or changing the current interpretation that Article 9 prohibits Japan from exercising the right of collective self-defense.[29] Second, postwar Japanese politicians have shrewdly used Article 9 to dodge the American demand for rearmament and to keep Japan away from US-led overseas military affairs so that Japan could concentrate on economic activities.

However, the most important factor allowing Japan to keep Article 9 intact is the lack of significant external threats. While West Germany had to face Warsaw Pact troops stationed on the demarcation line between East and West, Japan never faced an imminent threat of Soviet invasion during the Cold War. There were, of course, the Korean (1950–1953) and Vietnam (late 1960s–early 1970s) wars, but these regional wars were distant "fires across the sea" from Japan.[30] If Japan had had an imminent external threat, Japanese political leaders would not have been able to use Article 9 to dodge the US demand for rearmament, and the Japanese public would probably not have been able to adhere to the idealistic principle of Article 9. Had the Soviets posed an imminent threat, the Japanese would have had no choice but to give up Article 9 and fight side-by-side with US forces. But without such a threat, the Japanese were able to enjoy the luxury of Article 9.

Even after the Cold War, the relatively stable regional security environment in East Asia, along with continuing US alliance commitment to Japan as well as its strong interests in the Asia Pacific has allowed the Japanese to maintain Article 9. As a result of its "traumatic" experience of the Persian Gulf War of 1990–1991, the Japanese government changed its previous interpretation of Article 9 so that it could dispatch the SDF to overseas peacekeeping operations (PKOs) under UN authority in the early 1990s. The interpretation regarding collective self-defense, however, has remained intact. It is still unconstitutional for Japan to exercise the right of collective self-defense. And there has been no public support or government attempt to establish a court-martial in Japan.

(ii) Bureaucratic Politics (Diplomatic Institutions)
The notion that Japan should always closely follow US leadership is a long-established institutional norm within Japan's Ministry of Foreign Affairs (MOFA); whereas Germany's Foreign Office lacks such a norm.

Although the German Federal Foreign Office and Japan's MOFA are the bureaucratic organizations most responsible for foreign policymaking in their respective countries, neither of these organizations actually played a significant role in shaping their government's decisions regarding the Iraq War. In this section, I will first discuss the policy preferences of the MOFA and Federal Foreign Office regarding their countries' relations with the United States. Then, I will explain why the high-ranking officials within these two institutions had limited influence over their governments' policy toward the US attack on Iraq.

Japan: Ministry of Foreign Affairs

MOFA officials' policy preference regarding US-Japan relations is very clear. They regard the US-Japan Security Treaty to be unquestionably and critically important. This has been an established norm within the ministry for decades. MOFA officials who do not support this position do not receive promotions and, even worse, are sometimes forced out of the ministry altogether. Amaki Naoto (a former ambassador to Lebanon, 2001–2003), for example, protested the government's decision to support the US attack on Iraq in 2003 and was eventually forced to leave the ministry.

According to Amaki, Kuriyama Shōichi, former director of the US-Japan Security Treaty division within the MOFA, wrote a short brochure that provides a detailed description of Kuriyama's answers to questions posed to him by opposition parties in the Diet regarding the US-Japan Security Treaty. For example, in response to a question about whether the United States would really help Japan at the expense of its soldiers' lives, Kuriyama answered, "The United States is the only country that Japan can trust and [with which it] shares a common value. It is thus wrong in the first place to doubt whether or not the United States would really help us [in the event of a crisis], and raising such a question is disrespectful to the United States." This brochure has since been used by Kuriyama's successors, Amaki explains, as a "manual" (*tora no maki*) for dealing with such questions from the opposition.[31]

Amaki's claims about the uniformity of opinion within MOFA seem to be correct. All the MOFA officials with whom I conducted interviews not only stated that the US-Japan Security Treaty was a pillar of Japan's foreign policy, but also firmly backed the Japanese government's decision to support the US attack on Iraq. One of the high-ranking MOFA officials closest to Prime Minister Koizumi during the 2002–2003 Iraq crisis told me that at a December 2001 conference in Munich, he was informed by a foreign diplomat that the United States was certain to attack Iraq. Even at that time, the MOFA official noted, he knew that he would support the United States if it decided to attack Iraq.[32] Another high-ranking MOFA official said that, considering the security situation in present-day East Asia, Japan needed the United States, and, thus, it was thus unthinkable that Japan would not support the US attack on Iraq.[33] One senior LDP member of the lower house whom I interview called MOFA's policy norm "*beikoku ippento kotonakare shugi*,"[34] which means, "If Japan keeps a good relationship with the United States, everything will be fine."

Although these MOFA officials strongly held to their conviction that the US-Japan Security Treaty should be maintained and they, therefore, supported the US attack on Iraq, it is unclear whether these officials' conviction had a direct and significant influence on Prime Minister Koizumi's ultimate decision to support the US attack. It seems likely that Prime Minister Koizumi would have supported the US decision to attack Iraq, regardless of MOFA's policy preference. On the one hand, the high-ranking MOFA officials were certainly experts in foreign affairs and were clearly in a position to give advice to Prime Minister Koizumi. Indeed, MOFA officials had been telling Koizumi that Japan had no choice but to support the Iraq War since fall 2002. One high-ranking MOFA official even told Koizumi, "This is a good chance for us to get the United States indebted to Japan by supporting the United States at a time when the world is divided [over the Iraq issue]."[35] One retired MOFA official confidently suggested during an interview that Japan's foreign policy was made by MOFA itself. As he told it, policies made by MOFA would reach the prime minister through the MOFA, a MOFA vice minister, or an executive secretary to the prime minister in the Cabinet Secretariat (a high-ranking official sent from the MOFA).[36] MOFA officials may choose to give information to the prime minister as they see fit. This gives MOFA a great deal of power over the prime minister's foreign-policy decisions, as it limits the flow of information about the range of policy options.

Still, the prime minister is free to reject any and all of the policy options submitted by MOFA and to pursue a completely different course of action, should he so choose. Although Prime Minister Koizumi's decision to support the US attack on Iraq coincided with the preference within MOFA at the time, it is not clear Koizumi's choice directly reflected the advice of MOFA officials. Instead, it is just as likely the prime minister decided to support the US attack on Iraq simply because he might have thought that it was the right decision. Indeed, Prime Minister Koizumi is well known for ignoring advice from MOFA officials. He did, after all, choose to visit the Yasukuni Shrine every summer despite opposition from MOFA. The same high-ranking official who, as noted above, contended that Japan's foreign policy is set by MOFA, actually personally advised Koizumi to stop visiting the Yasukuni Shrine. Koizumi completely ignored him. The MOFA official remarked that Prime Minister Koizumi listens to what he chooses and ignores as he pleases.[37] Another MOFA official told me that although he personally believed that a prime minister should not visit the Yasukuni Shrine, he did not advise Koizumi against these visits, as he assumed that Koizumi would simply ignore him.[38] In addition, when then deputy minister for foreign affairs Tanaka Hitoshi told Koizumi about a number of problems that had arisen as a result of his visit to the Yasukuni Shrine, Koizumi replied, "Are you saying I should not visit Yasukuni Shrine because China told me not to?" When Tanaka further tried to convince him not to visit the shrine, Koizumi "at last burst into a fit of anger."[39]

Koizumi also demonstrated his willingness to ignore MOFA's advice by selecting a route for bringing the family members of the returned abductees back to Japan from North Korea through Chōsen Sōren (the General Association of Korean Residents in Japan), rather than the route that Tanaka had secretly been preparing, when he made a second visit to Pyongyang in 2004. When Koizumi heard that Tanaka was complaining about this choice, the prime minister called Tanaka and exclaimed, "Make no mistake. I am the Prime Minister. As long as I take full responsibility in negotiations with North Korea through my channel, this is the only diplomatic route we should pursue. You can't accuse your prime minister of being the source of dualistic diplomacy."[40] In this way, Koizumi made it clear that a prime minister can choose any policy he wants, regardless of advice from MOFA officials. When it came to deciding whether Japan should support the US decision to attack Iraq, Koizumi, of course, must have listened to the advice coming from MOFA officials. However, it seems he listened to them precisely because he thought they were giving him good advice. If he had disagreed with their advice, he would not have listened to them at all.

The FRG: Foreign Office

It seems that high-ranking officials within the German Federal Foreign Office did not have significant influence over the Social Democratic Party (SPD)-Green government's decision to oppose a US attack on Iraq for precisely the same reasons that MOFA officials' impact was limited. While high-ranking Foreign Office officials advise the chancellor and the foreign minister, the chancellor and foreign minister must prove willing to heed that advice before it can have any impact. In regard to the Iraq question, Chancellor Gerhard Schröder and Foreign Minister Joschka Fischer opposed a US attack, not because Foreign Office officials advised them to do so, but because they themselves judged that it was the right course of action to be taken at the time.

In the pages that follow, I will first discuss the institutional policy norms of the German Foreign Office. Then I will describe the overall stance of the Foreign Office toward the potential US attack on Iraq. Finally, I will discuss the limits of the Foreign Office's ability to influence the government's decision on this matter, as well as the government's foreign policymaking in general.

Although German Federal Foreign Office officials clearly believe that Germany's relations with the United States are very important, unlike Japan's MOFA, the Federal Foreign Office does not abide by the principle that Germany should follow the United States at any cost. There are two reasons why this is the case. First, it has been very difficult for the FRG to cope with regional threats by solely depending on the United States since the early Cold War period. To be sure, the US commitment to European security through NATO has been indispensable to German security. However, the United States has not been, and cannot be, Germany's only means of dealing with external threats. One high-ranking Foreign Office official, for example, told me that while Japan was able to be a "complacent ally" of the United States due to the relatively stable East Asian security environment, the Cold War division of Germany—as well as the post–Cold War civil war in former Yugoslavia—have made it difficult for the FRG to be so complacent. During the Cold War, he explained, FRG politicians and diplomats had to form "creative foreign policy" in order to alleviate the tension between the East and the West and to unite divided Germany. Because Germany could turn into a battlefield at seemingly any moment, the FRG could not totally rely on the United States in order to counter the threats from the Communist East. In the 1987 "Simulation of Security" study, for example, Chancellor Helmut Kohl realized that in the event of a nuclear war in Europe, Germany would be entirely destroyed. FRG political leaders therefore had to prepare for every contingency and had to create a distinctive policy toward the Soviet Union. Later, after the Cold War, German leaders grew concerned about instability in the Balkans, fearing that it might drag Europe back into a pre–World War security environment. Germans thus cannot be "complacent," this official argued, but must be active and creative in building European security.[41]

Another Foreign Office official also told me that the end of the Cold War shifted the FRG's foreign policy focus away from the United States and toward the European Union. Following German unification, German politicians and diplomats have begun to spend more energy on European integration than on maintaining Germany's transatlantic relations. The Europeanist became more powerful than the Atlanticist in the area of foreign policy, the official maintained.[42]

This sits in sharp contrast to Japan, which has not implemented a fundamental change in its security policy since the end of the Cold War. It continues to emphasize and rely on its alliance with the United States. To be sure, after the Cold War, Japanese leaders sought out security dialogues among countries in the Asia Pacific based on the 1991 Nakayama proposal that Japan pursue a more multilateral approach toward Asian regional security. The main purpose of the Nakayama proposal, however, was to ensure a continued US military presence in East Asia.[43] Moreover, in the hierarchical order of Japan's "multitiered" approach to Asian regional security, the bilateral US-Japan alliance has been placed at the very top of the "first tier," while the multilateral approach is considered the "third tier."[44] Therefore, while MOFA has continued to place its foreign-policy emphasis on the US-Japan alliance, the policy emphasis of the German Foreign Office has shifted from its transatlantic relations to its relationship with and role within the EU.

There is a second reason why German Foreign Office officials have never been as steadfastly committed to maintaining good relations with the United States as have their Japanese counterparts: The German government has been controlled by different political parties and coalitions over the years, while the Japanese government has been controlled by only the conservative, pro-US LDP since 1955 (with a short interruption in 1993–1994 and until 2009, when the Democratic Party of Japan finally defeated the LDP in the lower house election). After 1994, the LDP had to form a coalition with small parties in order to continue to control the government; yet it has remained the ruling party for the past six decades. It was thus relatively easy for MOFA officials to pursue the same pro-US policy without making any significant changes. On the other hand, the German government has been controlled by two different large parties—the Christian Democratic Union/Christian Social Union (CDU/CSU) and the SPD—with their small coalition partners. The CDU/CSU tends to be pro-US, whereas the SPD tends to pursue a course more independent of the United States (though it does not deny the importance of NATO). The changes in the ruling parties, therefore, have permitted a diversity of policy preferences among Foreign Office officials.

Although there is no conclusive data about the number of partisan supporters in the Foreign Office, it seems that a substantial number of SPD members or supporters remained in the Foreign Office during the long period of the CDU/CSU–FDP government control from 1982 to 1998. Interactions between the Foreign Office and the SPD continued throughout that period. One high-ranking Foreign Office official told me that he worked as an advisor for the SPD for three years in the middle of 1990s when the SPD was an opposition party. He noted that there is an informal custom by which the Foreign Office will rent its officials to political parties upon request, though parties have to pay the salary for the advisor.[45] (This custom does not exist in Japan.) When the Foreign Office official was working as an SPD advisor, his salary came from the SPD, not from the Foreign Office. His office was not in the Foreign Office, but in the Bundestag, and his direct boss was Karsten Voigt, foreign-policy spokesman of the SPD Bundestag Fraktion (Parliamentary Group).

By hiring a Foreign Office official as an advisor, parties can gain access to the rich information available in the Foreign Office. And the Foreign Office can, in turn, influence the parties. At the time he was hired by the SPD, this Foreign Office official in fact supported dispatching the Bundeswehr overseas. I asked him whether he was hired by Voigt because of this stance. He said, no, when he was hired, the issue of overseas dispatch was just one of many foreign-policy issues. But the issue of overseas dispatch did turn out to be the most significant foreign-policy concern later. In the middle of the 1990s, the majority of SPD Bundestag members opposed dispatching the Bundeswehr overseas, so this official worked to convince them how important it was for Germany to send its troops to PKOs. Although the Foreign Office official struggled tirelessly on this matter, he said that, ultimately, it was Karsten Voigt who convinced the SPD to change its position. In the end, however, it cost him his seat in the

Bundestag. The left wing of his local constituency told Voigt that they would not support him any longer.[46]

Although the Foreign Office official was hired by someone in the upper echelons of the SPD who already intended to try to change the party's position on overseas dispatch, this example shows how deep the relations between the Foreign Office and opposition party were. And more importantly, this example presents a striking contrast between the Foreign Office and MOFA in terms of their relations with opposition parties. While German Foreign Office officials had contacts with opposition parties and were willing to work for them, Japanese MOFA officials seem to have had little desire to maintain contact with the opposition parties, since it was not necessary to do so when there was no party turnover in government. When I asked one MOFA official whether he or other MOFA officials visited the offices of members of the opposition parties in the Diet in order to try to persuade them to support the Anti-Terrorism Special Measures Law (ATSML) in fall 2001, he looked at me with a hint of contempt and questioned whether I really had a basic knowledge of the legislative system in Japan. He told me that in order to pass legislation in the Diet, only a majority of votes was necessary. Some MOFA officials might have visited the opposition parties' offices; however, it effectively did not matter whether members of the opposition parties voted for or against the legislation. The LDP and its small coalition partner, the Kōmeito, controlled the government and dominated the majority of seats in both the lower and upper houses. All MOFA officials had to do, therefore, was talk to high-ranking members of the LDP and Kōmeito. Even if MOFA officials had met with members of the opposition parties, he continued, they would not have listened to MOFA's position anyway.[47] Because there was no opposition party that could replace the LDP in Japan (at least until September 2009), MOFA officials tended to regard the opposition parties as irrelevant in the process of foreign policymaking and have found no need to alter their fundamental commitment to the US-Japan alliance.

Regarding the Iraq question, most German Foreign Office officials seemed to agree with the government's decision to oppose the United States. One high-ranking German diplomat told me that there might be a few officials who expressed concerns about the government's decision; however, most Foreign Office officials agreed that the government's decision was right because: (1) the US action was a breach of the international law; (2) there was no proof that Iraq possessed weapons of mass destruction (WMD); and (3) the military attack was not the best way to change the Iraqi regime.[48] Stephen

F. Szabo also writes that neither the Foreign Office nor the intelligence establishment shared the US assessment of the threat posed by Saddam Hussein. They did not find any convincing evidence of the link between al-Qaeda and Iraq nor that Iraq possessed WMD. There was a consensus in the Foreign Office that the risks of a military attack on Iraq would outweigh the benefits by considering its impact, not just on Iraq, but also on neighboring states.[49] One German diplomat told Szabo:

> In the Foreign Office, we assessed a number of likely scenarios. We thought that a war would destabilize Iraq itself, as it was a fragile state that had always been run in a dictatorial manner. We worried about the impact of a Kurdish state on Turkey, Iran, and Syria. If Iraq fell apart, the strategic role of Iraq would be strengthened or a theocratic Shiite government would emerge, neither of which were desirable scenarios. Then there was the Israel factor—what would happen to the Palestinian-Israeli conflict? Would Saddam Strike at Israel? What would be the impact on Saudi Arabia, Jordan, and Egypt?[50]

My own interview with another high-ranking Foreign Office official also seems to reflect this overall consensus within the Foreign Office regarding Iraq. This official was Foreign Minister Fischer's closest advisor during the Iraq crisis of 2002–2003. He accompanied Fischer during his all foreign trips and constantly held informal talks with him over foreign-policy issues. He advised Fischer that while Iraq was a problem, there were many other problems that Germany should prioritize over Iraq, including the Israeli-Palestine conflict, Iran, North Korea, Pakistan, and Afghanistan.[51]

Although most Foreign Office officials agreed with the government's broad decision to oppose a US attack on Iraq in 2002, some high-ranking officials tried to slightly modify Chancellor Schröder's provocative stance. These officials worried that Schröder's policy would instigate American anger and, thereby, seriously damage Germany's relations with the United States. However, their attempts were not particularly successful. In an election speech in Hanover on August 5, 2002, for example, Chancellor Schröder remarked to the crowd, "Pressure on Saddam Hussein, yes. We must get the international inspectors into Iraq. But playing games with war and military intervention—against that I can only warn. This will happen without us...We are not available for adventures, and the time of checkbook diplomacy is finally at an end."[52] Following the delivery of these provocative (but appealing) words, Dieter Kastrup, a veteran diplomat working as a foreign-policy advisor to the Chancellor, urged Schröder to weigh his words carefully. Schröder responded that he understood what Kastrup meant. However, he added, "I have to win the election."[53] In fact, there was no full policy discussion of the German position within the government, even within the Chancellery or the Foreign Office. Schröder excluded his foreign-policy advisors and made the important decision largely on the recommendations of a few political advisers with little background in foreign policy.[54] Therefore, although high-ranking Foreign Office officials have the power to advise the chancellor, as well as the foreign minister, their influence on the German government's decision to oppose to a US attack on Iraq was ultimately quite limited.

In general, the position of Foreign Office officials vis-à-vis those of the chancellor and the foreign minister is weak, because the chancellor and the foreign minister have the power to influence the promotion of officials in the Foreign office. This may lead Foreign Office officials (whether consciously or not) to self-censor their advice and to avoid positions that seem controversial or to go against the grain. Naturally, when a new chancellor or foreign minister comes to office, he or she tries to surround him (or herself) with loyal bureaucrats and tends to reward those who demonstrate loyalty with promotions.[55] State Secretary Klaus Scharioth, for example, was supposed to be promoted to the position of ambassador to Washington, DC by Foreign Minister Joschka Fischer (the Greens) in April 2005.[56] However, after winning the September 2005 Bundestag election, new chancellor Angela Merkel (CDU) blocked Scharioth's nomination. The CDU considered Scharioth to be too critical of the United States and too close to the SPD.[57] In the end, Merkel dropped her objection to the nomination in December 2005,[58] and Merkel herself introduced Scharioth to US president G. W. Bush in January 2006.[59] However, this example shows how vulnerable the position of Foreign Office officials is to the power of the chancellor.

Finally, when I visited the German embassy in Washington, DC in the fall of 2008, I asked one diplomat, "What would Foreign Office officials do if they disagree with the government's decisions?" He answered that if a certain Foreign Office official disagrees with the government's decision, he or she has to keep silent, or—in an extreme case—he or she has to resign. He offered the example of Friedrich-Wilhelm von Prittwitz und Gaffron, who served as ambassador to the United States from 1927 to 1933. He resigned from the position of ambassador in April 16, 1933, following the National Socialist Party's (Nazi) takeover of the government. The German diplomat actually took me to a room where a picture of F. W. von Prittwitz und

Gaffron and a newspaper article about his resignation were displayed in the embassy. The story of von Prittwitz und Gaffron speaks to the limits placed on diplomats even in today's democratic political system. Diplomats are civil servants and have to be loyal to the chancellor and to the foreign minister.

In sum, the policy preferences of Japan's MOFA and Germany's Foreign Office toward the US attack on Iraq coincided with the decisions made by their respective top political leaders, namely Prime Minister Koizumi and Chancellor Schröder. Almost all MOFA officials supported the US military strike on Iraq, whereas German Foreign Office officials were against it. MOFA has a long-term, established institutional norm that calls on Japan to follow the United States, while the Foreign Office is not committed to the alliance with the US above all else. The difference in these policy norms has come from the regional security environments surrounding the two countries since the Cold War period and from the presence (or absence) of a large opposition party capable of taking over the government.

Yet the power of diplomats to influence the government's decision regarding how to respond to a possible US attack on Iraq was quite limited. They could advise the top political leaders; however, whether or not that advice would be heeded depended on the leaders' willingness to listen. In Japan's case, Prime Minister Koizumi listened to the advice coming from MOFA either because he found MOFA advice on this particular matter worth seeking or because MOFA's advice already coincided with his own opinion. If MOFA officials' advice had run counter to his own notions, Koizumi was free to ignore it. Similarly, Chancellor Schröder virtually excluded his foreign-policy advisors from the decision-making process concerning Iraq in summer 2002. Although most Foreign Office officials seemed to agree with the general decision made by the chancellor, they wanted Schröder to be careful about his wording during the election campaign, because his critical statements against the Bush administration were creating an atmosphere that allowed other SPD Bundestag members to publicly criticize the United States, further escalating the tension between the two countries.[60] Nevertheless, Schröder ignored their advice. As we see then, neither MOFA nor the Foreign Office had much influence on their respective governments' decision-making processes concerning the proposed US attack on Iraq.

(iii) Partisan Differences (Progressive versus Conservative)
The parties controlling the German government during the Iraq crisis were the progressive SPD and the Greens; whereas those controlling

the Japanese government were the conservative LDP and its small coalition partner, the Kōmeito.

Although some scholars have argued that the type of parties controlling the government—parties of the left or the right—is the most important explanatory variable for foreign-policy outcomes, it is not clear that the type of parties in office can sufficiently explain Japan and Germany's different responses to the US attack on Iraq. Brian C. Rathbun claims that, contrary to constructivist arguments, foreign-policy preferences of one country are not consistent over time. Instead, they vary according to what kind of party is controlling the government, because leftist and rightist parties make policies based on fundamentally different values. According to Rathbun, leftist parties' concept of national interests is inclusive, whereas rightist parties' concept is exclusive. Leftist parties pursue foreign policies that promote the welfare of other countries (such as economic development and the extension of basic human rights) as a part of their national interests, even though these policies would have few tangible consequences for their own countries. On the other hand, rightist parties narrowly define national interests and are concerned only about issues directly related to the well-being of their own countries. Thus, while leftist parties support humanitarian intervention, rightist parties oppose such interventions, particularly peace enforcement. In the 1990s, for example, while the German conservative CDU and CSU justified their policy to increase the Bundeswehr's involvement in overseas PKOs on humanitarian grounds, their real intention was to make Germany a "normal nation." And they supported involvement in the civil war in former Yugoslavia out of concern over the prospect of refugee flows into Germany, not the well-being of the people in the conflict area. Rathbun, therefore, concludes that the outcomes of German foreign policy depend on which parties—conservative CDU/CSU or leftist SPD-Greens—control the government.[61]

There are three reasons to doubt the explanatory power of the left-right party divide in the case of Japan and Germany's decisions regarding the Iraq War. First, it is questionable whether, as Rathbun claims, the CDU would have supported the United States and might even have participated in the Iraq War, had it won the September 2002 Bundestag elections. Rathbun writes:

> If the 2002 election had resulted in the predicted CDU victory, today's transatlantic crisis might largely have been avoided. If they had been elected, the Christian Democrats would certainly not have formed an axis of opposition with France and Russia, and would have thereby

deprived this coalition of resistance to US policy of its only genuinely principled and moralistic member. A CDU government might have even participated in the war effort, exposing the myth of "Kagan hypothesis" as well.[62]

To be sure, Angela Merkel, head of the CDU, stated that she would support a US-led military intervention if peaceful attempts to disarm Iraq failed. She even stated that if her party had controlled the government, Germany would have joined the eight European countries that declared their support for the United States in February 2003.[63] Still, no one can say for certain how the CDU would have reacted had it actually come to power at the time. Merkel expressed her strong support for the United States during the Iraq crisis when her party was in the opposition. Once she became chancellor in 2005, however, Merkel firmly resisted the US demand that Germany send its troops to southern Afghanistan, where intense battles between NATO forces and the Taliban were taking place.[64]

What is more, the answers I received from my German interview respondents to two counterfactual questions suggest that a CDU-controlled government would likely have made the same choices as did the SPD. I asked each respondent the following:

Suppose the CDU/CSU had won the September 2002 Bundestag election and controlled the government. Do you think that (1) the CDU/CSU government would have supported the Iraq War; and (2) the CDU/CSU government would have sent ground troops to Iraq?

Most replied that my questions were speculative and difficult to answer. However, they answered that even if a CDU-led coalition government had given verbal support for the US action, it still would have been very difficult to send ground troops to Iraq. If the CDU had controlled the government, the relationship between Germany and the United States would not have been as strained as it was under the SPD-Greens government. However, in the end, the CDU probably would have acted as did the SPD. Although the SPD opposed the US attack, it actually did everything it could do to help US forces fight against Iraq—such as protecting US bases in Germany and allowing US forces to use German air space—without actually sending the Bundeswehr to Iraq.

Moreover, my respondents suggested that it might even have been difficult for a CDU government to express verbal support for the US attack on Iraq, because it would have known that eventually the US would expect such support to go beyond mere lip service. Had the CDU government made an official statement supporting the US attack on Iraq, it would have become increasingly difficult for the CDU to resist US demands for German troops in Iraq. If a CDU government refused to send ground troops to Iraq after making a statement supporting the US action, Germany would lose credibility.[65]

Whichever party—whether the CDU or the SPD—controlled the government at the time would have faced the same difficult choice between (1) expressing verbal support for the United States and sending ground troops to Iraq later, or (2) opposing the US action and send no troops to Iraq. As I discuss in detail in the previous chapters, the possibility of Germany's entrapment into a US-led overseas war was much higher than that of Japan. The Japanese government could express its support for the US attack on Iraq because of the low risk of overseas entrapment. German political leaders, on the other hand, had to seriously consider the potentially serious consequences of providing even verbal support for the US action against Iraq.

Another reason to doubt the explanatory power of political parties in this case: the foreign-policy preferences of the CDU/CSU and the SPD are not as distinct as Rathbun suggests. Although Rathbun categorized the SPD as a leftist party, there are significant differences between the left wing and the right wing *within* the SPD over foreign-policy preferences. The right wing of SPD members generally shares foreign-policy preferences with the CDU/CSU. A member of the SPD right wing Seeheimer Circle insisted rather emphatically in my interview that the SPD was not a pacifist party. The SPD prefers diplomatic solutions to achieve peace, he argued. However, when diplomacy does not work, the SPD is willing to use force. When I raised the question of casualties among Bundeswehr soldiers in its operation in Afghanistan, he replied that 26 casualties were much less than he expected.[66] Soldiers from other countries such as the United States and Canada have died in much greater numbers than have German soldiers.[67] Right-wing SPD members thus do not hesitate to send troops abroad or to use force if it is necessary, and some might be even more aggressive than some CDU/CSU members. In fact, Chancellor Gerhard Schröder belonged to the right-wing SPD. He was a pragmatist, not an ideologically oriented politician, and he wielded primary power over foreign policymaking when he was in office.

The third reason why Rathbun's partisan argument cannot explain the difference between Germany's and Japan's responses to the US attack on Iraq is that there has been no credible leftist party to challenge the conservative LDP in Japan since 1955. The Japan Socialist

Party (JSP) was the largest opposition party until 1993. Yet it had never become large enough to take over the government and was considered a "permanent opposition party" (*mannen yatō*). During the Iraq crisis of 2002–2003, there were two leftist parties—the Social Democratic Party (SDP) (former JSP) and the Japan Communist Party (JCP)—but they had very few seats in the lower house (19 for the SDP and 20 for the JCP in 2002). The largest opposition party at that time was the Democratic Party of Japan (DPJ), and it held only 127 seats in the Diet. Therefore, no opposition parties—even if they all combined to form a coalition—were able to replace the LDP in 2002 (see tables 6.1 and 6.2).

More importantly, the DPJ is not a leftist party, though it contains some members who defected from the former Socialist Party (such as Yokomichi Takahiro). The leading DPJ leaders (such as Hatoyama Yukio and Ozawa Ichiro) were former LDP members, and DPJ policy preferences are quite similar to those of the LDP. As with the LDP, the DPJ has pursued a neoliberal policy agenda that stresses the independence and responsibility of the individual, as well as the nation. To solve the long-term economic recession, both parties asserted that Japan should restructure its economy by adopting neoliberal policies similar to those of Ronald Reagan and Margaret Thatcher during

Table 6.1 The Results of June 2000 and November 2003 Lower House Elections in Japan

Parties	Number of Seats		% of Seats	
	June 2000	Nov 2003	June 2000	Nov 2003
Liberal Democratic Party (LDP)	233	237	49	49
Kōmeito	31	34	6	7
Democratic Party of Japan (DPJ)	127	177	26	37
Japan Communist Party (JCP)	20	9	4	2
Social Democratic Party (SDP)	19	6	4	1
Liberal Party (Jiyūto)	22	n/a*	5	n/a
Others	28	17	6	4
Total	480	480	100	100

Note: * The Liberal Party was merged with the Democratic Party of Japan in 2003.
Source: The Ministry of Internal Affairs and Communication, http://www.soumu.go.jp/senkyo/senkyo_s/data/index.html#chapter2, accessed December 27, 2009; *Asahi Shinbun*, November 10, 2003.

Table 6.2 The Results of September 1998 and September 2002 Bundestag Elections in the FRG

Parties	Number of Seats		% of Seats	
	Sep 1998	Sep 2002	June 2000	Nov 2003
Social Democratic Party (SPD)	298	251	45	41.6
Alliance 90/The Greens	47	55	7	9.1
Christian Democratic Union (CDU)	198	190	30	31.5
Christian Social Union (CSU)	47	58	7	9.6
Free Democratic Party (FDP)	43	47	6	7.8
Party of Democratic Socialism (PDS)	36	2	5	0.3
Others	0	0	0	0
Total	669	603	100	99.9

Source: http://www.electionresources.org/de/, accessed January 6, 2010.

the 1980s. They advocated reducing government intervention in the economy, cutting public spending and taxes, and opening the domestic market to foreign competition.[68] In the realm of security policy, the leading members of the DPJ emphasized that Japan should shoulder greater responsibility for defending itself instead of free riding on the United States. For Japan to become a "normal country," they supported constitutional revision to legalize the SDF and enable it to engage in certain forms of military action abroad.[69] Given the lack of a leftist party capable of replacing the LDP, therefore, it is difficult to set up a counterfactual hypothesis to test Rathbun's thesis in case of Japan. If Rathbun's partisan thesis is applied to Japan's case, Japan supported the US action simply because the LDP was in office—period. However, we can learn little from such explanation. Rathbun's partisan argument is thus not very helpful in seeking to understand why Japan supported the US attack on Iraq.

In sum, the difference in the type of parties controlling the government is inadequate for explaining the two countries' divergent responses to the US attack on Iraq. It is difficult to predict exactly how the CDU/CSU would have acted if they won the 2002 Bundestag election since we cannot rerun the history. However, judging from both the data collected during my interviews with German politicians and Angela Merkel's policy choices since becoming chancellor in fall 2005, it seems unlikely that a CDU/CSU government would have sent ground troops to Iraq or even expressed verbal support for the US war against Iraq. In the end, the actual contents of Germany's support for the US effort to fight against Iraq would probably have been the same, regardless of whether the SPD or the CDU/CSU was in office. Additionally, the distinction between the CDU and the SPD in their foreign-policy preferences might not be as clear-cut as Rathbun suggests, because there are significant differences between the left wing and right wing within the SPD. The right-wing SPD members of the Bundestag have very similar foreign-policy preferences to the CDU/CSU. After all, as Franz-Josef Meiers observes, there is "a high-degree of continuity with the policies of the red-green government" even after the CDU took over the government in 2005.[70] When it was an opposition party, for example, the CDU criticized the SPD's military policy and insisted that the budget for the Bundeswehr should be increased[71]; however, German defense budget did not increase after Angela Merkel took office in 2005 (see figures 5.1 and 5.2). Finally, it is difficult to test Rathbun's partisan thesis in Japan's case due to the lack of credible leftist parties capable of replacing the conservative LDP.

3. Liberalism

(i) Timing of Election

There was a parliamentary election in the summer of 2002 in Germany, whereas there was no parliamentary election in Japan in 2002.

Although it is often said that the SPD exploited the Iraq issue in order to win the September 2002 Bundestag election, it seems that the SPD would have opposed the US attack on Iraq regardless of the timing of election. As a result of ailing economic conditions, prospects for an SPD victory were indeed gloomy. SPD members were assuming that they had already lost the election in July 2002. When SPD candidate Johannes Kahrs was giving an election speech between grapefruits and paprika at a market in Hamburg, for example, an old woman exclaimed, "Politicians are all criminals!"[72] The Iraq issue was, therefore, a gift from heaven for Chancellor Schröder and his fellow party members. The SPD's vocal opposition to a potential US attack on Iraq appealed to German voters (especially to nonpartisan voters), shifted attentions from the economy to foreign-policy issues, and eventually led to the SPD's victory over the CDU/CSU.[73]

Nevertheless, it is very likely that the SPD would have opposed the US-led war, even had there been no elections—though the tone of their opposition to the war might have been more moderate. As I just discussed in the section on partisan ideologies, the cost of entrapment into the US preventive war on Iraq was too high for either the SPD or CDU to risk, no matter what the domestic political environment. Had there been no election at the time, the SPD-Green government might have kept an uneasy silence on the Iraq issue for a while. However, they would have had to choose whether to oppose or to support the US by early 2003. And it is very likely that they would have chosen to oppose it, because, again, once they verbally supported the US, it would become increasingly difficult to avoid sending the Bundeswehr to Iraq.

In Japan's case, on the other hand, had a lower house election taken place in the summer of 2002, it seems unlikely that the Iraq issue would have become as contentious as it did in Germany. Foreign-policy issues revolving around the US-Japan Security Treaty have never become hot topics of debate during election campaigns. Even in the November 1960 lower house election, which took place only five months after the 1960 Security Treaty crisis,[74] the foreign-policy issue did not become salient in the campaign. Indeed, in the 1960 election, the LDP increased its number of seats by nine, whereas the JSP lost 21 seats.[75] In addition, some politicians told me that their voters were not interested in foreign-policy issues. Instead they were interested in economic issues such as taxes and social security. Even if politicians spend their energy and time on foreign-policy issues, they remarked, they cannot increase the number of votes. In terms of the Iraq question, these respondents suggested, if asked, Japanese voters would probably say they oppose the Iraq War. However, the Iraq War was a secondary issue for voters—one on which they did not base their votes in the November 2003 election.[76]

Of course, one of the reasons that Japanese voters were not interested in foreign-policy issues during the election campaign was that LDP politicians skillfully kept any issues that might negatively affect their campaign out of public discussion. During the November 2003 lower house election, for example, the Cabinet Secretariat refused to give a formal order to the Japan Defense Agency (JDA) to prepare for the dispatch of the SDF to Iraq, even though JDA director Ishiba Shigeru asked for one, because the Cabinet Secretariat did not want the SDF's dispatch to become a salient issue during the elections.[77]

However, issues surrounding the US-Japan Security Treaty have never become a contentious issue in past elections primarily because the majority of the Japanese public has been content with the security treaty, especially as Article 9 has worked as a safeguard against Japan's entrapment into US-led overseas war. Various polls indicate that in spite of the majority of the public's opposition to the Iraq War, it has continued to support the US-Japan Security Treaty. According to a poll taken by the Cabinet Office, throughout the years 1978–2003 more than 60 percent of respondents "agreed" or "moderately agreed" that the US-Japan Security Treaty had contributed to Japan's peace and security. Another poll taken by the Cabinet Office over the same period shows that over 60 percent of respondents preferred to continue to defend Japan with "the US-Japan security system and the SDF," while very few endorsed the views that "Japan should abolish the US-Japan Security Treaty and defend itself" or that "Japan should abolish the security treaty and reduce or abolish the SDF."[78]

A December 2003 NHK (*Hihon hōsō kyōkai*: Japan Broadcasting Corporation) opinion poll produced similar findings. Asked what Japan should do about the US-Japan alliance based on the security treaty, 49.9 percent answered that "Japan should maintain the status quo," 19.7 percent that "Japan should decrease the extent of its cooperation [with the United States]," 15.5 percent that "Japan should strengthen its alliance with the US," and only 5 percent said that "Japan should abolish the US-Japan Security Treaty." Of the respondents who answered that "Japan should maintain the status quo" or that "Japan should strengthen its alliance with the United States," 30.4 percent did so "because the United States plays an important role in maintaining peace in Asia," 30.2 percent "because if Japan failed to maintain good relations with the United States, that would affect the Japanese economy," 26.1 percent "because the US-Japan alliance contributes to Japan's security," and 21.8 percent "because it will complement Japan's defense."[79]

Japanese public support for the US-Japan Security Treaty, however, does not mean that the Japanese people are willing to participate in US-led overseas military affairs. Rather, public support depends on the condition that the Japanese government will keep the current interpretation of Article 9 and the right of collective self-defense, and that Article 9 will continue to keep Japan out of overseas entanglements. The public's strong desire to avoid war abroad is reflected in its negative attitude toward a possible revision of Article 9. Although many LDP and DPJ politicians have been advocating constitutional revision, the public is still skeptical about revising Article 9. In the December 2003 NHK opinion poll, 43.9 percent answered that "it is not necessary to revise Article 9," versus 36.5 percent who answered that revision was "necessary." Among the respondents who favored revision, 52.9 percent averred that "Article 9 should be revised in order to make the SDF constitutional, and the SDF should be used for national defense and UN peacekeeping operations." A total of 25.6 percent believed that "Article 9 should be revised in order to make the SDF constitutional, and the SDF should participate in UN-led military operations," and 16 percent thought that "Article 9 should be revised to make the SDF constitutional, and the SDF should participate in military operations to help its allies." Those who support the SDF's participation in overseas military activities are thus still a minority, even among those who prefer the revision of Article 9.[80]

The public is also skeptical about changing the current interpretation of the right of collective self-defense. The Japanese government's interpretation holds that although Japan possesses the right of collective self-defense, Article 9 does not allow it to exercise this right. In other words, Article 9 does not allow Japan to attack a third country in defense of a Japanese ally. Although many LDP and DPJ politicians have asserted that Japan should have the ability to exercise the right of collective self-defense, a substantial segment of the public still does not support such changes in the current interpretation. The same December 2003 NHK opinion poll found that 35.4 percent wanted the government to maintain the current interpretation of the right of collective self-defense; 21.1 percent preferred that the government not recognize this right at all, while 29.9 percent wanted the government to revise Article 9 or to change its interpretation so that Japan could exercise the right of collective self-defense. Therefore, as long as the government does not attempt to revise Article 9 or change the current interpretation of the right of collective self-defense, it is unlikely that the issues surrounding the US-Japan Security Treaty and specific US foreign policies will become contentious during an election campaign in Japan.

4. Constructivism

(i) Differences between the Two Countries' Antimilitarist Cultures

There might have been differences between the two countries in terms of the ideas and principles of their political-military cultures.

There are some questions regarding how to determine the way in which the cultures of antimilitarism influenced the two countries' divergent policies toward the US war against Iraq. First of all, do "cultures of antimilitarism" really exist in Japan and Germany? If so, are the ideas, beliefs, and values of antimilitarism in Japan the same as those in Germany? If they are different, how did the difference between the two countries' cultures of antimilitarism affect their policies toward the Iraq War?

Judging from public opinion polls in Japan and Germany, it seems that there is deep skepticism on the efficacy of use of force to solve international problems among the public in the two countries. Not only did the majority of the public in both Japan and Germany oppose the US war in Iraq in spring 2003, but they also opposed their countries' possible involvement in the US military action in Afghanistan in fall 2001 (see chapter 2). However, similar to Jennifer Lind, who observed the stark difference between German and Japanese conservatives in terms of their response to their government's contrition over the past atrocities against neighboring countries,[81] I recognized that there were differences between the two countries in terms of how elites perceived and interpreted their countries' past—the devastating experience of World War II—from a number of interviews that I conducted with key political actors in the two countries. In order to overcome the past, German elites try to make a clear distinction between the present and the past—present democratic Germany is different from Nazi Germany. They try to sever themselves from the past by being conscious of the past. On the other hand, Japanese elites try to overcome their country's past by recreating positive stories about prewar Japan. Unlike their German counterparts, Japanese elites do not distinguish the present from the past because they do not see prewar Japan as something negative. Instead of severing themselves from the past, Japanese elites yearn for prewar Japan and do not hesitate to bring its elements into present Japan.

When I conducted interviews in Germany, some of my German respondents told me about their family members' experiences of World War II (and World War I) and stated: "We know what war is." Even a young SPD Bundestag member in his late thirties made the same remarks.[82] Additionally, most of my German respondents (politicians and diplomats) who were around 60 years old had experienced the mandatory 18-month military service when they were young. Even after World War II ended, the war did not really end for the Germans—until the Berlin Wall finally came down in late 1989. On the other hand, none of my Japanese respondents talked about their family members' experiences of war or expressed antiwar sentiment. Moreover, there was no mandatory conscription in Japan during the Cold War since a Soviet invasion was unlikely. In fact, the Japanese might have enjoyed peace and security more than any other nation under US protection during the Cold War. For this reason, a notion of war seems somewhat distant for the Japanese elites, compared to their German counterparts. Although Japanese conservative elites have argued that the principles of pacifism based on Article 9 of the constitution is unrealistic, their nostalgic idea to transform present Japan into prewar Japan based on the concept of prewar *kokutai* (a nation state as a family with an emperor at the top) seems also fairly philosophical because they have never experienced a real threat of war since 1945.[83]

When I conducted an interview with a vice admiral in the MSDF Fleet Headquarters in Yokosuka, he stressed how great admirals of the prewar Japanese Imperial Navy (such as Yamamoto Isoroku, commander-in-chief during the World War II) were.[84] So a few months later, when I had a chance to visit his German counterpart in the German Navy Fleet Headquarters in Flensburg, I asked him whom he respected the most. The German vice admiral did not mention any name of admirals of the prewar *Kriegsmarine*. Instead, he gave me some names of the people he actually worked with in Germany and Norfolk, Virginia, in the United States.[85] In addition, when I met a German vice admiral who recently retired, I asked him the same question. Again, he did not give me any name of prewar *Kriegsmarine* admirals. Instead, he told me that Karl Dönitz (commander-in-chief of the *Kriegsmarine* during World War II) was a part of the history of German Navy. But he was not part of a tradition of the present German Navy (*Bundesmarine/Deutsche Marine*). The tradition of the present German Navy started in 1956. The prewar *Kriegsmarine* does not fit into the present democratic system. He also added that he was proud of his father (a U-boat officer) who died in the North Atlantic in 1944. He died for the duty as a navy officer. However, the retired vice admiral said that he could not be proud of the cause for which his father fought and died.[86]

I also learned how German elites perceived the past differently from their Japanese counterparts when I visited the Federal Ministry of Defense (MOD) in Berlin. There was a large carpet showing the air map of Berlin in 1944—a city totally destroyed by the allied air raids—in the center of the MOD's building. It was surprising that not only did German political elites put such a carpet in the center of the building to remember the devastating history of their country, but they also try to embrace the lessons of history. It is unimaginable that the Japanese Ministry of Defense would put a carpet (or whatever art objects) showing, for example, the ground zero of Hiroshima or Nagasaki in the center of its building. Both Hiroshima and Nagasaki are the symbol of Japanese pacifism as well as of Japan's total defeat and surrender to the United States, which contradicts the positive images of prewar Japan that Japanese elites have believed. Such an art object will surely raise an embarrassing question to the Japanese conservatives: How can Japanese people respect prewar Japanese leaders (like Commander-in-Chief Admiral Yamamoto Isoroku) who led Japan to such a destructing defeat? The carpet in the German MOD indicates that the gap between the Left and the Right in their interpretation of the past is much wider in Japan than in Germany. In Germany, the antimilitarist cultures are mostly shared by both the conservatives and progressives; whereas, in Japan, they are not shared by Japanese conservative elites, namely LDP politicians and SDF officers.

As we can see then, while the public opinion in both Japan and Germany were against the war on terrorism in Afghanistan and the Iraq War, there are substantial differences between the German and Japanese elites in terms of how they have interpreted the history of World War II, as well as of how they have understood the relations between the past and the present. Nevertheless, it is uncertain how this difference in the nature of political-military cultures between the two countries influenced their different policy toward the Iraq War. It is true that most Japanese elites do not share the principles of pacifism based on Article 9. However, as long as they have to go through elections every four years to become a Diet member, their behavior cannot totally deviate from the public preference. As I discussed in the previous section about the timing of election, the issues revolving around the US-Japan Security Treaty have never become salient in the past elections because the Japanese voters tacitly understood that as long as Article 9 was kept intact, the likelihood of Japan's entrapment into US-led overseas military affairs was low. No matter how conservative LDP politicians have yearned for prewar Japan and claimed that Japan should revise the present constitution, they cannot go against the public preference due to potential electoral punishment. That was the very reason why the Cabinet Secretariat tried to keep the issue of the SDF dispatch to Iraq out of public discussion during the fall 2003 lower house election.

Therefore, Japan supported the Iraq War, whereas Germany opposed it, not so much because the natures of their antimilitarist cultures were different. Instead, the Japanese public—that embraced the culture of antimilitarism much like its German counterpart—understood that the likelihood of Japan's entrapment into the Iraq War was low, and thereby being tolerant of their government's token support for the war in order to maintain the overall US-Japan alliance system. Not only had the Japanese never experienced negative effects of US unilateralism (due to the relatively stable regional environment in East Asia in the 1990s), but Japan's participation in any US-led war would also be fairly limited due to the restriction in place under Article 9. Indeed, the legal grounds on which the SDF-Iraq Bill of July 2003 (which enabled Japan to dispatch the SDF to Iraq) was passed did not stem from its obligation under the security treaty. Rather, it was a special law made effective for a very limited time, and the purpose of the SDF dispatch was to help postwar reconstruction efforts in Iraq, not to help US counter-insurgency combat operations. For this reason, the Japanese public was relatively silent concerning the Iraq War compared to the Germans because the likelihood of Japan's entrapment into the Iraq War was much lower than was Germany's—not because they were any less "antimilitarist" than the Germans. If the Japanese had had a negative experience with US unilateralism, and if Japan had had the same kind of alliance obligation with the United States as did Germany, the Japanese surely would have been spoken out more vocally against the Iraq War.

7

Conclusion

US unilateralism emerged after the collapse of Soviet Union in 1990 was not as problematic to Japan as to Germany because the likelihood of Japan's entrapment into US-led overseas war was lower than that of Germany for three reasons. First, although regional tensions existed in East Asia in the 1990s, none of them developed into an actual military conflict. East Asia was in fact more stable than Europe where EU countries had to call in an aid of the US forces to stop civil wars in former Yugoslavia. While Germany had a negative experience of emerging US unilateralism in the military operation against Serbia in 1999, Japan did not have such an experience since there was no military conflict in East Asia. Additionally, while its interest in European affairs declined, the United States continued to show its strong interest in the Asia Pacific as well as its security commitment to Japan even after the end of the Cold War, thereby keeping Japan's fear of abandonment by the United States relatively low in spite of the presence of regional tensions. In contrast, Germany was not completely free from the fear of abandonment by the United States despite the disappearance of the Soviet threat.

Second, Germany's alliance obligation under NATO was much higher than that of Japan under the US-Japan Security Treaty. Although the collective security guarantee of NATO's Article 5 is not automatic, the member states cannot help but exercise the right of collective self-defense in order to maintain the credibility of NATO should one of their member states be attacked by a third country or party. Moreover, the purpose of NATO was expanded from the territorial defense of member states to out-of-area peacekeeping operations (PKOs), while that of the US-Japan Security Treaty has remained primarily defense of Japan (at least from Japan's point of view). German political leaders and officials were so anxious to be consulted by Americans about their plans and activities in overseas military operations because US behavior would bring about significant consequence to German politics. On the other hand, wherever the US forces go or whatever they do in the world, that was not basically Japan's business because Japan is not obliged to exercise the right of collective self-defense or to contribute its forces to US-led overseas operations under the US-Japan Security Treaty. The attitudes of the two countries' political actors toward 9/11 and the Iraq War in my interviews discussed in Chapter 3 are endorsing this difference. Japanese interviewees were indifferent to 9/11 and apathetic about the Iraq War, whereas German interviewees were very emotional and responsive to questions regarding these subjects.

Third, all the three forces of the Bundeswehr have been under NATO command since it was established in 1955. Not only are they capable of fighting combat operations alongside of other NATO forces, but they have also developed a strong sense of camaraderie toward the allied forces (including the US forces) through working together under NATO for many decades. On the other hand, while the Maritime Self-Defense Force (MSDF) has been integrated into the US Seventh Fleet, thereby having developed a sense of camaraderie toward the US Navy, the Ground Self-Defense Force (GSDF) has been an isolated military entity without significant foreign contacts since the Cold War period, thereby having little sense of camaraderie toward foreign forces. (The Air Self-Defense Force [ASDF] is somewhat between the MSDF and the GSDF, although it closes to the GSDF.) Moreover, because the ground troops are more likely to have a risk of casualties than the navy and the air force, the constitutional restrictions on use of force and absence of a court-martial in Japan have further discouraged the GSDF to send its servicemen to overseas PKOs that are likely to endanger their lives. The GSDF's conservatism on overseas dispatch is strikingly different from the German Army, which is willing to participate in overseas PKOs despite of the risk of casualties. The characteristics of the GSDF, therefore, have contributed to the low likelihood of Japan's entrapment into US-led overseas war.

These variables explaining the difference in the two countries' alliance security dilemma with the United States can also explain the difference in their normalization process since the early 1990s. Germany is much more advanced than Japan in the process of normalization. Germany has sent thousands of ground troops not only to former Yugoslavia but also to Afghanistan, whereas Japan has never deployed such a large number of ground troops overseas. Unlike Germany where serious discussion took place on whether or not it should take part in NATO's air campaign against Serbia in order to stop ethnic cleansing in Kosovo in 1999, Japan did not have to consider whether to participate in a US-led regional military operation for the absence of military conflict in the region. The regional environment in East Asia seems to further slow the process of Japan's normalization in the future. While the rise of China and its future uncertainty have been serious concerns for Japan, the strategic importance of Japan for the United States—especially of its military bases in Japan—has also increased as the power of China rises because the United States does not want to lose its dominant maritime position in the Asia Pacific. For this reason, Japan does not have to be seriously concerned about abandonment by the United States; as a consequence, its slow normalization process seems to continue in the future.

Japan's exclusive focus on its territorial defense under the US-Japan Security Treaty has also contributed to its slow process of normalization. While the scope of the US-Japan alliance seems to be expanded to entire Asia-Pacific region as a result of the 1996 US-Japan Revised Defense Guidelines followed by Japan's 1999 Defense Guidelines bill (*shūhen jitaihō*) and the revisions to the SDF Law, Japan's alliance obligation is still limited.[1] On principle, for Japan, the purpose of the US-Japan Security Treaty is to defend its national territory. Japan has never shared the US global security agenda, and has had little intention to transform the US-Japan Security Treaty accordingly. As Christopher Hughes suggests, Japan is by no means the "Great Britain of the Far East." Japan did not share the US antiterrorism agenda following 9/11. Consequently, it did not show the same degree of commitment in the war on terror in Afghanistan or in the fight against weapons of mass destruction (WMD) in Iraq as did the UK. Japan rather used the war on terror to justify its long-planned military security policy to cope with the traditional security challenges in the region, namely North Korea and China.[2] Japan's primary concern has remained its national territorial defense, and this has been reflected in Oros's concept of "security identity" and Midford's "attitudinal defensive realism" among the Japanese public. There is a widespread political-strategic norm in Japan that a military is necessary only for the sake of territorial defense. The public is skeptical about efficacy of offensive use of force, and oppose the SDF's participation in overseas war.[3]

The low likelihood of the constitutional revision and establishment of a court-martial have also worked (and will work) as a significant obstacle for the process of Japan's normalization. Although many Japan specialists expected the constitutional revision would be likely when Abe Shinzo became a prime minister in 2006, such an expectation turned out to be premature for the lack of public support.[4] As long as Article 9 is kept intact, not only can Japan not exercise the right of collective self-defense, but the SDF will remain as *defensive* forces. The SDF cannot become regular armed forces since there is no court-martial in Japan. In addition, the absence of a court-martial has discouraged the SDF to participate in overseas operations since SDF servicemen are afraid of the consequence of their use of force. Without legal protection on their use of force, it is difficult for the SDF to send its servicemen to overseas operations. Yet, the prospect of establishing a court-martial in Japan seems to be very dim.

Along with the legal restrictions, the GSDF's lack of camaraderie toward foreign forces has further slowed (will slow) Japan's normalization process. Although the United States has demanded Japan make "human contributions" to overseas PKOs since the 1990–1991 Persian Gulf War, the US Army has never tried to integrate the GSDF into its strategic structure or created some kind of institutional structure that would foster camaraderie between the US Army and the GSDF, as the US Navy did to the MSDF. As I explained in chapter 5, not only is the size of the US Army Japan (USARJ) in the Camp Zama small, but those in the USARJ are not combat troops but administrative staffs. The US Army I Corps in Fort Lewis, Washington, was supposed to move to the Camp Zama according to the 2006 Defense Policy Review Initiative (DPRI), which was designed to upgrade the functions and interoperability of the US-Japan alliance; however, that plan was cancelled later.[5] Therefore, the GSDF will continue to be an isolated military institution with few contacts with foreign troops. In addition, considering that it requires a substantial period of time to foster camaraderie between military institutions, it is hard to expect that the GSDF will develop a strong sense of camaraderie for foreign troops in the near future.

Finally, the relative decline of US credibility as a result of the Iraq War will also slow Japan's normalization. Although the US-Japan Security Treaty has been (and will continue to be) a pillar of Japan's security policy, Japan is likely to become more cautious about its support for US-led overseas wars than before as a result of its experience of the Iraq War. As I explained in Chapter 3, although the Japanese government officially expressed its support for the US invasion of Iraq in March 2003, the support of Liberal Democratic Party (LDP) politicians and government officials for the war was not necessarily sincere. Most of them thought that even if they suggested Americans not to go to war against Iraq, Americans would not listen to them. In addition, when I conducted interviews with some LDP politicians, they attributed Japan's support for the Iraq War to an individual decision made by Prime Minister Koizumi (*koizumi-san ga kimeta koto*), implying that they were not responsible for that decision.[6] After all, Japanese politicians and officials were able to be irresponsible for Japan's support for the war because the likelihood of Japan's entrapment in the war was low. Later, however, they were embarrassed by the statements by US presidents George W. Bush and Barack Obama that the Iraq War was a mistake. When I asked a former SDF chief of staff, "Why do you think the Iraq War turned out to be a failure?", he strongly denied the word I used: "a failure [*shippai*]." He insisted that the Iraq War was not a "failure."[7] The Japanese government officially does not regard the Iraq War as a "failure" or a "mistake [*machigai*]." If the government admitted that the Iraq War was a failure or a mistake, then it has to be responsible not only for its support for the war, but also for its dispatch of the SDF to Iraq. However, it is so awkward for the Japanese government to keep saying that the Iraq War was not a failure, while the two US presidents admitted that the war was a mistake. It was fortunate that no SDF servicemen died in Iraq, and all of them returned to Japan safely. If the SDF had suffered casualties in Iraq, Japanese politicians and officials could not have remained as irresponsible as they were. After having the embarrassing experience over the Iraq War, therefore, Japanese politicians and officials are likely to become more cautious about making their decision to support for US-led war abroad in the future.

NOTES

1 INTRODUCTION

1. Hans W. Maull, "Germany and Japan: The New Civilian Power," *Foreign Affairs* 61, no. 1 (Winter 1990/91): 91–106; Thomas U. Berger, *Culture of Antimilitarism: National Security in Germany and Japan* (Baltimore, MD: John Hopkins University Press, 1998).
2. Glenn H. Snyder, "Alliance Theory: A Neorealist First Cut," *Journal of International Affairs* 44, no. 1 (Spring/Summer 1990): 103–123.
3. Peter J. Katzenstein, *A World of Regions: Asia and Europe in the American Imperium* (Ithaca, NY: Cornell University Press, 2005).
4. World Bank, Gross Domestic Product (Current US$, 2010), http://data.worldbank.org, accessed December 7, 2011.
5. Stockholm International Peace Research Institute, Military expenditure, Constant (2009) US$, http//www.sipri.org, accessed September 15, 2011.
6. Berger, *Culture of Antimilitarism*. Peter J. Katzenstein, ed., *The Culture of National Security: Norms and Identity in World Politics* (New York: Columbia University Press, 1996); Peter J. Katzenstein, *Cultural Norms and National Security: Police and Military in Postwar Japan* (Ithaca, NY: Cornell University Press, 1996); Maull, "Germany and Japan."
7. Paul Midford, *Rethinking Japanese Public Opinion and Security: From Pacifism to Realism?* (Stanford, CA: Stanford University Press 2011), 2.
8. Hanns W. Maull, "German Foreign Policy, Post-Kosovo: Still a 'Civilian Power?'" *German Politics* 9, no. 2 (August 2000): 1–24; Adrian Hyde-Price, *Germany and European Order: Enlarging NATO and the EU* (Manchester, UK: Manchester University Press, 2000), 148, 166–168; Peter Rudolf, "Germany and the Kosovo Conflict," in Pierre Martin and Mark R. Brawley, eds., *Alliance Politics, Kosovo, and NATO's War: Allied Force or Forced Allies?* (New York: Palgrave, 2000), 131–143; Sebastian Harnisch and Kerry Longhurst, "Understanding Germany: The Limits of 'Normalization' and the Prevalence of Strategic Culture," in Stuart Taberner and Paul Cooke, eds., *German Culture, Politics, and Literature into the Twenty-First Century Beyond Normalization* (Rochester, NY: Camden House, 2006), 49–60; Franz-Josef Meiers, "The German

Predicament: The Red Lines of the Security and Defence Policy of the Berlin Republic," *International Politics* 44 (2007): 623–644; Allister Miskimmon, "Falling into Line? Kosovo and the Course of German Foreign Policy," *International Affairs* 85, no. 3 (2009): 561–573.
9. Harnisch and Longhurst, "Understanding Germany," 54.
10. Rainer Baumann and Gunther Hellmann, "Germany and the Use of Military Force: 'Total War,' the 'Culture of Restraint' and the Quest for Normality," *German Politics* 10, no.1 (2001): 64.
11. Ibid., 62.
12. Ibid., 71.
13. Richard Samuels, *Securing Japan: Tokyo's Grand Strategy and the Future of East Asia* (Ithaca, NY: Cornell University Press, 2007), 86.
14. Michael J. Green, *Japan's Reluctant Realism: Foreign Policy Challenges in an Era of Uncertain Power* (New York: Palgrave, 2003); Christopher W. Hughes, "Japanese Military Modernization: In Search of a 'Normal' Security Role," in Ashley J. Tellis and Michael Wills, eds., *Strategic Asia 2005–06: Military Modernization in an Era of Uncertainty* (Seattle, WA: National Bureau of Asian Research, 2005), 105–134; Christopher W. Hughes, *Japan's Re-emergence as a 'Normal' Military Power* (New York: Routledge, 2005); Christopher W. Hughes, "Japan's Military Modernisation: A Quiet Japan-China Arms Race and Global Power Projection," *Asia-Pacific Review* 16, no. 1 (2009): 84–99; Christopher W. Hughes, *Japan's Remilitarisation* (London: Routledge, 2009); Christopher W. Hughes and Ellis S. Krauss, "Japan's New Security Agenda," *Survival* 49, no. 2 (Summer 2007): 157–176; Kenneth B. Pyle, "Abe Sinzo and Japan's Change of Course," *NBR Analysis* 17, no. 4 (October 2006); Richard Samuels, *Securing Japan: Tokyo's Grand Strategy and the Future of East Asia* (Ithaca, NY: Cornell University Press, 2007).
15. Hughes and Krauss, "Japan's New Security Agenda," 157.
16. Ibid., 158.
17. Hughes, "Japanese Military Modernisation," 120–121.
18. Ibid., 117–118, 131; A similar argument was also made by Handa Shigeru. See "Jieitai ga kaiken naku gunntai o ishiki suru hi [The day when the SDF will become military forces without constitutional revision]," *Gendai* (October 2004), 130–138.
19. Hughes, "Japan's Military Modernisation," 85.
20. Pyle, "Abe Sinzo," 9.
21. Andrew L. Oros, *Normalizing Japan: Politics, Identity and the Evolution of Security Practices* (Stanford, CA: Stanford University Press 2008); Midford, *Rethinking Japanese Public Opinion*.
22. Oros, *Normalizing Japan*, 5–6.
23. Ibid., 171.
24. Ibid., 180.
25. A formal translation of the law is: Act on Special Measures concerning Humanitarian Relief and Reconstruction Work and Security Assistance in Iraq.

26. Oros, *Normalizing Japan*, 182.
27. Ibid., 183.
28. Midford, *Rethinking Japanese Public Opinion*, 16.
29. Ibid., 172–173.
30. Ibid., 14.
31. Ibid., 146–170.
32. http://icasualties.org/OEF/index.aspx, accessed December 12, 2011.
33. Miskimmon, "Falling into Line," 565.
34. http://icasualties.org/OEF/index.aspx, accessed December 12, 2011.
35. Snyder, "Alliance Theory," 104.
36. Ibid., 110.
37. Ibid., 113.
38. Yasuhiro Izumikawa, "Explaining Japanese Antimilitarism: Normative and Realist Constraints on Japan's Security Policy," *International Security* 35, no. 2 (Fall 2010): 123–160.
39. According to Izumikawa, the domestic political norm of "antitraditionalism" reflects the Japanese public's strong desire to protect and promote democracy and to resist the traditionalist's attempt to bring Japan back to the prewar era. For Japanese people, the question of security policy is also a question of democracy at home because people who pursue active security policies (e.g., Kishi Nobusuke, Nakasone Yasuhiro, etc.) are traditionalists who try to bring Japanese society back to the prewar era. The public believes that undemocratic practices promoted by the prewar Japanese government (such as forcing citizens to be deferential to and obey authority through legal punishment and education) is the very source of the rise of Japan's prewar militarism, and therefore, the traditionalists' ambitions for active security policies should be restrained.
40. Izumikawa, "Explaining Japanese Antimilitarism," 132.
41. Ibid., 152.
42. Christopher W. Hughes, "Not Quite the 'Great Britain of the Far East': Japan's Security, the US-Japan Alliance and the 'War on Terror' in East Asia," *Cambridge Review of International Affairs* 20, no. 2 (June 2007): 336.
43. Thomas Berger, "Set for Stability? Prospects for Conflict and Cooperation in East Asia," *Review of International Studies* 26 (2000): 405–428; Muthiah Alagappa, "Introduction: Predictability and Stability Despite Challenges," in Muthiah Alagappa, ed., *Asian Security Order: Instrumental and Normative Features* (Stanford, CA: Stanford University Press, 2003), 1–30; David C. Kang, "Getting Asia Wrong: The Need for New Analytical Frameworks," *International Security* 27, no. 4 (Spring 2003): 57–85.
44. Alagappa, "Introduction," 4.
45. Berger, "Set for Stability?" 405; Alagappa, "Introduction," 21.
46. Alagappa, "Introduction," 19.
47. Victor D. Cha, "Abandonment, Entrapment, and Neoclassical Realism in Asia: The United States, Japan, and Korea," *International Studies Quarterly* 44, no. 2 (June 2000): 263.

48. Berger, "Set for Stability?" 411.
49. Alagappa, "Introduction," 22.
50. Michael Mastanduno, "Incomplete Hegemony: The United States and Security Order in Asia," in Muthiah Alagappa, ed., *Asian Security Order: Instrumental and Normative Features* (Stanford, CA: Stanford University Press, 2003), 157.
51. Berger, "Set for Stability?" 408, 416.
52. Yoichi Funabashi, *Alliance Adrift* (New York: Council on Foreign Relations Press, 1999).
53. Christopher W. Hughes, "North Korea's Nuclear Weapons: Implications for the Nuclear Ambitions of Japan, South Korea, and Taiwan," *Asia Policy* 3 (January 2007): 88–89.
54. Josef Janning and Thomas Bauer, "Into the Great Wide Open: The Transformation of the German Armed Forces After 1990," *Orbis* (Summer 2007): 531.
55. Hyde-Price, *Germany and European Order,* 143.
56. Ibid., 156, 160.
57. Rudolf, "Germany and the Kosovo Conflict," 132.
58. Maja Zehfuss, *Wounds of Memory: The Politics of War in Germany* (Cambridge, UK: Cambridge University Press, 2007), 4–13; Paul Hockenos, *Joschka Fischer and the Making of the Berlin Republic: An Alternative History of Postwar Germany* (Oxford, UK: Oxford University Press, 2008), 266–274.
59. Detlef Puhl, "Kosovo and German Public Opinion," in Wolfgang-Uwe Friedrich, ed., *The Legacy of Kosovo: German Politics and Policies in the Balkan* (Washington DC: American Institute for Contemporary German Studies, 2000), 51–55.
60. Jeffrey Lantis, "The Moral Imperative of Force: The Evolution of German Strategic Culture in Kosovo," *Comparative Strategy* 21, no. 21 (2002): 29, 33.
61. Regina Kapp, "Germany: a 'Normal' Global Actor?" *German Politics* 18, no.1 (March 2009): 25.
62. Helga Haftendorn, *Coming of Age: German Foreign Policy since 1945* (Oxford, UK: Rowman & Littlefield Publisher, 2006), 1.
63. Meiers, "German Predicament," 638; Rudolf, "Germany and the Kosovo Conflict," 133–134; Hyde-Price, *Germany and European Order*, 136, 144; Anja Dalgaard-Nielsen, "Gulf War: The German Resistance," *Survival* 45, no. 1 (Spring 2003): 102.
64. Rainer Baumann, "German Security Policy within NATO," in Volker Rittberger ed., *German Foreign Policy since Unification* (Manchester, UK: Manchester University Press, 2001), 143; Peter Rudolf, "The Myth of the 'German Way': German Foreign Policy and Transatlantic Relations," *Survival* 47, no.1 (Spring 2005): 135.
65. Paul C. Latawski and Martin A. Smith, *The Kosovo Crisis and the Evolution of Post–Cold War European Security* (Manchester, UK: Manchester University Press, 2003), 40.

66. Benjamin S. Lambeth, *NATO's Air War for Kosovo: A Strategic and Operational Assessment* (Santa Monica, CA: Rand, 2001), 205.
67. Lambeth, *NATO*, 206.
68. Ibid., 168.
69. Latawski and Smith, *Kosovo Crisis*, 47.
70. Interview with a retired, high-ranking German Federal Foreign Office official, October 4, 2011.
71. Hyde-Price, *Germany and European Order*, 160.
72. Ivo H. Daalder and Michael E. O'Hanlon, *Winning Ugly: NATO's War to Save Kosovo* (Washington DC: Brookings Institution Press, 2000), 182–226; Lambeth, *NATO*, 219–250; Jeffrey Simon and Sean Key, "Beyond European Security: Europe, the United States, and NATO," in Ronald Tiersky and Erik Jones, eds., *Europe Today: A Twenty-First Century Introduction* (Lanham, MD: Rowman & Littlefield Publishers, 2007), 415–416.
73. Ivo Daalder and James Goldgeier, "Global NATO," *Foreign Affairs* 85, no. 5 (September-October 2006):105–113; Thomas Fedyszyn, "Saving NATO: Renunciation of the Article 5 Guarantee," *Orbis* (Summer 2010): 374–386.
74. For the development of the ESDP after the Kosovo War, please see Latawski and Smith, *Kosovo Crisis*, 120–142; Marco Overhaus, "Civilian Power under Stress: Germany, NATO, and the European Security and Defense Policy," in Hanns W. Maull, ed., *Germany's Uncertain Power: Foreign Policy of the Berlin Republic* (New York: Palgrave, 2006), 66–78.
75. "German Troops to Join Terror War," *CNN*, November 6, 2001, http://articles.cnn.com/2001-11-06/world/ret.germany.troops_1_terror-war-german-troops-fight-against-international-terrorism?_s=PM:WORLD, accessed January 7, 2012.
76. Interview with a senior, high-ranking SPD member of the Bundestag Foreign Relations Committee, May 29, 2007; Interview with a German Air Force officer, August 22, 2008.
77. Hughes, *Japan's Re-emergence*, 98–105.
78. Kawaguchi Hajime and Otsuka Eiji, *Jieitai no Iraq hahei sashitomem soshō: hanketsubun wo yomu* [A law suit to stop the SDF dispatch to Iraq: Reading the court judgment] (Tokyo: Kadokawa shoten, 2009), 150–152.
79. Svein Vigeland Rottem, "The Ambivalent Ally: Norway in the New NATO," *Contemporary Security Policy* 28, no. 3 (December 2007): 619–637.
80. Interview with a retired, high-ranking, Bundeswehr officer, December 15, 2011.
81. Interview with a retired, high-ranking German Federal Foreign Office official, October 4, 2011.
82. For full discussion on the 1996 revised US-Japan Guidelines for Defense Cooperation, see Christopher W. Hughes, *Japan's Re-emergence*, 98–105.

83. For details about the 1991 NATO Strategic Concept, see chapter 4 of this book.
84. For a detailed account, see chapter 5 of this book.
85. Asahi Shinbun "Jieitai 50-nen" Shuzaihan, *Jieitai: Shirazareru henyo* [SDF: Unknown transformation] (Tokyo: Asahi Shinbun Sha, 2005), 38–41; Handa, *Tatakaenai guntai* [Troops that cannot fight] (Tokyo: Kodansha, 2005), 50–53.
86. Charles C. Ragin, *The Comparative Method: Moving Beyond Qualitative and Quantitative Strategies* (Berkeley, CA: University of California Press, 1987), 48.
87. Ragin, *Comparative Method*, 47.
88. Alexander L. George and Andrew Bennett, *Case Studies and Theory Development in the Social Science* (Cambridge, MA: MIT Press, 2005).
89. Kenneth N. Waltz, *Man, the State and War: A Theoretical Analysis* (New York: Columbia University Press, 1954); Kenneth N. Waltz, *Theory of International Politics* (Reading, MA: Addison-Wesley, 1979); Kenneth N. Waltz, "Structural Realism after the Cold War," *International Security* 25, no.1 (Summer 2000): 5–41.
90. Graham Allison, *Essence of Decision: Explaining the Cuban Missiles Crisis* (Boston, MA: Little, Brown, 1971); William Grimes, "Institutionalized Inertia: Japanese Foreign Policy in the Post–Cold War World" in G. John Ienberry and Michael Mastanduno, eds., *International Relations Theory and the Asia-Pacific* (New York: Columbia University Press, 2003).
91. Yakushiji Katsuyuki, *Gaimu sho: gaiko kyouka e no michi* [Ministry of Foreign Affairs: the means for strengthening foreign relations] (Tokyo: Iwanami shoten, 2003).
92. Brian C. Rathbun, "The Myth of German Pacifism," *German Politics and Society* 79, no. 24 (Summer 2006): 69.
93. John R. Oneal and Bruce M. Russett, *Triangulating Peace: Democracy, Interdependence, and International Organizations* (New York: Norton, 2001).
94. Immanuel Kant, *Perpetual Peace: A Philosophical Sketch* [1795]. Reprinted in Kant's *Political Writings*, edited by Hans Reiss (Cambridge, UK: Cambridge University Press, 1970).
95. John Gerard Ruggie, "What Makes the World Hang Together? Neo-Utilitarianism and the Social Constructivist Challenge," *International Organization* 52, no. 4 (Autumn 1998): 855–885; Katzenstein, ed., *Culture of National Security*; Alexander Wendt, *Social Theory of International Politics* (Cambridge, UK: Cambridge University Press, 1999).
96. Berger, *Culture of Antimilitarism*; Katzenstein, ed., *Cultural Norms and National Security*.
97. Berger, *Cultures of Antimilitarism*, 15.
98. Ibid., 16.
99. Ibid., 26.

2 Background

1. Thomas U. Berger, *Culture of Antimilitarism: National Security in Germany and Japan* (Baltimore, MD: John Hopkins University Press, 1998), 23.
2. World Bank, Gross Domestic Product (Current US$, 2010), http://data.worldbank.org, accessed January 6, 2012.
3. Klaus Becher, "German Forces in International Military Operations," *Orbis* (Summer 2004): 397–408.
4. Tanaka Hitoshi and Tahara Soichiro, *Kokka to gaiko* [State and foreign relations] (Tokyo: Kodansha, 2005), 216–219.
5. Rainer Baumann and Gunther Hellmann, "Germany and the Use of Military Force: Total War, the Culture of Restraint and the Quest for Normalcy," in Douglas Webber, ed., *New Europe, New Germany, Old Foreign Policy?* (Portland, OR: Frank Cass, 2001), 67; Jeffrey S. Lantis, *Strategic Dilemmas and the Evolution of German Foreign Policy since Unification* (Westport, CT: Praeger 2002), 149–150.
6. Gerhard Kümmel and Nina Leonhard, "Casualties and Civil-Military Relations: The German Polity between Learning and Indifference," *Armed Forces and Society* 31, no. 4 (Summer 2005): 513–536.
7. "Schröder on Sept. 11 and Afghanistan: I Remember My Own Tears," *Spiegel Online*, October 25, 2006, http://www.spiegel.de/international/0,15818,444689,00.html, accessed January 16, 2007.
8. Yomiuri shinbun seijibu, *Gaiko o kenka ni shita otoko: Koizumi gaiko 2000 nichi no shinjitsu* [A man who turned diplomacy into quarrel: The truth of 2000 days of Koizumi's diplomacy] (Tokyo: Shinchosha, 2006), 123–125.
9. German Bundeswehr website, http://www.bundeswehr.de/portal/a/bwde/kcxml/04_Sj9SPykssy0xPLMnMz0vM0Y_QjzKLd443Dgo ESYGZASH6kTCxoJRUfV-P_NxUfW_9AP2C3IhyR0dFRQD -G0VU/delta/base64xml/L2dJQSEvUUt3QS80SVVFLzZfQ180M kQ!?yw_contentURL=%2FC1256EF4002AED30%2FW264VFT243 9INFODE%2Fcontent.jsp, accessed October 5, 2009.
10. The MSDF's fuel support was officially ended in December 2009.
11. Verlang für Demoskopie Allensbach am Bodensee, *Allensbacher Jahrbuch der Demoskopie 1998–2002* (München: K.G. Sauer, 2002), 995.
12. Ibid., 992.
13. Wilhelm Haumann and Thomas Petersen, "German Public Opinion on the Iraq Conflict: A Passing Crisis with the USA or a Lasting Departure?" *International Journal of Public Opinion Research* 16, no. 3 (2004): 319.
14. George W. Bush, "Address before a Joint Session of the Congress on the State of the Union," January 29, 2002, http://www.presidency.ucsb.edu/ws/index.php?pid=29644#, accessed October 6, 2009.
15. Phillip H. Gordon and Jeremy Shapiro, *Allies at War: America, Europe and the Crisis over Iraq* (New York: McGraw-Hill, 2004), 59–61, 83–91.

16. Accessed October 7, 2009, http://www.usembassy.it/file2002_08/alia/a2082601.htm.
17. Gordon and Shapiro, *Allies at War*, 96–103.
18. Robert Rohrschneider and Dieter Fuchs, "It Used to Be the Economy: Issues and Party Support in the 2002 Election," *German Politics and Society* 21, no.1 (Spring 2003): 76–94.
19. Gordon and Shapiro, *Allies at War*, 108–114.
20. Ibid., 152.
21. Ibid., 115–125, 146–154.
22. *Asahi Shinbun* [Asahi newspaper], December 11, 2001.
23. Ibid., December 8, 2001.
24. Ibid., March 19, 2003.
25. Yomiuri shinbun seijibu, *Gaiko*, 152–153.
26. *Asahi Shinbun*, September 27, 2002.
27. Ibid., February 12, 2003.
28. Ibid., February 14, 2003.
29. Yomiuri shinbun seijibu, *Gaiko*, 150.
30. Ibid., 150.
31. *Japan Times*, February 20, 2002.
32. Ibid., February 19, 2002.
33. *Asahi Shinbun*, March 14, 2003.
34. Ibid., October 1, 2002.
35. Ibid., September 10, 2002.
36. Ibid., August 9, 2002.
37. Ibid., February 16, 2003.
38. Ibid., March 13, 2003.
39. Ibid., March 21, 2003.
40. Ibid., March 26, 2003.
41. Ibid., April 18, 2003.
42. *Japan Times*, July 18, 2003.

3 REGIONAL SECURITY ENVIRONMENTS AND US SECURITY COMMITMENT: EAST ASIA VERSUS EUROPE

1. Thomas Berger, "Set for Stability? Prospects for Conflict and Cooperation in East Asia," *Review of International Studies* 26 (2000), 411.
2. Muthiah Alagappa, "Introduction: Predictability and Stability Despite Challenges," in Muthiah Alagappa, ed., *Asian Security Order: Instrumental and Normative Features* (Stanford, CA: Stanford University Press, 2003), 22.
3. Michael Mastanduno, "Incomplete Hegemony: The United States and Security Order in Asia," in Muthiah Alagappa, ed., *Asian Security Order: Instrumental and Normative Features* (Stanford, CA: Stanford University Press, 2003), 157.

NOTES

4. Helga Haftendorn, *Coming of Age: German Foreign Policy since 1945* (Oxford, UK: Rowman & Littlefield Publisher, 2006), 23, 66, 75.
5. Ibid., 83.
6. Wolfram F. Hanriender, *Germany, America, Europe: Forty Years of German Foreign Policy* (New Heaven, CT: Yale University Press, 1989), 64–65; Michael Mandelbaum, *The Nuclear Revolution: International Politics Before and After Hiroshima* (Cambridge, UK: Cambridge University Press, 1981), 154–155.
7. Haftendorn, *Coming of Age*, 86–89.
8. Hanriender, *Germany, America, Europe*, 72.
9. Mandelbaum, *Nuclear Revolution*, 157–158; Hanriender, *Germany, America, Europe*, 13, 71–78; Haftendorn, *Coming of Age*, 242.
10. Hanriender, *Germany, America, Europe*, 48. [Translated from Wilhelm G. Grewe, *Rückblenden, 1976–1951* (Frankfurt am Main: Propyläen, 1979), 684.]
11. Hanriender, *Germany, America, Europe*, 199.
12. Haftendorn, *Coming of Age*, 163–164.
13. Lawrence S. Kaplan, *NATO Divided, NATO United: The Evolution of an Alliance* (Westport, CT: Praeger, 2004), 81–83; Haftendorn, *Coming of Age*, 240–243.
14. Chief of Staff Bundeswehr General Klaus Naumann, "The Transformation of NATO and the Shaping of European Security," A paper presented at XII NATO Workshop on Political-Military Decision Making, Dresden, Germany 18–22 June 1995, http://www.csdr.org/95Book/95Workshop/htm, accessed July 21, 2008.
15. Peter Struck, "Defense Policy Guidelines," Federal Ministry of Defense, May 21, 2003.
16. John S. Duffield, *World Power Forsaken: Political Culture, International Relations, and German Security Policy after Unification,* (Stanford, CA: Stanford University Press, 1998), 119–124.
17. For detailed descriptions of the background of the conflicts in Yugoslavia and Germany's response to them, see Jeffrey S. Lantis, *Strategic Dilemmas and the Evolution of German Foreign Policy since Unification* (Westport, CT: Praeger 2002), 79–163.
18. Duffield, *World Power Forsaken*, 46.
19. Ibid., 243.
20. Günter Joetze, "Pan-European Stability: Still a Key Task?" in Hans W. Maull, ed., *Germany's Uncertain Power: Foreign Policy of the Berlin Republic* (New York: Palgrave, 2006), 162–163.
21. Duffield, *World Power Forsaken*, 44, 120.
22. Ibid., 122–124; Peter Rudolf, "The Transatlantic Relationship: A View from Germany," in Hanns W. Maull, ed., *Germany's Uncertain Power: Foreign Policy of the Berlin Republic* (New York: Palgrave, 2006), 140–141.
23. Lantis, *Strategic Dilemmas*, 144.

24. For detail about the Kosovo War, see http://www.pbs.org/wgbh/pages/frontline/shows/kosovo, accessed April 19, 2009; Lantis, *Strategic Dilemmas*, 143–145.
25. Adrian Hyde-Price, "German Perceptions," in Mary Buckley and Sally N. Cummings, ed., *Kosovo: Perception of War and Its Aftermath* (London, UK: Continuum, 2001), 108–109.
26. Paul Latawski and Martin A. Smith, *The Kosovo Crisis and the Evolution of Post Cold War European Security* (Manchester, UK: Manchester University Press, 2003), 143–169.
27. Peter Rudolf, "Germany and the Kosovo Conflict," in Pierre Martin and Mark R. Brawley, eds., *Alliance Politics, Kosovo, and NATO's War: Allied Force or Forced Allies?* (New York: Palgrave, 2000), 133–134.
28. Rainer Baumann and Gunther Hellmann, "Germany and the Use of Military Force: 'Total War', the 'Culture of Restraint' and the Quest for Normality," *German Politics* 10, no.1 (2001), 64; Maja Zehfuss, *Wounds of Memory: The Politics of War in Germany* (Cambridge, MA: Cambridge University Press, 2007), 4–13; Paul Hockenos, *Joschka Fischer and the Making of the Berlin Republic: An Alternative History of Postwar Germany* (Oxford, UK: Oxford University Press, 2008), 266–274.
29. Rudolf, "Germany and the Kosovo Conflict," 138.
30. "Schröder on Kosovo: The Goal was Exclusively Humanitarian," *Spiegel Online*, October 25, 2006, http://www.spiegel.de/international/0,1518,444727,00.html, accessed January 16, 2007.
31. Interview with a retired, high-ranking German Federal Foreign Office official, October 4, 2011.
32. Ibid.
33. Latawski and Smith, *Kosovo Crisis*, 40.
34. Benjamin S. Lambeth, *NATO's Air War for Kosovo: A Strategic and Operational Assessment* (Santa Monica, CA: Rand, 2001), 181, 205.
35. Ibid., 206.
36. Ibid., 168.
37. Latawski and Smith, *Kosovo Crisis*, 47.
38. Interview with a retired, high-ranking German Federal Foreign Office official, October 4, 2011.
39. Detlef Puhl, "Kosovo and German Public Opinion," in Wolfgang-Uwe Friedrich, ed., *The Legacy of Kosovo: German Politics and Policies in the Balkan* (Washington DC: American Institute for Contemporary German Studies, 2000), 51–55; Lantis, "Moral Imperative of Force," 29, 33.
40. Roger Choen, "Crisis in the Balkans: Diplomacy, Schroder's Blunt 'No' to Ground Troops in Kosovo Reflects Depth of German Sensitivities," *New York Times*, May 20, 1999.
41. Duffield, *World Power Forsaken*, 113–143.
42. Rudolf, "Germany and the Kosovo Conflict," 138–139; Joetze, "Pan-European Stability," 158–159.
43. Joetze, "Pan-European Stability," 158.

44. "Schröder on Kosovo."
45. Regarding the development of the ESDP after the Kosovo War, please see Latawski and Smith, *The Kosovo Crisis*, p. 120–142; Marco Overhaus, "Civilian Power under Stress: Germany, NATO, and the European Security and Defense Policy," in Hanns W. Maull, ed., *Germany's Uncertain Power: Foreign Policy of the Berlin Republic* (New York: Palgrave, 2006), 66–78.
46. Rudolf, "The Transatlantic Relationship," 140.
47. For example, Germany sent its navy ships to EU-led Operation Atalanta to control pirates off the coast of Somalia in December 2008.
48. Kaplan, *NATO Divided*, 147.
49. Peter Rudolf, "US Leadership and the Reform of Western Security Institutions: NATO Enlargement and ESDP," in Bernhard May ed., *The Uncertain Superpower: Domestic Dimensions of US Foreign Policy after the Cold War* (Leske + Budrich, Opladen, 2003), 98–99.
50. Interview with a SPD member of the Bundestag, May 24, 2007.
51. Roger Boyes, "Greens Urged to Save Schroder Coalition" *The Times London*, November 16, 2001.
52. Steven Erlanger, "Pressing Greens, German Leader Wins Historic Vote on Sending Troops to Afghanistan," *New York Times*, November 17, 2001.
53. Stephen F. Szabo, *Parting Ways: The Crisis in German-American Relations* (Washington DC: Brookings Institution Press, 2004), 16.
54. Sebastian Harnisch, "German Non-Proliferation Policy and the Iraq Conflict," *German Politics* 13, no. 1 (March 2004): 6.
55. Heiko Borchert and Mary N. Hampton, "The Lessons of Kosovo: Boon Or Bust for Transatlantic Security?," *Orbis* (Spring 2002): 374.
56. Ibid., 373.
57. Szabo, *Parting Ways*, 17–18; Bob Woodward, *Bush at War* (New York: Simon and Schuster, 2002), 179–180.
58. Kaplan, *NATO Divided*, 136.
59. Interview with a senior SPD member of the Bundestag Foreign Relations Committee, May 29, 2007.
60. Interview with a high-ranking official of the German Federal Foreign Office, January 29, 2008; Interview with a SPD member of the Bundestag Defense Committee, June 5, 2008;
61. Matthias Gebauer, "Twisting and Turning over German Troops," *Spiegel Online*, November 29, 2006, http://www.spiegel.de/international/0,1518,451359,00.html, accessed July 25, 2008; Susanne Koelbl and Alexander Szandar, "Germany Faces Taliban Pincer in Afghanistan," *Spiegel Online*, December 17, 2007, http://www.spiegel.de/international/0,1518,523805,00.html, accessed March 15, 2008; (Author unknown) "NATO Asks Germany to Send Combat Troops to Afghanistan," *Spiegel Online*, January 29, 2008, http://www.spiegel.de/international/world

/0,1518,531841,00.html, accessed July 18, 2008; Susanne Koelbl and Alexander Szandar, "US Demands More German Troops at Taliban Front," *Spiegel Online*, February 1, 2008, http://www.spiegel.de/international/0,1518,532476,00.html, accessed July 18, 2008.
62. Interview with a senior German Air Force officer, August 22, 2008.
63. Interview with a CDU member of the Bundestag Defense Committee, June 19, 2008; Interview with a high-ranking SPD member of the Bundestag Foreign Relations Committee, July 1, 2008; Interview with a high-ranking Foreign Office official, November 17, 2008.
64. Susanne Koelbl and Alexander Szandar, "US Demands More German Troops at Taliban Front," *Spiegel Online*, February 1, 2008, http://www.spiegel.de/international/0,1518,532476,00.html, accessed July 18, 2008.
65. Ralf Beste, Konstantin von Hammerstein, and Alexander Szander, "Shrinking Solidarity in Afghanistan?: Debate Flares Anew about German Military Mission," *Spiegel Online*, May 28, 2007, http://www.spiegel.de/international/germany/0,1518,485289,00.html, accessed July 25, 2008.
66. Szabo, *Parting Ways*, 18.
67. Interview with a CDU member of the Bundestag Defense/Foreign Relations Committee, June 24, 2008.
68. Interview with a retired, high-ranking German Army officer, September 23, 2008.
69. Interview with a CDU member of the Bundestag Defense/Foreign Relations Committee, June 19, 2008.
70. Interview with a high-ranking FDP member of the Bundestag, June 20, 2008.
71. Interview with a high-ranking Bundeswehr officer, June 11, 2008.
72. Interview with a retired, high-ranking German Air Force officer, August 13, 2008.
73. Interview with a German Army officer, September 17, 2008.
74. D. Robert Worley, *Waging Ancient War: Limits of Preemptive Force* (Carlisle, PA: US Army War College, February 2003), 20.
75. Szabo, *Parting Ways*, 65.
76. Ibid., 22.
77. Ibid., 27.
78. Interview with three different FDP members of the Bundestag, June 4, 17, and 20, 2008.
79. Interview with a high-ranking FDP member of the Bundestag, June 20, 2008.
80. Interview with a FDP member of the Bundestag Foreign Relations Committee, June 4, 2008.
81. Interview with a CDU member of the Bundestag Defense Committee, June 24, 2008.
82. Interview with a CDU member of the Bundestag Defense Committee, May 29, 2008.

83. Interview with a CDU member of the Bundestag Defense Committee, June 24, 2008; Harnisch, "German Non-Proliferation Policy," 13.
84. Interview with a high-ranking Bundeswehr officer, June 11, 2008.
85. "Germany Would Aid US in Case of Kuwait Attack by Iraq: Junior Minister," *Agence France Presse*, November 23, 2002.
86. "Roundup: US Pressure on Iraq Straining Berlin Coalition," *Deutsche Pressure Agentur*, November 25, 2002.
87. "German Government to Examine US Request for Support in Iraq: Defense Minister," *Spiegel Online*, November 24, 2002.
88. "Roundup: US Pressure on Iraq Straining Berlin Coalition," *Deutsche Pressure Agentur*, November 25, 2002.
89. Geir Moulson, "German Defense Minister Suggests Future Deployment in Iraq is Possible, But Government Says Refusal to Send Troops to Iraq," *The Associated Press*, October 13, 2004.
90. Ibid.
91. Ibid.
92. "German Greens Criticize Defense Minister's Talk of Possible Iraq Mission," *BBC Monitoring Europe*, October 14, 2004.
93. Richard Bernstein and Michael R. Gordon, "Berlin File Says Germany's Spies Aided US in Iraq," *New York Times*, March 2, 2006.
94. "German MPs Learn Navy Escorted US Warships during Iraq War," *BBC Monitoring Europe*, November 10, 2006.
95. Erich Follath, John Goetz, Marcel Rosenbach and Holger Stark, "The Real Story of Curveball: How German Intelligence Helped Justify the US Invasion of Iraq," March 22, 2008, http://www.spiegel.de/international/world/0,1518,542840,00.html, accessed March 21, 2009.
96. "Those Guys are Heroes: How German Agents Helped Pave the Way into Iraq," *Spiegel Online*, December 16, 2008, http://www.spiegel.de/international/world/0,1518,596584,00.html, accessed March 21, 2009.
97. "US General on Berlin Agents in Baghdad: The Germans Were Invaluable to US," *Spiegel Online*, December 16, 2008, http://www.spiegel.de/international/world/0,1518,596537,00.html, accessed March 21, 2009.
98. "The World from Berlin: Germany Was against the War, But Also Slightly Involved," *Spiegel Online*, December 19, 2008, http://www.spiegel.de/international/world/0,1518,597536,00.html, accessed March 21, 2009.
99. "US Military Praise Ludicrous: Steinmeier Rejects Doubts about Agents in Iraq," *Spiegel Online*, December 18, 2008, http://www.spiegel.de/international/world/0,1518,597403,00.html, accessed March 21, 2009.
100. "The World from Berlin: Germany Was against the War, But Also Slightly Involved," *Spiegel Online*, December 19, 2008, http://www

.spiegel.de/international/world/0,1518,597536,00.html, accessed March 21, 2009.
101. Berger, "Set for Stability?" 405; Alagappa, "Introduction," 21.
102. Alagappa, "Introduction," 19.
103. Berger, "Set for Stability?" 411.
104. Alagappa, "Introduction," 22.
105. Mastanduno, "Incomplete Hegemony," 157.
106. Berger, "Set for Stability?" 408, 416.
107. Christopher W. Hughes, "North Korea's Nuclear Weapons: Implications for the Nuclear Ambitions of Japan, South Korea, and Taiwan," *Asia Policy* 3 (January 2007): 88–89.
108. Kenneth B. Pyle, *The Japanese Question: Power and Purpose in a New Era* (Washington, DC: AEI Press, 1996), 25.
109. John Welfield, *An Empire in Eclipse: Japan in the Postwar American Alliance System—A Study in the Interaction of Domestic Politics and Foreign Policy* (London, UK: Athlone One Press, 1988), 80, 354, 356.
110. Michael Schaller, *Altered States: The United States and Japan since the Occupation* (New York: Oxford University Press, 1997), 22.
111. Welfield, *Empire in Eclipse*, 40–41.
112. Ibid., 51–52.
113. Pyle, *Japanese Question*, 29.
114. Welfield, *Empire in Eclipse*, 78.
115. Ibid., 48, 90–92, 148; Pyle, *Japanese Question*, 19, 123.
116. Paul Midford, "Japan's Leadership Role in East Asian Security Multilateralism: The Nakayama Proposal and the Logic of Reassurance," *The Pacific Review* 13, no. 3 (2000): 370.
117. Pyle, *Japanese Question*, 28.
118. Ibid., 129.
119. Kenneth B. Pyle, *The Making of Modern Japan* (Lexington, MA: D.C. Heath and Company, 1996), 239.
120. Pyle, *Japanese Question*, 87; Welfield, *Empire in Eclipse*, 144–145.
121. Michael J. Green, *Japan's Reluctant Realism: Foreign Policy Challenges in an Era of Uncertain Power* (New York: Palgrave, 2003), 111–130.
122. Funabashi Yoichi, *Dōmei hyōryū* [Alliance Adrift] (Tokyo: Iwanami shoten, 1997), 42–45.
123. Yoichi Funabashi, *The Peninsula Question: A Chronicle of the Second Korean Nuclear Crisis* (Washington, DC: Brookings Institution Press, 2007), 88.
124. Ibid., 88.
125. Interview with a retired, high-ranking MOFA official, March 12, 2008.
126. Funabashi, *Peninsula Question*, 66.
127. Ibid., 59.
128. Green, *Japan's Reluctant Realism*, 77–92.

129. Funabashi, *Dōmei hyōryū*, 389–393, 422–424.
130. Yinan He, "History, Chinese Nationalism and the Emerging Sino-Japanese Conflict," *Journal of Contemporary China* 16, no. 50 (2007): 1–24.
131. Tanaka Hitoshi and Tahara Soichiro, *Kokka to gaiko* [State and foreign relations] (Tokyo: Kodansha, 2005), 133–134.
132. Takemi Keizo, "Iraku eno haken: nichibei doumei to nihon no kokueiki no tameni hitsuyouda [SDF dispatch to Iraq: What do we need for the U.S.-Japan alliance and Japan's national interest?]," *Ronza*, December 2003, 53.
133. Pyle, *Japanese Question*, 15.
134. Ibid., 130.
135. Natsuyo Ishibashi, "The Dispatch of Japan's Self-Defense Forces to Iraq: Public Opinion, Election, and Foreign Policy," *Asian Survey* 47, no. 5 (September/October 2007): 772.
136. Ibid., 771–772.
137. Interview with a DPJ member of the Lower House Foreign Relations Committee, Iraq Committee, and Security Committee, January 31, 2008.
138. Richard J. Samuels, "Politics, Security Policy, and Japan's Cabinet Legislation Bureau: Who Elected These Guys, Anyway?," *JPRI Working Paper*, no. 99, March 2004.
139. Interview with a retired, high-ranking CLB official, February 28, 2008.
140. Interview with a high-ranking MOD official, January 30, 2008.
141. Interview with a high-ranking MOF official, March 13, 2008. According to the MOF official, US military personnel sprinkled water around yard without limit and run an air conditioner throughout night. While Japanese citizens are living in small houses and buildings in overcrowded areas around the US bases, they are living in large houses and enjoying a higher standard of living. When the high-ranking MOFA official went to US bases to examine how the host nation's support was used in 2000, one US military officer threatened him by saying that if the MOF official cut the host nation's support, the US officer would report to the US embassy in Tokyo. Then, the US embassy would report to the White House. The White House would in turn complain to a Japanese prime minister. (And, finally the Japanese prime minister would fire the MOF official.) However, the MOF official did not back down. He (as well as the MOF as a whole) had never intended to destroy the US-Japan alliance system; however, he thought that the reduction of host nation support was necessary in order to make the two countries' relationship healthy and to make the security treaty acceptable to the Japanese public.
142. Interview with a DPJ member of the Lower House/ Foreign policy expert, February 7, 2008.

143. Mike M. Mochizuki, *Toward a True Alliance: Restructuring U.S.-Japan Security Relations* (Washington, DC: Brookings Institution Press, 1997), 19–20.
144. Thomas J. Christensen, "China, the U.S.-Japan Alliance, and the Security Dilemma in East Asia," *International Security* 23, no. 4 (Spring 1999), 57–58, 80.
145. Robert Ross, "The Geography of the Peace: East Asia in the Twenty-first Century," *International Security* 23, no. 4 (Spring 1999), 115.
146. Funabashi, *Peninsula Question*, 86–87.
147. Interview with a retired, high-ranking MOFA official, March 12, 2008.
148. Interview with a retired, high-ranking MOFA official, February 12, 2008; Interview with a high-ranking MOFA official, March 18, 2008.
149. Interview with a retired, high-ranking MOFA official, February 12, 2008.
150. Interview with a senior, high-ranking LDP member of the Lower House/ a former minister of defense, February 15, 2008.
151. Katayama Satsuki, "Zaimusho tanto shukeikann karano kiteki: Jieitai nimo kōzō kaikaku ga hitsuyūda [Warning from a MOF budget examiner: The SDF needs to restructure]," *Chuokoron* (January 2005), 156–163.
152. Funabashi, *Dōmei hyōryū*, 385–439.
153. Yomiuri shinbun seijibu, *Gaiko o kennka ni shita otoko: Koizumi gaiko 2000 nichi no shinjitsu* [A man who turned diplomacy into quarrel: The truth of 2000 days of Koizumi's diplomacy] (Tokyo: Shinchosha, 2006), 254.
154. Interview with a high ranking MOD official, January 30, 2008.
155. Interview with a high ranking MSDF officer, January 23, 2008.
156. Pyle, *Japanese Question*, 128; Okamoto Susumu, "Taibei shien maenomeri jijō: Torauma ni noru Koizumi [A reason for Japan's support for the United States: Koizumi rides on trauma]," *Asahi Shinbun Weekly AERA*, October 8, 2001.
157. Interview with a retired, high-ranking MOFA official, February 1, 2008.
158. Interview with a DPJ member of the Lower House, February 5, 2008.
159. Interview with a senior high-ranking LDP member of the Lower House, February 20, 2008.
160. Interview with a LDP member of the Lower House Foreign Relations Committee, February 5, 2008.
161. Interview with a senior high-ranking LDP member of the Lower House/ a former minister of defense, February 15, 2008.
162. Interview with a retired, high-ranking MOFA official, February 1, 2008.

163. Author's interview with a high-ranking METI official, February 12, 2008.
164. Interview with a retired, high-ranking MOFA official, February 1, 2008.
165. Shinoda Tomohito, *Kantei gaikō: Seiji rīdāshippu no yukue* [Cabinet Secretariat's diplomacy: the future of its political leadership] (Tokyo: Asahi shinbunsha, 2004), 85–86; *Asahi Shinbun*, February 20, 2002; Interview with a high-ranking senior LDP member of the Lower House, February 20, 2008.
166. Asahi Shinbun, March 19, 2003.
167. Interview with a high-ranking MOD official, January 30, 2008; Yomiuri shinbun seijibu, *Gaikō*, 154–156.
168. Koizumi Junichiro, "Koizumi soridaijin kasha kaiken: Iraku mondai ni kannsuru taiou ni tsuite [Prime Minister Koizumi: About Japan's dealing with the Iraq issue]," March 20, 2003, http://www.kantei.go.jp/jp/koizumispeech/2003/03/20kaiken.html, accessed February 19, 2009.
169. Handa Shigeru, "Jeitai no Honne Uzumaku Shiwaku [The real intention of the GSDF]," *Ronza,* January 2004, 34–39.
170. Interview with a retired, high-ranking GSDF officer, February 27, 2008.
171. "Shin sakimori ko henbou suru jieitai: daiichibu iraku haken no jitsuzo, <2> ninnmu kettei [New thinking on soldiers for defense—changes in the SDF: The first part—the reality of the SDF dispatch to Iraq <2> decision on duty]," *Tokyo Shinbun*, January 11, 2007, http://www.tokyo-np.co.jp/feature/sakimori/news/070111.html, accessed September 23, 2007; Handa Shigeru, "Jieitai iraku hakenn ga motarashitamono [A consequence of the SDF dispatch to Iraq]," *Magazin 9-jo Konohitoni kikitai*, http://www.magazine9.jp/interv/handa/index.html, accessed May 30, 2009; *Asahi Shinbun* "Jieitai gojyu nen" shuzaihan, *Jieitai shirarezaru henyo* [The SDF unknown transformation] (Tokyo: Asahi Shinbunsha, 2005), 82–83, 113–114.
172. Samawah was not bombed by the United States. The buildings and roads in the city were just old. So the GSDF repaired those infrastructures. See Watai Takeharu, "Jieitai haken kara hantoshi: Samawa no genjitsu to genso [A half year since the SDF was dispatch to Iraq: the reality and illusion of Samawah]," *Ronza,* September 2004, 94–101; Handa, "Jieitai iraku hakenn ga motarashitamono."
173. Interview with a high-ranking MOFA official, March 18, 2008.
174. Asakura Toshio, "Watashitachi wa naze bei-nihon seifu wo shiji shitaka [The reason that I supported the governments of Japan and the United States]," *Ronza*, November 2003, 69–75.

4 Alliance Institutions: NATO versus US-Japan Security Treaty

1. Peter Rudolf, "The Myth of the 'German Way': German Foreign Policy and Transatlantic Relations," *Survival* 47, no.1 (Spring 2005): 143.

2. John Welfield, *An Empire in Eclipse: Japan in the Postwar American Alliance System—A Study in the Interaction of Domestic Politics and Foreign Policy* (London, UK: Athlone One Press, 1988), 62.
3. Kawaguchi Hajime and Otsuka Eiji, *Jieitai no Iraq hahei sashitomem soshō: hanketsubun wo yomu* [A law suit to stop the SDF dispatch to Iraq: Reading the court judgment] (Tokyo: Kadokawa shoten, 2009), 150–152.
4. Handa Shigeru, "Naze jieikan wa indoyō e ittaka [Why did the MSDF ships go to the Indian Ocean?]," *Sekai*, January 2002, 28.
5. *Japan Times*, September 21 and 22, 2007.
6. Handa Shigeru, *Senchi haken: kawaru jieitai* [Dispatch to war field: Changing SDF] (Tokyo: Iwanami shoten, 2009), 72.
7. Kawaguchi and Otsuka, *Jieitai*, 106–164; Handa Shigeru, "Jieitai wa beigun shien: kūji wa iraku de nani wo hakonde iruka [Reality was to support US forces: What is the ASDF transporting in Iraq?], *Sekai*, October 2007, 20–24.
8. Handa, "Jieitai wa beigun shien," 22.
9. Interview with a retired, high-ranking ASDF officer, April 19, 2011.
10. *Japan Times*, October 28, 2007.
11. Lawrence S. Kaplan, *NATO Divided, NATO United: The Evolution of an Alliance* (Westport, CT: Praeger, 2004), 4–5.
12. Jeffrey S. Lantis, *Strategic Dilemmas and the Evolution of German Foreign Policy since Unification* (Westport, CT: Praeger 2002), 108–109; Author unknown, "Important NATO Cases at the Constitutional Court," *Spiegel Online*, July 4, 2007, http://www.spiegel.de/international/germany/0,1518,492304,00.html, accessed July 25, 2008.
13. Kaplan, *NATO Divided*, 5.
14. Interview with a retired, high-ranking German Federal Foreign Office official, October 4, 2011.
15. Svein Vigeland Rottem, "The Ambivalent Ally: Norway in the New NATO," *Contemporary Security Policy* 28, no. 3 (December 2007) 619–637.
16. Interview with a retired, high-ranking, Bundeswehr officer, December 15, 2011.
17. Interview with a retired, high-ranking German Federal Foreign Office official, October 4, 2011.
18. Susanne Koelbl and Alexander Szander, "Not Licensed to Kill: German Special Forces in Afghanistan Let Taliban Commander Escape," *Spiegel Online*, May 19, 2008, http://www.spiegel.de/international/world/0,1518,554033,00.html, accessed July 25, 2008.
19. Susanne Koelbl and Alexander Szandar, "Gates Wants More from Berlin: US Demands More German Troops at Taliban Front," *Spiegel Online*, Februrary 1, 2008, http://www.spiegel.de/international/world/0,1518,532476,00.html, accessed July 18, 2008; Konstantin von Hammerstein and Alexander Szandar, "NATO Turns Screws on Germany:

The Coming Afghanistan Showdown," *Spiegel Online*, February 11, 2008, http://www.spiegel.de/international/world/0,1518,534524,00.html, accessed July 25, 2008.
20. Timo Noetzel and Benjamin Schreer, "All the Way? The Evolution of German Military Power," *International Affairs* 84, no. 2 (2008): 211–221; Matthias Gebauer, "Angela Merkel in Riga: Diplomacy, Criticism and Roast Goose," *Spiegel Online*, November 30, 2006, http://www.spiegel.de/international/0,1518,451628,00html, accessed July 25, 2008.
21. Joseph Legold, "NATO's Post–Cold War Collective Action Problem," *International Security* 23, no. 1 (Summer 1998): 81–82.
22. Legold, "NATO's Post–Cold War," 97.
23. The Strategic Concept is "an official document that outlines NATO's enduring purpose and nature and its fundamental security tasks. It also identifies the central features of the new security environment, specifies the elements of the Alliance's approach to security and provides guidelines for the further adaptation of its military forces." Four different Strategic Concepts were written during the Cold War, and two after the end of the Cold War. All the Strategic Concepts (except MC 14/3) were approved by the North Atlantic Council (NAC) composed of the representatives from all the member states. See http://www.nato.int/cps/en/natolive/topics_56626.htm, accessed October 16, 2009.
24. S. Neil MacFarlane, "Challenges to Euro-Atlantic Security," in Pierre Martin and Mark R. Brawley, eds., *Alliance Politics, Kosovo, and NATO's War: Allied Force or Forced Allies?* (New York: Palgrave, 2001), 27–40; *The Alliance's New Strategic Concept, November 7–8, 1991*, http://www.nato.int/cps/en/natolive/official_texts_23847.htm, accessed July 5, 2009; *The Alliance's Strategic Concept, April 24, 1999*, http://www.nato.int/cps/en/natolive/official_texts_27433.htm, accessed July 5, 2009.
25. *Prague Summit Declaration*, November 21, 2002, http://www.nato.int/docu/pr/2002/p02–127e.htm, accessed July 5, 2009.
26. Kaplan, *NATO Divided*, 146.
27. Strobe Talbott, "From Prague to Baghdad: NATO at Risk," *Foreign Affairs* (November/December 2002): 46–57.
28. Struck, "Defense Policy Guidelines."
29. Rolf Mützenich, "Die NATO in der Krise: Brauchen wir 40 Jahre danach einen neuen Harmel-Bericht?" December 14, 2007, http://www.rolfmuetzenich.de, accessed July 4, 2009.
30. Interview with a high-ranking CDU member of the Bundestag/ a former parliamentary secretary of the Federal Ministry of Defense, May 29, 2008.
31. Richard Bernstein, "The German Question," *New York Times*, May 2, 2004.
32. Interviews with a retired, high-ranking German Army officer, September 23, 2008; and a retired, high-ranking German Air Force officer, August 13, 2008.

33. For full discussion on the 1996 revised US-Japan Guidelines for Defense Cooperation, see Christopher W. Hughes, *Japan's Re-emergence as a "Normal" Military Power* (New York: Routledge, 2006), 98–105.
34. Hughes, *Japan's Re-emergence*, 126–128.

5   Military Institutions: Bundeswehr versus Self-Defense Forces (SDF)

1. As of October 2011, the number of casualties suffered by the US Army in Operation Enduring Freedom (OEF) stood at 9,710 (67.9 percent of all US casualties in OEF); whereas the US Marine suffered 4,036 (28 percent), the US Navy 279 (1.9 percent), and the US Air Force 317 (2.2 percent). Similarly, of the 53 casualties suffered in Afghanistan among the Bundeswehr, 47 come from the army; "iCasualties.org: Operation Enduring Freedom," http://icasualties.org/OEF/Index.aspx, accessed January 27, 2012.
2. Peter Struck, "Defense Policy Guidelines," Federal Ministry of Defense, May 21, 2003, 4.
3. Interview with a retired, high-ranking German Air Force officer, August 13, 2008.
4. Interview with a senior German Air Force officer, August 22, 2008.
5. Interview with a high-ranking German Navy officer, July 3, 2008.
6. Douglas C. Peifer, *The Three German Navies: Dissolution, Transition, and New Beginnings, 1945–1960* (Gainesville, FL: University Press of Florida, 2002).
7. Tristan Nichols, "Germany Honors UK Naval Dead," *Evening Herald (Plymouth)*, May 19, 2008.
8. Interview with a retired, high-ranking German Navy officer, August 18, 2008.
9. Interview with a senior German Army officer, September 17, 2008.
10. For the German military officers working in Bonn (the former capital of the FRG), Brussels is not far away at all. It is an easy trip by car. Indeed, the distance between Bonn and Brussels is less than that between Bonn and Berlin.
11. Interview with a senior German Army officer, September 11, 2008.
12. The joint exercises took place only in autumn and winter because they had to minimize the damage to the farmland. After harvest was over, the tanks could run over the farmland.
13. Interview with a retired, high-ranking German Army officer, September 23, 2008.
14. Interview with an SPD member of the Bundestag Defense Committee, June 5, 2008.
15. Interview with a senior German Army officer, September 17, 2008.
16. Interview with a senior German Army officer, September 11, 2008.

17. James Fallow, "The Invasion of Iraq," *Frontline*, http://www.pbs.org/wgbh/pages/frontline/shows/invasion/interviews/fallows.html, accessed June 14, 2009.
18. Interview with a retired, high-ranking German Army officer, September 23, 2008.
19. Author unknown, "German Navy Warship Salutes USS Winston S. Churchill," September 14, 2001, http://www.ingratia.org/stories/USSChurchill.html, accessed June 15, 2009.
20. Interview with a retired, high-ranking German Navy officer, August 18, 2008.
21. Interview with a high-ranking German Navy officer, July 3, 2008.
22. US Department of Defense, "Global War on Terrorism: Casualties by Military Service Component," http://siadapp.dmdc.osd.mil/personnel/CASUALTY/gwot_component.pdf, accessed February 25, 2012.
23. Interview with a retired, high-ranking German Air Force officer, August 13, 2008.
24. Interview with a senior Leftist Party member of the Bundestag Foreign Relations Committee, June 25, 2008.
25. Interview with a senior German Air Force officer, August 22, 2008.
26. Interview with a retired, high-ranking German Army officer, September 23, 2008.
27. Toby Helm, "German Commando Fears Bloodbath," *The Ottawa Citizen*, September 24, 2001.
28. Interview with a retired, high-ranking German Army officer, September 23, 2008.
29. Interview with a senior German Army officer, September 11, 2008.
30. Interview with a senior German Army officer, September 17, 2008.
31. For details about the Bundeswehr reform, see, von Bastian Giegerich, "Mugged by Reality? German Defense in Light of the 2003 Policy Guidelines," *Düsseldorfer Institut für Außen- und Sicherheitspolitik* (12.10.2003); Kerry Longhurst, *Germany and the Use of Force* (Manchester, UK: Manchester University Press, 2004), 107, 108, 111, 112, 113.; Josef Janning and Thomas Bauer, "Into the Great Wide Open: The Transformation of the German Armed Forces After 1990," *Orbis* (Summer 2007): 529–541. Timo Noetzel and Benjamin Schreer, "All the Way? The Evolution of German Military Power," *International Affairs* 84, no. 2 (2008): 211–223.
32. Franz-Josef Meiers, "The Reform of the Bundeswehr: Adaptation or Fundamental Renewal?" *European Security* 10, no. 2 (Summer 2001): 1–22.
33. Struck, "Defense Policy Guidelines," 4.
34. Ibid., 3.
35. Ibid., 12.
36. Giegerich, "Mugged by Reality?," 10; Janning and Bauer, "Into the Great Wide Open," 532; Longhurst, *Germany and the Use of Force*, 98,

114, 115, 125; Martin Agüera, "Reform of the Bundeswehr: Defense Policy Choices for the Next German Administration," *Comparative Strategy* 21 (2002): 184.
37. Mandy Kirby, "Defense Minister Rubbishes Policy Conflict as Cause of German Military Chief's Resignation," *World Markets Analysis*, January 21, 2004.
38. Author unknown, "Nervige Nadelstiche," *Der Spiegel*, October 11, 2003.
39. Friedrich Kuhn, "German Army Inspector Contradicts Minister in Plan for Future," *BBC Monitoring Europe*, September 2, 2003; Author unknown, "German Generals Challenging Defense Minister over Austerity Plans," *BBC Monitoring International Reports*, September 1, 2003.
40. Timo Noetzel and Benjamin Schreer, "German Special Operations Forces: The Case for Revision," *SWP Comments* 26, November 2006.
41. Interview with a FDP member of the Bundestag, June 17, 2008.
42. Noetzel and Schreer, "German Special Operations Forces," 1–4.
43. Interview with a Leftist Party member of the Bundestag, June 25, 2008.
44. Interview with an SPD member of the Bundestag Foreign Relations Committee, July 1, 2008; Interview with an SPD member of the Bundestag Foreign Relations Committee, June 26, 2008.
45. Noetzel and Schreer, "German Special Operations Forces."
46. Alexander Szandar, Marcel Rosenbach, Susanne Koelel and John Goetz, "Beer, Brats and Bad Behavior: German Elite Troops in Afghanistan Marred by Reports of Misconduct," *Spiegel Online*, October 1, 2007, www.spiegel.de/international /germany/0,1518,508800,00.html, accessed July 25, 2008.
47. Author unknown, "Kurnaz Lawyer Worried: German Army Estroyed Secret Files about Foreign Missions," *Spiegel Online*, June 26, 2007, www.spiegel.de/international/germany/0,1518,490782,00.html, accessed on July 25, 2008.
48. NATO went to war against Serbia without a clear UN mandate in 1999.
49. I omit the Air Self-Defense Force (ASDF) from my discussion because the characteristics of the ASDF are close to those of the GSDF, and therefore the ASDF does not well contrast with the GSDF. It is true that the ASDF is purchasing air planes from the United States and sending its servicemen to the United States for training. In addition, the headquarters of US Forces Japan (USFJ) is located at the Yokota Air Base, and a head of USFJ has been held by an air force officer. However, as with the case of the GSDF, the ASDF has not been integrated into the overall strategic structure of the US Air Force (USAF). The task of the ASDF has been clearly separated from that of the USAF. The ASDF has focused on Japan's air defense, while the USAF is supposed to carry out offensive attack outside of Japan. And the ASDF is not supposed to go out of Japan to assist the USAF's overseas operations.

50. Asahi Shinbun "Jieitai 50-nen" Shuzaihan, *Jieitai: Shirazareru henyo* [SDF: Unknown transformation] (Tokyo: Asahi Shinbun Sha, 2005), 283–319.
51. *Asahi Shinbun*, June 2, 2004.
52. NHK Hodo kyoku, *Kaijō jieitai wa koushite umareta: Y-bunsho ga akasu sousetsu no himitsu* [How the MSDF was born: Secret that Y-document reveals] (Tokyo: Nihon housoukyoku shuppankai, 2003), 211–264.
53. Satō Keizo, "Kaijō jieitai kinmu kaiso [Memoir of my working in the MSDF]," in Nagomi kai, ed., *Kaijo jietai to watashi tachi* [The MSDF and us] (Chiba, 2004), 26–31.
54. Interviews with three different high-ranking MSDF officers, February 14, 2008, January 19, 2011, and February 4, 2011.
55. Interview with a retired high-ranking MSDF officer, January 19, 2011.
56. Agawa Naoyuki, *Umino yūjō* [camaraderie on the sea] (Tokyo: Chuokoronsha, 2001), 88–112.
57. Interview with a senior GSDF officer, March 17, 2008.
58. Interview with a high-ranking MSDF officer, February 4, 2011.
59. Interview with a senior MSDF officer, January 23, 2008.
60. Interview with a high-ranking MSDF officer, February 14, 2008.
61. Hisae Masahiko, *9–11 to nihon gaiko* [9/11 and Japanese foreign policy] (Tokyo: Kodansha, 2002), 60–64; Yomiuri shinbun seijibu, *Gaiko o kennka ni shita otoko: Koizumi gaiko 2000 nichi no shinjitsu* [A man who turned diplomacy into quarrel: The truth of 2000 days of Koizumi's diplomacy] (Tokyo: Shinchosha, 2006), 131–134.
62. Yomiuri shinbun seijibu, *Gaiko*, 132; Handa, *Tatakaenai guntai* [Troops that cannot fight] (Tokyo: Kodansha, 2005), 46–47.
63. The Japan Coastal Guard usually takes care of this job.
64. NHK Hodo kyoku, *Kaijō jieitai*, 64–69.
65. Ibid., 63. Hisae, *9–11*, 70–73.
66. Yomiuri shinbun seijibu, *Gaiko*, 142–144.
67. Interview with a high-ranking MSDF officer, February 14, 2008.
68. Interview with a retired, high-ranking German Navy officer, August 18, 2008.
69. Ibid.
70. *Japan Times*, September 21 and 22, 2007.
71. Ibid., October 28, 2007.
72. US Department of Defense, "Global War on Terrorism: Casualties by Military Service Component," http://siadapp.dmdc.osd.mil/personnel/CASUALTY/gwot_component.pdf, accessed June 28, 2009.
73. "iCasualties.org: Operation Enduring Freedom," http://icasualties.org/oef/byNationality.aspx?hndQry=Germany, accessed June 28, 2009.
74. Interview with a senior GSDF officer, March 17, 2008.
75. Interview with a retired, high-ranking GSDF officer, February 24, 2011.
76. Interview with a senior GSDF officer, March 17, 2008.

77. Interview with a retired, high-ranking GSDF officer, February 24, 2011.
78. Handa, *Tatakaenai guntai*, 48–50.
79. Interview with a senior GSDF officer, March 17, 2008.
80. For example, according to a poll taken by *Asahi Shinbun* on April 9, 1993, 47 percent of respondents answered "the SDF is constitutional," while 28 percent "the SDF is unconstitutional."
81. "Jieitai 50-nen" Shuzaihan, *Jieitai*, 38–41; Handa, *Tatakaenai guntai*, 50–53.
82. Handa, *Tatakaenai guntai*, 52.
83. Interview with a retired, high-ranking German Army officer, September 23, 2008.
84. Konrad Freytag, "Outside View: Afghanistan Report," *United Press International*, May 26, 2004.
85. Handa Shigeru, "Jieitai no Honne Uzumaku Shiwaku [The real intention of the GSDF]," *Ronza*, January 2004, 34–39; Handa, *Tatakaenai guntai*, 57–59.
86. "Jieitai 50-nen" Shuzaihan, *Jieitai*, 75–77.
87. Ibid., 112–113.
88. Ibid., 124.
89. Handa, *Tatakaenai guntai*, 70; "Jieitai 50-nen" Shuzaihan, *Jieitai*, 82–83.

6 Alternative Explanations

1. World Trade Organization, http://stat.wto.org/CountryProfiles, accessed February 13, 2007.
2. Interview with a high-ranking official of the German Federal Ministry of Economic and Technology, June 12, 2008.
3. Federal Ministry of Economics and Technology, http://www.bmwi.de/BMWi/Navigation/Aussenwirtschaft/aussenhandelsdaten, did=193940.html
4. World Trade Organization, http://stat.wto.org/CountryProfiles, accessed February 13, 2007.
5. Ibid.
6. *Asahi Shinbun,* February 14, 2003.
7. Interview with a senior LDP politician / a former minister of defense, January 16, 2008.
8. Interview with a LDP member of the lower house, February 5, 2008.
9. Interview with a DPJ member of the lower house, January 31, 2008. Interview with a DPJ member of the lower house, February 7, 2008.
10. *Asahi Shinbun,* March 9, 2003.
11. Interview with a high-ranking METI official, February 13, 2008.
12. Interview with a senior LDP member of the lower house / a former minister of defense, February 15, 2008.

13. Interview with a high-ranking METI official, February 22, 2008. According to the METI official, there were four different ways of manufacturing defense products: (1) pure, "made-in-Japan," in which Japanese companies develop products and manufacture them in Japan (e.g., Mitsubishi type-90 tank); (2) codevelopment and manufacture, in which Japanese companies develop products with foreign companies and manufacture them in Japan or overseas (e.g., F-2 fighter aircraft codeveloped and manufactured by Mitsubishi and Lockheed Martin); (3) license production, in which Japanese companies manufacture defense products in Japan that were developed by foreign companies by paying a license fee to those companies. (License production is better than a simple assembly, because Japanese companies can learn something by manufacturing new weapons by themselves in Japan. However, it is not so useful in terms of learning new technologies, because they cannot access to the information to manufacture the most important part of the product.); and (4) simple assembly, in which Japanese companies simply assemble products in Japan that were developed and manufactured overseas.
14. Interview with a METI official, March 14, 2008.
15. "Germany Fears Boycott over Iraq War," *Automotive News*, February 24, 2003.
16. "Survey: War Won't Spoil US Appetite for German Cars," *Automotive News*, March 10, 2003.
17. John N. Frank, "New Strategies Needed for French and German Goods Product Boycotts," *PR Week* (US), April 14, 2003.
18. This is a striking difference between the German and Japanese business associations. Japanese business associations such as the Japan Business Federation (*keidanren*) have provided financial support for political parties, particularly to the LDP, and actively participate in politics.
19. According to the high-ranking business official, however, things were different when he talked with American politicians. American politicians, regardless of whether they were the Democrats or Republicans, tried to put pressure on German business leaders (including him) and demanded they support the US war on Iraq. I asked him why the German business leaders did not succumb to the American demand. He replied that the American politicians put too much pressure on them. Americans were too pushy when they demanded the German business leaders support the Iraq War. When they asked the German business leaders to support the Iraq War, they should have been more polite and gentle. But their attitude toward the Germans was very condescending. Interview with a former high-ranking member of the Association of German Chambers of Commerce and Industry, July 8, 2008.
20. Interview with a high-ranking official of the Federal Ministry of Economics and Technology, June 12, 2008.
21. Agency for Natural Resources and Energy (Japan), http://www.enecho.meti.go.jp/topics/hakusho/2008energyhtml/2–1–1.htm, accessed September

12, 2009.Federal Ministry of Economics and Technology, accessed April 7, 2008, http://www.bmwi.de/BMWi/Navigation/Energie/mineraloelve rsorgung.html.
22. Cabinet Office (Japan), http://www5.cao.go.jp/j-j/sekaI_chouryuu/sh03 -01/sh03-02-02-07z.html, accessed September 12, 2009.
23. Agency for Natural Resources and Energy, http://www.enecho.meti .go.jp/topics/hakusho/2007energyhtml/html/2-1-3-1.html,accessed September 12, 2009.
24. Federal Ministry of Economics and Technology, http://www.bmwi.de /BMWi/Navigation/Energie/mineraloelversorgung,did=159820.html
25. Asahi Shinbun "wangan kiki" shuzaihan, *Wangan sensō to nihon* [The Gulf War and Japan] (Tokyo: Asahi Shinbunsha, 1991), 16–19; Kunimasa Takeshi, *Wangan sensō toiu tenkanten* [The Gulf War as a turning point] (Tokyo: Iwanami shoten, 1999), 30–31.
26. Interview with a senior METI official, March 10, 2008.
27. Interview with a senior METI official, February 12, 2008.
28. Interview with a senior researcher in the Institute of Energy Economics Japan, February 20, 2008.
29. Natsuyo Ishibashi, "The Dispatch of Japan's Self-Defense Forces to Iraq: Public Opinion, Elections, and Foreign Policy," *Asian Survey*, 47, no. 5 (September/October 2007): 771–772.
30. Thomas R. H. Havens, *Fire Across the Sea: The Vietnam War and Japan, 1965–1975* (New Jersey: Princeton University Press, 1987).
31. Amaki Naoto, *Saraba gaimusho!: Watashi wa Koizumi shushō to baikoku kanryō wo yurusanai* [Goodbye the MOF!: I will not forgive Prime Minister Koizumi and officials who sold Japan] (Tokyo: Kōdansha, 2004), 64–66.
32. Interview with a retired, high-ranking MOFA official, February 1, 2008.
33. Interview with a high-ranking MOFA official, March 18, 2008.
34. Interview with a senior LDP member of the lower house / a former defense minister, January 16, 2008.
35. Yomiuri shinbun seijibu, *Gaiko o kennka ni shita otoko: Koizumi gaiko 2000 nichi no shinjitsu* [A man who turned diplomacy into quarrel: The truth of 2000 days of Koizumi's diplomacy] (Tokyo: Shinchosha, 2006), 159.
36. Interview with a retired, high-ranking MOFA official, March 12, 2008.
37. Ibid.
38. Interview with a retired, high-ranking MOFA official, February 1, 2008.
39. Yoichi Funabashi, *The Peninsula Question: A Chronicle of the Second Korean Nuclear Crisis* (Washington, DC: Brookings Institution Press, 2007), 48.
40. Ibid., 47.
41. Interview with a high-ranking Foreign Office official, September 8, 2008.
42. Interview with a Foreign Office official, November 17, 2008.

43. Paul Midford, "Japan's Leadership Role in East Asian Security Multilateralism: The Nakayama Proposal and the Logic of Reassurance," *Pacific Review* 13, no. 3 (2000): 367–397.
44. Kuniko Ashizawa, "Japan's Approach toward Asian Regional Security: From 'Hub-and-Spoke' Bilateralism to 'Multi-Tiered,'" *Pacific Review* 16, no. 3 (2003): 361–382.
45. It is very expensive to hire a Foreign Office official as an advisor, so it is totally up to the political parties whether they choose to make such a hire.
46. Interview with a high-ranking Foreign Office official, September 8, 2008.
47. Interview with a MOFA official, November 29, 2006.
48. Interview with a high-ranking Foreign Office official, January 29, 2008.
49. Stephen F. Szabo, *Parting Ways: The Crisis in German-American Relations* (Washington DC: Brookings Institution Press, 2004), 44–45.
50. Ibid., 45.
51. Interview with a high-ranking Foreign Office official, November 17, 2008.
52. Szabo, *Parting Ways*, 23.
53. Ibid.
54. Ibid., 23, 137.
55. Interview with a high-ranking SPD member of the Bundestag/ Foreign policy expert, July 19, 2007.
56. "Germany Fischer Planning to Reward Ministry Loyalists," *BBC Monitoring International Reports*, April 11, 2005. (Translated from German newspaper *Welt am Sonntag* web site on April 10, 2005).
57. *Washington Post*, November 30, 2005. In October 2002, for example, Sharioth compared the new US strategic doctrine of preventive military strikes with the 1968 Brezhnev Doctrine by which the Soviet Union legitimized its invasion of Prague. At that time, the Soviets called the uprising in Prague "a threat to world peace." See "German Top Officials Criticize New U.S. Security Doctrine," *BBC Monitoring International Reports*, October 8, 2002.
58. "German Govt Taps Foreign Min Offl as Ambassador to US," *Market News International*, December 20, 2005.
59. "Germany's Merkel Wins over a High-Powered Crowd," *Washington Post*, January 18, 2006.
60. For example, Justice Minister Herta Däubler-Gmelin compared US G. W. Bush with Hitler in her election campaign speech. See Szabo, *Parting Ways*, 29.
61. Brian C. Rathbun, *Partisan Interventions: European Party Politics and Peace Enforcement in the Balkans* (Ithaca, NY: Cornell University Press, 2004), 15–45.
62. Brian C. Rathbun, "The Myth of German Pacifism," *German Politics and Society* 79, no. 24 (Summer 2006): 69.
63. *The Economist*, February 22, 2003.

64. Matthias Gebauer, "Angela Merkel in Riga: Diplomacy, Cynicism and Roast Goose," *Spiegel Online*, November 11, 2006, http://www.spiegel.de/international/germany/0,1518,451628,00.html, accessed July 25, 2008; Konstantin von Hammerstein and Alexander Szander, "NATO Turns Crews on Germany: The Coming Afghanistan Showdown," *Spiegel Online*, February 11, 2008, http://www.spiegel.de/international/germany/0,1518,534524,00.html, accessed July 25, 2008.
65. Interviews with a FDP member of the Bundestag, June 4, 2008; a Leftist Party member of the Bundestag, June 25, 2008; a SPD member of the Bundestag, June 26, 2008; a FDP member of the Bundestag, June 17, 2008; a CDU member of the Bundestag, June 19, 2008; a CDU member of the Bundestag, June 24, 2008; a former high-ranking member of the Association of German Chambers of Commerce and Industry, July 8, 2008; a high-ranking member of the American Jewish Committee, July 10, 2008; a high-ranking German Army officer, September 17, 2008; a former high-ranking German Army officer, September 23, 2008; and an official of the German Federal Foreign Office, November 17, 2008.
66. As of summer 2008 when I conducted the interview, 26 Bundeswehr soldiers had died in Afghanistan.
67. Interview with an SPD member of the Bundestag, June 19, 2008.
68. Otake Hideo, "Rinen Naki Manifesuto de Seiji wa Kawaranai [Manifesto without ideas cannot change politics]," *Ronza* (December 2003), 8–13; Leonard Schoppa, "Neoliberal Economic Policy Preferences of the 'New Left': Home-Grown or an Anglo-American Import?" in Rikki Kersten, ed., *The Left in the Shaping of Japanese Democracy* (London: Routledge, 2006), 117–39.
69. Natsuyo Ishibashi, "The Dispatch of Japan's Self-Defense Forces to Iraq: Public Opinion, Election, and Foreign Policy," *Asian Survey* 47, no. 5 (September/October 2007), 776–779.
70. Franz-Josef Meiers, "The German Predicament: The Red Lines of the Security and Defence Policy of the Berlin Republic," *International Politics* 44 (2007), 623–644.
71. Beverly Crawford, *Power and German Foreign Policy: Embedded Hegemony in Europe* (New York: Palgrave Macmillan, 2007), 95.
72. Arno Heissmeyer, Kayhan Oezgenc, Burkhard von Pappenheim, and Thomas Wiegold, "SPD: Wider den Genossen-Frust," *Focus Magazin*, August 5, 2002.
73. Robert Rohrschneider and Dieter Fuchs, "It Used to Be the Economy: Issues and Party Support in the 2002 Election," *German Politics and Society* 21, no.1 (Spring 2003): 76–94.
74. A massive number of university students surrounded the Parliament building to protest Prime Minister Kishi Nobusuke's attempt to revise the US-Japan Security Treaty in June 1960. Because of the massive students' protest, US president Eisenhower cancelled his visit to Japan.
75. George R. Packard, *Protest in Tokyo: The Security Treaty Crisis of 1960* (New Jersey: Princeton University Press, 1966).

76. Interview with a DPJ member of the lower house, January 23, 2008; an LDP member of the lower house, February 5, 2008; and a DPJ member of the lower house, February 7, 2008.
77. Handa, "Jieitai no Honne," 34–39; Ishibashi, "Dispatch," 774–776.
78. Cabinet Office, Government of Japan, http://www8.cao.go.jp/survey, accessed May 6, 2012.
79. Naikaku sōri daijin kanbō, *Seron Chōsa Nenkan* [Annual Public Opinion] (Tōkyō: Ōkurashō insatsukyoku, 2004), 522–524.
80. Ibid., 522–524.
81. Lind observes that German conservatives have never protested against their government's contrition over what Nazi Germany had done to neighboring countries during World War II, whereas there has been always severe backlash from Japanese conservatives when their government apologized to its neighbors for past aggression. Lind traces the lack of conservative backlash in Germany to the strategic constraints placed on West Germany to achieve its goals: reunification, rearmament, and integration with the West. See Jennifer Lind, *Sorry States: Apologies in International Politics* (Ithaca: Cornell University Press, 2008), 4–6, 181–183.
82. Interview with an SPD member of the Bundestag, July 22, 2008.
83. Prime Minister Mori Yoshiro (in office 2000–2001), for example, remarked at a meeting of lawmakers and Shinto religious leaders in Tokyo on May 15, 2001, "We hope the Japanese people acknowledge that Japan is a divine nation centering on the emperor...Education reform led by regional (Shinto) guardian deities and shrines should be carried out." See Scott Stoddard, "Prime Minister: Japan a Divine Nation Revolving around Emperor," *Associated Press Worldstream*, May 16, 2000; Koizumi's successor Prime Minister Abe Shizo's (in office 2006–2007) concept of "Beautiful Country" also shows the typical nostalgia for prewar Japan among the conservatives. He published a book titled "Beautiful Country" in 2006, in which he casted doubt on the legitimacy of the Tokyo war crimes tribunal during the US occupation (1945–1952), and claimed that it is legitimate for Japanese prime minister to visit the Yasukuni Shrine, which is dedicated to the war dead, including Class A war criminals. In addition, he insisted that Japan should change the current interpretation of the right of collective self-defense in order to become an equal alliance partner to the United States. See Chisaki Watanabe, "Japan's Abe Publishes Book Outlining Political Views Ahead of Premier Race," *Associated Press Worldstream*, July 19, 2006; Hiroko Nakata, "Missile Crisis Put Abe in Leader Spotlight: Kozumi Kept to Overseas Sidelines as Probable Successor Took Center Stage, *Japan Times*, July 21, 2006; Anthony Faliola, "Party Leader on a Mission to Instill Pride in Japanese: Poised to Rule as Primeminister, Shinzo Abe Wants Nation to Shake Its Postwar Pacifism," *The Houston Chronicle*, September 21, 2006; and Takehiko Kambayashi, "Japan Rethinks Military Role under New Head: Abe Seeks to Step Up US Ties," *The Washington Times*, September 29, 2006.

84. Interview with a high-ranking MSDF officer, February 14, 2008.
85. Interview with a high-ranking German Navy officer, July 3, 2008.
86. Interview with a retired, high-ranking German Navy officer, August 18, 2008.

7 Conclusion

1. Christopher W. Hughes, *Japan's Re-emergence as a "Normal" Military Power* (New York: Routledge, 2005), 98–105.
2. Christopher W. Hughes, "Not Quite the Great Britain of the Far East: Japan's Security, the US-Japan Alliance and the War on Terror in East Asia," *Cambridge Review of International Affairs* 20, no. 2 (June 2007): 325–338.
3. Andrew L. Oros, *Normalizing Japan: Politics, Identity and the Evolution of Security Practices* (Stanford, CA: Stanford University Press 2008), 5; Paul Midford, *Rethinking Japanese Public Opinion and Security: From Pacifism to Realism?* (Stanford, CA: Stanford University Press 2011), 29.
4. Midford, *Rethinking Japanese Public Opinion*, 146–170.
5. Handa Shigeru, *Boei yokai: Shishin naki nihonno anzen hosho* [Meltdown of defense: Japan's security without direction] (Tokyo: Junposha, 2010), 156.
6. Interviews with an LDP member of the lower house Foreign Relations Committee, February 5, 2008 and a former chairman of LDP General Council, February 20, 2008.
7. Interview with a former SDF chief of staff, February 17, 2011.

INDEX

Adenauer, Konrad, 43
Afghan secret service organization (NDS), 94
Agency for Natural Resources and Energy (ANRE), 145–146
Air Self-Defense Force (ASDF), 4, 7, 18, 40, 89, 90–91, 122–123, 143, 172, 194, 198
Alagappa, Muthiah, 10
Allison, Graham, 24
Al-Qaeda, 14, 33, 42, 53, 55, 58, 79, 113, 120–121, 155
Amaki, Naoto, 148
Anti-Terror Special Measure Law (ATSML), 30, 77–78, 88, 90, 101, 123, 127, 154
Armitage, Richard, 36–37, 39, 40
Arnold, Rainer, 59
Article 5 (NATO Charter), 5, 11, 14, 16, 30, 91–93, 95, 97, 103, 171, 181
Article 9 (Japanese Constitution), 15–16, 18, 23, 28, 69–70, 78, 87–91, 100, 102–103, 122–124, 126–127, 131–135, 146–147, 165–166, 168–170, 174
Article 24 (German Basic Law), 92
Asakura, Toshio, 83
Association of German Chambers of Commerce and Industry, 143

Bauer, Thomas, 11
Baumann, Rainner, 3, 6
Berger, Thomas U., 2, 25–26
Brandt, Willy, 44

buryoku kōshi, 15, 88, 93
Bush, George W. (US President, 2001–2008), 32–34, 37–40, 48, 51, 53–56, 59, 67, 72, 78–80, 85, 111, 114, 156–157, 175

Cabinet Legislation Bureau (CLB), 70
Cabinet Secretariat, 30, 40, 77, 79–81, 123, 149, 164, 169
Cha, Victor, 10
Cheney, Dick (US vice president), 34
Chirac, Jacque (French president), 33, 35
Christian Democratic Union (CDU), 6, 21, 24, 29, 35, 43, 45, 54–57, 82, 97, 153, 156, 158–160, 162–164
Christian Social Union, (CSU), 24, 29, 35, 55–57, 82, 153, 158–160, 162–163
Chōsen Sōren, 150
Chūō kōron, 65
CIA, 59–60
Conference on Security and Cooperation in Europe (CSCE), 50
Constitutional court decision (1994 in Germany), 29, 92, 95, 120
Constructivism, 2, 25, 139, 166
Coordinated Joint Outline Emergency Plan (CJOEP), 122, 128, 131
Costal Safety Force (CSF), 123
C130 (transport aircraft), 89

Defense Guidelines bill (1999) [*shūhen jitaihō*], 17, 75, 100, 173
Defense Policy Guidelines (DPG) [authored by Peter Struck], 46, 96, 107, 117
Defense Policy Review Initiative (DPRI) (2006), 174
de Gaulle, Charles, 43
Democratic Party of Japan (DPJ), 69–71, 78, 90, 141, 161–162, 165–166
Die Welt, 60
Dönitz, Karl, 168

Ebihara, Shin, 37
Erler, Gernot, 58
European Security and Defense Identity (ESDI), 50
European Security and Defense Policy (ESDP), 14, 50–51, 75

Fallujah, 89
Federal Foreign Office, 21, 23, 58, 148, 151–157
Federal Intelligence Service (Bundesnachrichtendienst [BND]), 57, 59–60
Federal Ministry of Economics and Technology, 144
Federal Republic of Yugoslavia (FRY), 5, 11–12, 19, 29, 46, 50, 62, 140, 151, 158, 171–172
Fischer, Joschka, 3, 6, 48, 52, 151, 155–156
Flag Officer Sea Training (FOST), 108
Flexible response, 43–44, 65
France, 13, 20, 35–36, 43, 45, 49, 83, 86, 112, 114, 121, 140, 158
Franks, Tommy, 60
Free Democratic Party (FDP), 29, 55, 57, 82, 120, 153
Fukuda, Yasuo, 81
F-22 fighter aircraft, 143

Gates, Robert, 54, 111, 126–127
German Army, 18–19, 105–106, 109–113, 115–119, 121–122, 128–129, 132–135, 172
German Special Force (KSK), 94, 106, 116–117, 120–121, 134–135
Glos, Michael, 57
Gordon, Philipp H., 33
Green, Michael J., 3
Green Party, 52, 58–59
Grewe, Wilhelm, 44
Grimes, William, 24
Ground Self-Defense Force (GSDF), 18–19, 40, 74, 77–81, 89–90, 105–106, 122–123, 128–136, 146, 172, 174
Gotōda, Masaharu, 69
Gudera, Gert, 118–119, 133
Guidelines for Japan-US Defense Cooperation, 123
Günzel, Reinhard, 116–117

Handa, Shigeru, 88
Hanning, August, 57
Harnisch, Sebastian, 3
Hashimoto, Ryutaro, 67
Hatoyama, Yukio, 161
Hellmann, Gunther, 3
Host nation's support, *See* Sympathy budget
Hughes, Christopher W., 3, 4, 9, 173
Hussein, Saddam, 33–34, 37, 55, 57, 79, 110, 112–13, 155
Hyde-Price, Adrian, 3

Institute of Energy Economics Japan, 146
International Security Assistance Forces (ISAF), 7, 15, 31, 54, 94, 114, 121, 134–135
Iraq Special Measures Law (ISML 2003), 4, 17; *See also* SDF-Iraq Bill

INDEX

Ishiba, Shigeru, 80, 164
ittaika, 15, 88, 93
Izumikawa, Yasuhiro, 8–9

Janning, Josef, 11
Japan Coast Guard (JCG), 123
Japan Communist Party (JCP), 161
Japanese Imperial Navy, 123–124, 168
Japan Socialist Party (JSP), 161, 164
Jung, Franz Josef, 54

Kahrs, Johannes, 163
Kant, Immanuel, 25
Kastrup, Dieter, 155
Katayama, Satsuki, 74
Katzenstein, Peter J., 2, 25
Kawaguchi, Yoriko, 37
Keidanren (Japan Business Federation), 142
Kennan, George, 91
Kennedy, Paul M., 76
Kennedy, John F., 43
Kim Jon Il, 66
Klose, Hans-Ulrich, 58
Kobayashi, Yōtarō, 74
Kohl, Helmut, 151
Koizumi, Jun'ichiro, 3, 4, 20, 30–31, 37–40, 74, 79–81, 85, 125, 149, 150, 157, 175
Kōmeito, 23, 40, 126, 154
Kono, Yohei, 39–40
Korean Peninsula Energy Development Organization (KEDO), 72–73
Korean War, 28, 87, 123–124
Kosaka, Masataka, 65
Kosovo Conflict, *See* Kosovo War
Kosovo Force (KFOR) [NATO-led], 29, 110
Kosovo Liberation Army (KLA), 48
Kosovo War, 3, 6–7, 12–14, 29, 42, 46–50, 52–53, 56, 61, 72, 75, 82, 109, 110, 121, 140, 173
Krauss, Eliss, 3
Kriegsmarine, 168
Kujat, Harald, 126–127

Kuriyama, Shōichi, 148
Kyuma, Fumio, 141

Lepgold, Joseph, 95, 97
Liberal Democratic Party (LDP), 4–5, 19, 23, 38–40, 65, 68–70, 73, 78, 125–126, 133, 141–142, 145, 149, 152, 154, 160–166, 169, 174
License production, 142
Lind, Jennifer, 167
Longhurst, Kerry, 3

Mainichi Shinbun, 65
Maritime Self-Defense Force (MSDF), 3, 5, 7, 18, 30–31, 66, 74–75, 77, 88–90, 101, 122–129, 133–134, 168, 172, 174
Marks, James, 60
Massaki, Hajime, 135–136
Maull, Hans W., 3
Meiers, Franz-Josef, 3, 163
Merkel, Angela, 6, 156, 159, 163
Midford, Paul, 4–6, 173
Milosevic, Slobodan, 12, 14, 47–48, 50
Ministry of Economy, Trade, and Industry (METI), 79, 142–143, 145–146
Ministry of Finance (MOF), 70, 71, 74
Ministry of Foreign Affairs (MOFA), 23–24, 30, 36–37, 66–67, 72–73, 76, 78–79, 81, 123, 148–154, 157
Miskimmon, Alister, 3
Miyazawa, Kiichi, 39, 69
Most similar nations design, 19
"Mr. X" (North Korean agent), 67
Müller, Kerstin, 58
Multilateralism, 3, 12–13
Mützenich, Rolf, 97

Nachtwei, Guenter, 59
Nagoya High Court, 89, 91
Nakatani, Gen (Defense Agency Director General), 36

Nakatani, Masahiro (GSDF Chief of Staff), 133–134
Nakasone, Yasuhiro, 39
Nakayama proposal, 152
National Defense Program Guideline (NDPG 2004), 4
Naumann, Klaus, 45
Nixon, Richard, 65
Nixon Doctrine, 123
Nixon Shock, 65
Nomura, Kichizabro, 123
Normalization, 2–6, 8, 65–66, 172–174
Norway, 20
Nuclear Non-Proliferation Treaty (NPT), 68

Okuda, Hiroshi, 74, 142
One-country pacifism (*ikkoku heiwa shugi*), 64
Oneal, John R., 24
Operation Allied Force (OAF), *See* Kosovo War
Operation Enduring Freedom (OEF), 7, 30–32, 52, 59, 77, 90, 94, 100, 114, 120, 125–128, 133–134
Organization of Petroleum Exporting Countries (OPEC), 145
Oros, Andrew L., 4, 6, 173
Ostpolitik, 44–45
Ozawa, Ichiro, 161

Peace Depot, 88–89, 127–128
Pecos (US Navy oiler), 89, 127
Persian Gulf War (1990–1991), 27–29, 76
PKO (Peacekeeping operation) law (1992), 17, 29, 69
Powell, Collin, 57, 59, 111
Prague summit meeting (2002), 96
Preemptive vs. preventive war, 56, 79
Process-tracing method, 21

Public opinion, 1, 4, 5, 12, 21, 25, 31, 167, 169
Puhl, Detlef, 12
Pyle, Kenneth B., 3

"Quints" (in the Kosovo War), 13, 49

Racak massacre, 48
Rathbun, Brian C., 24, 158, 160, 162–163
Realism, 2, 5–6, 22, 139, 173
Reischauer, Edwin, 65
Rudolf, Peter, 3
Rumsfeld, Donald, 36, 53, 111
Russet, Bruce M., 24
Russia, 10, 16, 35, 46–47, 50, 68, 83, 93, 108, 112, 145, 158

Samuels, Richard J., 3
Sato, Eisaku, 9, 65
Schäfer, Paul, 59
Scharioth, Klaus, 156
Scharping, Rudolf, 117, 126, 134
Schmidt, Helmut, 45
Schröder, Gerhard, 3, 6, 12, 30–31, 33–34, 48, 50, 52–53, 55–57, 82, 85, 110, 112–113, 151, 155–157, 160, 163
SDF-Iraq Bill, 40, 78–79, 101, 170; *See also* Iraq Special Measures Law
Seeheimer Circle, 160
Sekai (magazine), 78
Senkaku Islands, 67
Seventh Fleet, 18, 124–125, 127, 129–131, 172
Shapiro, Jeremy, 33
Shinseki, Eric, 110–112, 135
Shinzo, Abe, 4
Short, Michael, 13, 49
Shūhen jitaihō, 17, 75, 100, 173
Six-Party Talks, 73
Snyder, Glenn H., 1, 8
Social Democratic Party (SDP: *Shamintō*), 161